PRODUCTION AND OPERATIONS MANAGEMENT

PRODUCTION AND OPERATIONS MANAGEMENT

Anand Kumar Sharma

ANMOL PUBLICATIONS PVT. LTD.
NEW DELHI - 110 002 (INDIA)

ANMOL PUBLICATIONS PVT. LTD.
H.O.: 4374/4B, Ansari Road, Darya Ganj,
New Delhi-110 002 (India)
Ph.: 23261597, 23278000
B.O.: No. 1015, Ist Main Road, BSK IIIrd Stage
IIIrd Phase, IIIrd Block,
Bangalore - 560 085 (India)
Visit us at: www.anmolpublications.com

Production and Operations Management

First Published, 2006

PRINTED IN INDIA

Published by J.L. Kumar for Anmol Publications Pvt. Ltd., New Delhi - 110 002 and Printed at Mehra Offset Press, Delhi.

Contents

Preface

"Production and Operstions Management" as a paper is being taught at M.Com., M.B.A. and Other Management Courses at various universities and institutions. This book is designed as an introductory text to the above paper, encompassing vital information on all pertinent aspects. Thus the material presented here would be of interest as well as of great use to the students, teachers and professionals of Management Courses. This book will provide complete knowledge of location and layout planning, materials handling, production planning and control techniques, product design and development, work study, material management, quality control, purchase management, stores management, statistical quality control, maintenance management etc. to the students.

The major topics dealt in this book are—Nature and Scope of Production Management; Faculty Location and Layout Planning; Materials Handling; Production Planning and Control Techniques; Scheduling; Product Design and Development; Management Control; Productivity and Work Study; Materials Management; Quality Control; Material Planning Budgeting; Purchase Management; Stores Management and Control; Statistical Quality Control; Quality Assurance and Maintenance Management etc.

It is hoped that all those will benefit from the contents of this book for whom it is meant. The author will feel amply rewarded, if motive is achieved.

Editor

1

Nature and Scope of Production Management

HISTORICAL DEVELOPMENT OF PRODUCTION AND OPERATIONS MANAGEMENT

Production process responsible for producing goods and services in desired quantities have developed rapidly both in size and quality. Well known economist Adam Smith was the first person to introduce the concept of production economies in factory system by emphasizing the importance of division of labour in his pioneering work. The Wealth of Nations in the year 1776. Gradually the people started realising the advantage of large scale industrial establishments and the role of specialisation in improving the quality and quantity of goods and services produced. It was observed that specialised efforts on machines and tools were more useful and productive. Charles Babbage in his book "The Economic and Manufacture published in 1883 also agreed with the Adam Smith concept of division of labour but he also advocated the principle of limiting skills as a basis for pay fixation. The industrial revolution in U.K. after the second world war found the techniques of Operation Research of great use in the solution of many industrial problems, The application of these techniques provided scientific basis to production management.

Frederik Winslow Taylor is known as the father of scientific management. He studied the factory problems of his day scientifically and popularised the notion of efficiency—getting the desired result with the least waste of time, effort, or materials.

Taylor was born in 1856 in Pennsylvania, the son of a prosperous attorney. With a plan to follow in his father's professional footsteps, he attended preparatory school and applied such energy in his studies that he gradually impaired his eyesight. Although he passed the entrance exams to Harvard Law School with honours, his poor health prevented him from continuing in the legal profession. He turned instead to a fouryear apprentice programme for pattern makers and machinists. It was here in industry that Taylor found outlets for his interest-scientific investigation, experimentation, and improving and reforming things on the basis of fact. Taylor found industrial conditions that he could not tolerate—worker soldering (loafing), poor management, and lack of harmony between workers and managers.

It was realised that in planning a production process, some degree of risk and uncertainty is always associated. This risk and uncertainty can be analysed with the help of probability. Moreover due to many uncontrollable factors there is always unpredictable variation in the output. Probability and statistical methods were considered to be appropriate tools to measure and analyse such variations. Many production problems in present set up can be solved by using the concept of probability and statistics. With development in technology and expansion of enterprises the production process became more complex. Many interrelated factors came into existence and that made the analysis very difficult. To solve the problems suitable mathematical techniques were needed. FW Harris in 1914 evolved economic lot size method to control the inventory of an enterprise. The method was further developed by FE Raymond but application of the method in practice was not general. There were two new development of great significance in 1930's namely.

(i) Introduction of statistical quality control by Walter Shewart in 1931.

(ii) Development of sampling theory by L.H.C. Tippet in 1934. Statistical quality control was introduced in controlling the quality of the product during World War II whereas the sampling techniques found application in production analysis in 1950. There was rapid development in the concepts, theory and techniques of production after management after World War II. The operation research techniques evolved during defence operations in World War II found useful application in industrial operations *e.g.*, linear programming and net work analysis. Queuing theory, inventory analysis, replacement methods found useful avenues in the formalisation and analysis of various production problems. Advent of computers introduced the field of automation. The demand of manpower in defence operations in second world was necessitated to evolve production systems requiring lesser labour force. This resulted in detailed time and motion studies and standard machine tool designs to improve the efficiency of reduced work force.

If we assess the past, covering a period of 200 years after Adam Smith, it can be observed that total production capacity as well as productivity have expanded considerably. Production Management has become an empirical applied science. Undoubtedly during this period, we have responded to the expansion of markets and large scale business units by using the concepts of division of labour and progressive mechanisation in order to achieve economies of large scale production. There has been continuous improvement in design, layout and equipment of production processes by:

(i) With efficient use of labour, material and equipment economies in production.

(ii) Using sophisticated production control technique to produce goods and services of desired specifications at the desired time and with minimum cost.

(iii) Improvement in production line *e.g.*, automation in industries.

Meaning of Production System

Production System and Manufacturing system (types or methods) are used interchangeably. A system is composed of a number of components. These components are combined together for the accomplishment of same predetermined goals. Any manufacturing organisation can be termed as production system to produce goods and services. There are three main components of this system namely inputs, transformation process and output. But these components can be further divided into a number of Sub Components, operations and activities. Inputs can be men, material operations. Transformation process involves many activities and operations necessary to change inputs into outputs. The operations and activities can be mechanical, chemical, inspection and control, material handling operations etc. Output is ill the form of goods and services. Thus a combination of all activities and operations to produce some goods and services is known as manufacturing system. The system depends on a number of factors *viz.*, policies of the organisation, types of production, size of production etc. However. the production method, its organisation and operations differ from company to company.

TYPES OF PRODUCTION SYSTEM

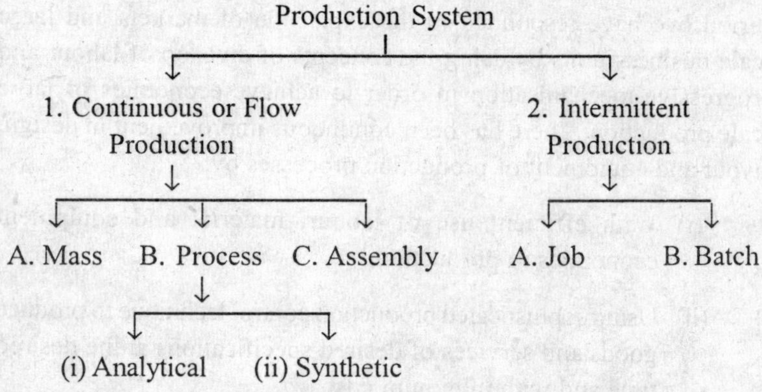

I. CONTINUOUS SYSTEM OR FLOW PRODUCTION

In this system the items are produced for the stocks and not for specific orders. Before planning manufacturing to stock, a sales forecast is made to estimate likely demand of the product and a master schedule is prepared to adjust the sales forecast according to past orders and level of inventory. Here the inputs are standardised and a standard set of processes and sequence of processes can be adopted. Due to this routing and scheduling for the whole process can be standardised.

After setting of master production schedule, a detailed planning is carried on. Basic manufacturing information and bills of materials are recorded. Information for machine load charts, equipment, personnel and material needs is tabulated. In continuous manufacturing systems each production run manufacturers in large lot sizes and the production process is carried on in a definite sequence of operations in a predetermined order. In process storage is not necessary which in turn reduces material handling and transportation facilities. First in first out priority rules are followed in the system.

In short, here the input-output characteristics are standardised allowing for standardisation of operations and their sequence.

Production Control Mechanism for Continuous Manufacturing System

In this system the control mechanism is not as elaborate and complex as for intermittent system. In continuous system large quantities of standardised products are produced using standardised production process.

Following points of control mechanism are worth noting for such a system:

(i) This system does not involve diverse work, due to which routing standardised route and schedule sheets are prepared.

(ii) In case of standard products meant for mass production, master route sheets are prepared for more effective coordination of various departments.

(iii) Scheduling is required to rate the output of various standard products in their order to priority, operations and correct sequence to meet/sales requirements.

(iv) Work relating to dispatching and follow-up is usually simple. Dispatch schedules can be prepared well in advance in such systems.

Continuous system can be divided into three types of production, namely

(a) Mass Production. Standardisation is the fundamental characteristic of this system. Here items are produced in large quantities and much emphasis is not given to consumers orders. In fact the production is to stock and not to order. Standardisation is there w.r.t. materials and machines. Uniform and uninterrupted flow of material is maintained through predetermined sequence of operations required to produce the product. The system can produce only one type of product at one time.

These days, mass production system is generally used to manufacture sub-assemblies or particular parts/components of an item. These parts are assembled together by the enterprise to get the final product. One distinct advantage of this approach is that different combinations of sub-assemblies or parts can be used to manufacture different kinds of products. Specialisation and standardisation in manufacturing single component also leads to economies in production and product diversification to meet specific demands of consumers.

(b) Process Production. This system is analogous to Mass production system with more stress on automation in production process. The volume of production is very high. This method is used for manufacturing those items whose demand is continuous and high *e.g.*, petroleum products, particular brand of medicines, heavy chemical industries, plastic industries etc. Here single raw material can be transformed into different kinds of product at different stages of the production process *e.g.*, in processing of crude oil in refinery one gets kerosene, gasolene etc. at different stages of production.

In mass and processing systems planning and scheduling for materials and finished products is done well in advance. The loading chart gives information about the availability of adequate equipment. The requirement of labour and equipment to produce desired quantity of items is known in advance and knowing the plant capacity, planning can be done for arranging shifts system. The procurement schedule can be also be planned in advance.

Production control operations are done during the production process. Minor adjustment can be done in case of emergency. The whole system is designed to produce some specific type of product only.

(c) Assembly Production. Assembly line is a type of flow production which developed in the automobile industry in the U.S.A. A manufacturing unit prefers to develop and employ assembly line because it helps to improve the efficiency of production. The use of flow production methods results in cost reduction.

Assembly line is particularly useful when a limited variety of similar products is to be produced on a mass scale or in fairly batches on a regular or continuous basis.

In any production system the most vital decision is the proper layout of assembly line. The design of assembly line involves the proper balancing of technology and other manufacturing facilities so as to develop a rational approach for optimisation of results. The assembly line design depends largely upon product design and location of production. In order to develop an assembly line machines are positioned keeping in view the following considerations:

(i) The rate of flow of work.

(ii) The direction of manufacturing operations.

(iii) The convenience and comfort of operators or workers.

(iv) The availability of service facilities like water, electricity, compressed air, oxygen, etc.

(v) The supply and demand of materials.

In an assembly line, each machine must directly receive material from the previous machine and pass it on directly to the next machine. Therefore, the location of machines is automatically regulated by the sequence of operations. Machines and equipment should be arranged in such a manner that every operator has a free and safe access to each machine. Space should be provided (or free movement of fork lifts, trucks, etc. which deliver materials and collect finished products. The passage should not be blocked and workers must not be in danger of being hit by the moving trollies, etc. At the same time there should be economical utilisation of floor space.

These days assembly line process is employed in assembling automobiles, radios, televisions, computers, videos and other electrical and electronic products.

Advantages and Disadvantages of Continuous Production

Advantages :

(i) Direct labour content is reduced.

(ii) High Accuracy.

(iii) Control process simple.

(iv) Storage at different stages of operation not necessary.

(v) Reduced Material Handling.

(vi) Investment in material can be more rapidly translated into income from sales.

(vii) Work in progress is at a minimum.

(viii) Any weakness in the system is easily located.

Disadvantages

Continuous system however is very rigid and if there is a fault in one operation, the entire process is disturbed.

II. INTERMITTENT PRODUCTION

According to Buffa "intermittent production situations are those where the facilities must be flexible enough to handle a variety of products and sizes, or where the basic nature of the activity imposes change of important characteristics of the input (*e.g.* change in production design). In instances such as these, no single sequence pattern of organisations is appropriate, so the relative location of the operation must be a compromise that is best for all inputs considered together. Under intermittent production, the basic product design changes from time to time. Therefore, facilities should be flexible enough to handle a wide variety of products and of different shapes and sizes. Production facilities are arranged according to their functions so that functional skills and expertise can be concentrated to a specialised operation. Job type machine shops, batch type chemical operations are examples of intermittent model.

Intermittent production may be of two types:

(a) Job-Production. Job or 'make complete' production of single complete unit by one operate or a group of operators *e.g.*, bridge building, dam construction, ship building etc. Here whole project is considered as one operation and work is completed on each product before passing on to the next. Each product is a class by itself and requires a distinct and separate job for production purposes. The system requires versatile and highly skilled labour with high capital investments. Control of operations is relatively simple.

In this system the goods are produced to definite customer's orders. There is no assurance of continuous demand for specific items and the manufacturing depends on the receipt of orders from customers.

Merits. Job Production involves comparatively small investments in machinery and equipment. It is flexible and can be adapted easily to change in product design. A fault is one operation does not results into complete stoppage of the entire process.

Demerits. Job shop manufacturing is the most complex system of production. For instance, in building a ship thousands of individual parts must be fabricated and assembled a compels schedule of activities is required to ensure smooth flow of work without any bottleneck. Many parts require operation time on the small machines even though the operations in the manufacturing cycle take place at the different points of time Optimum machine loading is therefore, a very difficult problem.

Raw material and work in progress inventories are high due to the uneven and irregular flow of work. Therefore, large storage space is required and material handling costs are high. Highly skilled machine operators are required for the efficient performance of setting up and operating tasks. Work loads are unbalanced. Labour and equipments must be flexible to accommodate the continuously changing production. There is often inefficient utilisation of labour and plant. Speed of work is slow and unit costs are high.

(b) Batch Production. In the system of batch production, any product is divided into parts or operations and that each operation is to be completed throughout the whole batch before the next operation is undertaken. In other words, here after the production of one batch, the plant and machines become available to other batch of similar type of production. One can employ more specialised labour for each operation with comparatively low investment. But organisation and planning is more complicated in this system. It is characterised by the irregularity in the increase of work added to the basic material. The best example of batch production system is of chemical industry, where different medicines are manufactured in batches. Other examples can be production of electronic instruments, machine tools, printing press etc.

In this system a batch is not passed to next operation until the work on the previous operation is complete for the whole batch and no new batch enters the production line, till all the operations for manufacturing any product are completed. This results in considerable idle time for various operational centres.

A common characteristic of Job-Batch systems is that items are produced to definite customer orders and not for stock. There appears to be no significant deviation in planning and scheduling processes in both these systems. In general diagrams are used for functions, rectangles for documents and solids for raw or semifinished goods.

Here production planning is not based on sales forecasts but one has to estimate or evaluate the requirements on the basis of general business conditions, past information and future sales promotion programmes of the organisation.

MEANING OF PRODUCTION AND OPERATIONS MANAGEMENT

Production and Operations Management (POM) is the management of an organisation 5 production system, which converts inputs into the organisation's products and services.

A production system takes inputs-raw materials, personnel, machines, buildings, technology, cash, and other resource and converts them into outputs products and services. This conversion process is the heart of what is called production and is the predominant activity of a production system. Because managers in POM, whom we shall simply call operations managers, manage the production system, their primary concern is with the activities of the conversion process or production.

Managers in the marketing function are responsible for creating a demand for an organisation's products and services. Managers in the finance function are responsible for achieving the financial objectives of the firm. Businesses cannot succeed without production, marketing, or finance. Without production, no products or services could be produced; without markeuing, no products or services could be sold; and without finance, financial failure would surely result. Whereas production, marketing, and finance act independently to achieve their individual functional goals, they act together to achieve the organisation's goals. Achievement of the organisational goals of profitability, survival, and growth in a dynamic business climate requires cooperative teamwork among these primary business functions. While managers in production, marketing, and finance have much in common, the decisions that they make can distinctly different.

WHAT IS PRODUCTION/OPERATIONS MANAGEMENT (POM)?

Any organisation can be represented by a hierarchy of input/ output diagrams. At the base of the hierarchy is a simple diagram which shows that a customer's needs flow into the organisation which then transforms them into that which satisfies the consumer (Fig. 1.1).

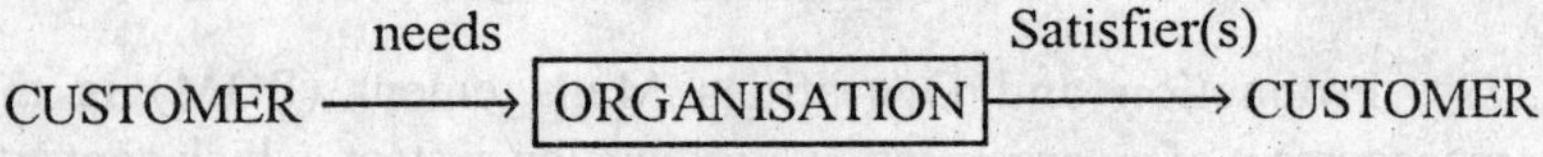

Fig.1.1 The Customer needs and satisfiers.

Since the output returns to the origin, the input/output diagram can be represented as a closed loop (Fig. 1.2).

This basic diagram may be broken down into five sequential input! output diagrams. In the first the customer's needs are identified and translated into a statement of explicit forecasts [Fig. 1.3(i)], which in turn becomes the inputs to the second diagram where they are analysed and integrated to become a statement of resource plans [Fig. 1.3(ii)].

These resource plans are satisfied from suppliers, either internal or external, and generate the inputs which move into the transformation *facility* [Fig. I.3(iii)], which produces outputs either physical

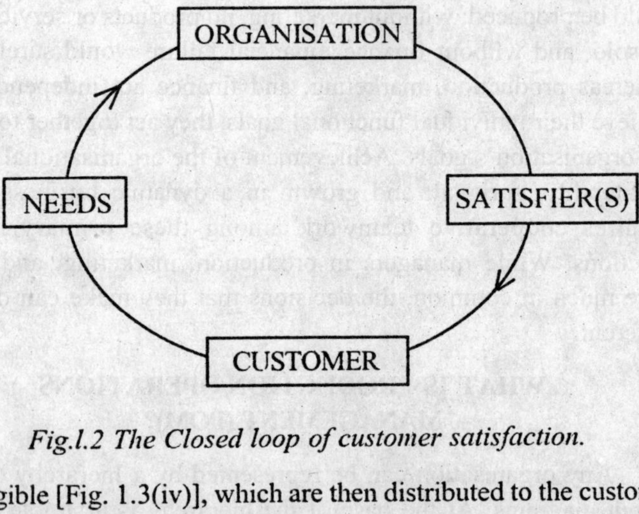

Fig.l.2 The Closed loop of customer satisfaction.

or tangible [Fig. 1.3(iv)], which are then distributed to the customers providing the satisfaction originally required [Fig. 1.3(v)].

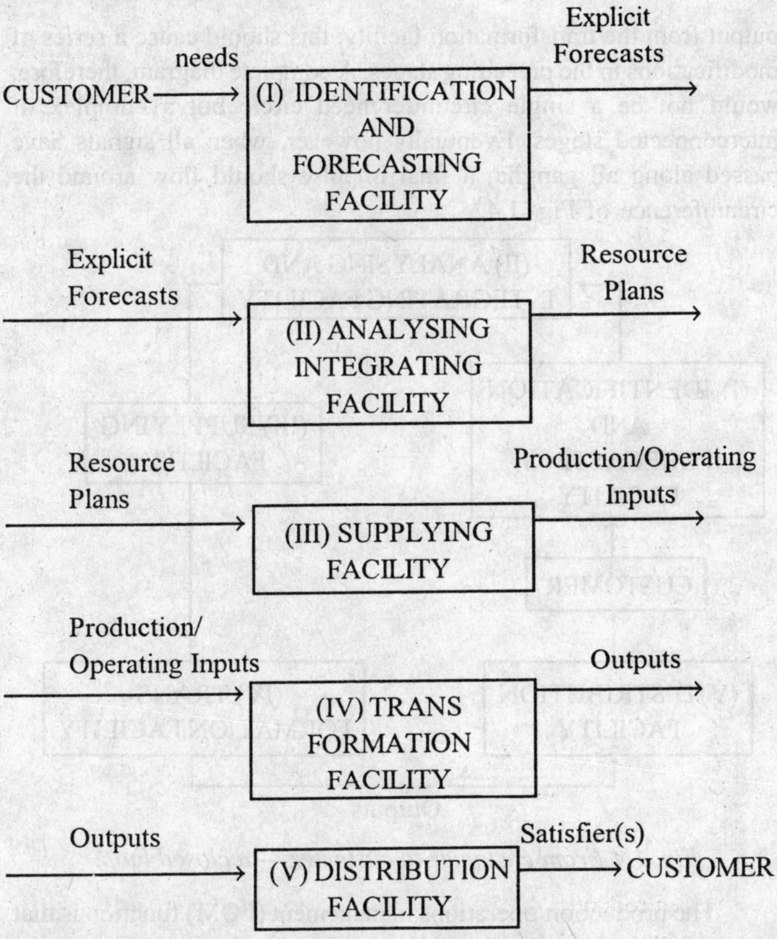

Fig.1.3 Five Input/output diagrams for customer satisfaction.

Since the output from anyone diagram represents input to the next, and as the last output returns to the start, the total diagram can be represented as a closed loop. (Fig. 1.4).

This diagram is, of course, grossly simplified. For example, when forecasts are analysed it may be found that within the facilities available they are unachievable . A reverse reaction should then cause the forecasts to be modified, and a second iteration will take place. Equally, distribution facilities may be inadequate for clearing the output from the transformation facility: this should cause a series of modifications in the preceding stages. A complete diagram, therefore, would not be a single circumferenced circle but a complex of interconnected stages. Eventually however, when all signals have passed along all gangila, a final impulse should flow around the circumference of Fig. 1.4.

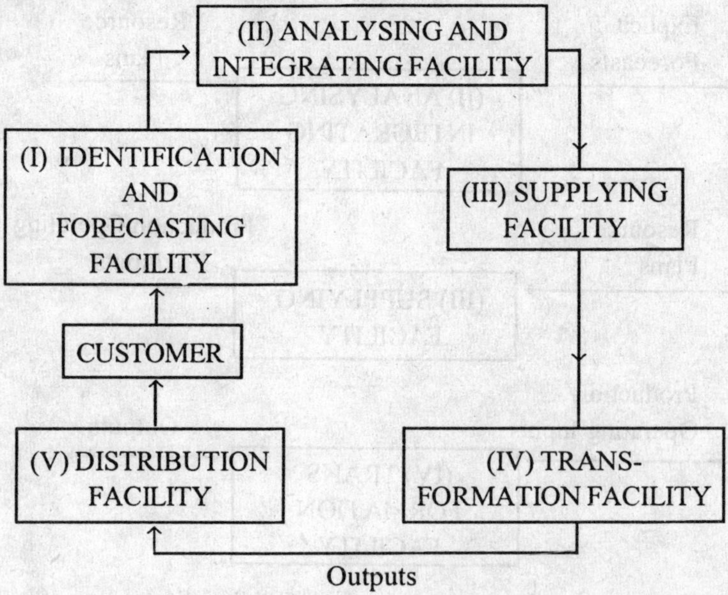

Fig. 1.4 From customer to customer — a closed loop.

The production/operations management (POM) function is that which covers the second, third and fourth of these input/output diagrams, namely the analysis, supply and transformation facilities [Figs 1.3(ii)-(iv)]. Since these are extremely closely linked it is not uncommon to regard them as one facility and the production/operation manager or director can then be regarded as the manager of the whole transformation process (Fig. 1.5).

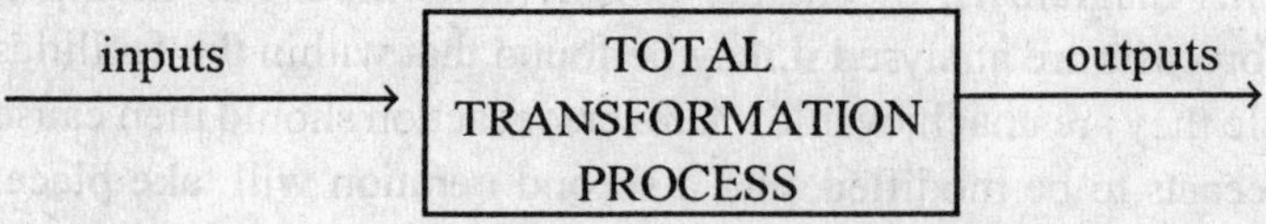

Fig. 1.5 Transformation-Inputs to Outputs

Similarly, the identification and forecasting facility and the distribution facility are also very closely linked and may be regarded as a single one, called marketing. In some situations the distribution facility may be linked to production/operating rather than marketing; in others—for example retailing—the transformation facility may become vestigial or disappear altogether. Despite these possibilities, the fundamental tasks of any organisation may be said to be 'Marketing' and 'Production/Operations.

The relationship between these two major functions is crucial to the success — that is, the survival — of the whole organisations. The closer together they approach, the greater the likelihood of success, and it is interesting to realise that at the beginning of any organisation the marketing/operations functions are usually carried out by one and the same person. Separation of these two functions or a reduction of their inter-connections increases the likelihood of disaster.

FACTORS AFFECTING POM TODAY

Of the many factors impinging on POM today, six stand out in their impact:

(i) Reality of global competition;

(ii) Quality, customer service, and cost challenges;

(iii) Rapid expansion of advanced production technology;

(iv) Continued growth of the service sector;

(v) Scarcity of production resources;

(vi) Social-responsibility issues.

A key impact of these factors on operations managers is that a country's borders no longer provide protection from foreign imports. Competition has become intense and is increasing. To succeed in global competition, companies must make a commitment to customer responsiveness and continuous improvement toward the goal of quickly developing innovative products that have best combination of exceptional quality, fast and on time delivery, and low prices and costs. And this competition dictates that operations managers use more sophisticated production methods made possible by rapidly expanding advanced production technology.

And as if the challenges of global competition to POM were not enough, operations manager's jobs are complicated by the need for more effective management of the expanding service sector, scarcity of capital, materials, and other resources for production; and the need for operations managers to exercise more social responsibility. Given these factors, how can operations managers cope and succeed today?

These factors do indeed create an interesting and challenging opportunity for those who would be operations managers or who would study POM.

Is There a Difference Between Production and Operations?

Earlier it was stated that some of the outputs from the transformation facility might in fact be intangible. Thus, instead of being artefacts they may be a service for the customer. An example of such a situation mi' ' be a club where the needs of the custemer are that s(he) shall be entertained by providing an opportunity for social intercourse. Here the transformation processes results in the provision of an ambience which will allow the social intercourse to take place. The manager of such an enterprise conceptually carries out the same tasks as the manager of an enterprise producing artefacts. Equally, loaqing jobs on to a set of equipment is not significantly different from providing passenger accommodation on a range of train services. The replenishment of stock in a factory has many of the characteristics of the problems of replenishing staff in a aircraft. This co-existence of structure between tasks in parallel disparates organisations enables a used study of POM to be carried out.

The interesting fact which has emerged over the last few years is that the well-established tools of the production manager, that is one who produces artefects, are equally applicable to the manager of an "intangible' enterprise. That is not to say that every technique is applicable in every circumstance, but that there is a 'tool kit' of techniques and methods which is available to operations/production managers, and which should be known in order to be able to choose the appropriate tool. A domestic tool kit might very well contain a range of screwdrivers of different sizes. Depending on the circumstances, the appropriately sized screwdriver is chosen. Similarly in POM the tool kit will contain techniques which are not always used, but which are available to be used when appropriate.

FUNCTIONS OF PRODUCTION MANAGEMENT

The main functions of production management can be listed as:

(i) Specification and procurement of input resources namely management, material and land, labour, equipment and capital.

(ii) Product design and development to dctermine the production process for transforming the input factors into output of goods and services.

(iii) Supervision and control of transformation process for efficient production of goods and services.

In modern times production management has to perform a variety of functions namely

(i) Design and development of production process.

(ii) Production planning and control.

(iii) Implementation of the plan and related activities of various components and departments responsible for producing the necessary goods and services.

THE CRITERIA OF PERFORMANCE FOR THE PRODUCTION AND OPERATIONS MANAGEMENT SYSTEM

Three objectives or criteria of performance of the production and operations management system may be identified.

(a) Effectiveness

(b) customer satisfaction

(c) Efficiency.

The case for 'efficiency' or 'productive' utilisation of resources is clear. Whether, the organisation is in the private sector in the public sector, is a 'manufacturing' or a 'service' organisation, or a 'profit-making' or a 'non-profit' organisation, the productive or optimal utilisation or resource inputs is always a desired objective. However, effectiveness has more dimensions to it. It involves an optimality in the fulfillment of multiple objective, with a possible prioritisation within the objectives. This is not difficult to imagine because modern production and operations management has to serve the so-called target customers, the people working within, as also the region, country or society at large. In order to survive, the production/ operations management system, has not only to be 'profitable' and/or 'efficient', but, must necessarily satisfy many more 'customers'. This effectiveness has to be again viewed in terms of the short and long-time horizons (depending upon the operations system's need to remain active for short or long time horizons)—because, what may seem now like an 'effective' solution may not be 'all that effective in the future'. In fact the effectiveness of the operations system may depend not only upon a multi-objectives satisfaction but also on its flexibility or adaptability to changed situations in the future so that it continues to fulfil the desirable objectives set while maintaining optimal efficiency.

Meaning and Definition of Product

The concept of a product is a complex one and requires careful consideration. A refrigerator (a physical product), a haircut, a train journey (services), family planning, good use of cooking gas (ideas) are all products. A lot of research and experience in the market place have shown that the marketer must treat the product as 'a bundle of utilities' offered to the customers rather than considering it merely as a physical item. For example, the customer of a refrigerator wants a trouble free, spacious machines, at a reasonable price and a good after sales service alongwith. This means that he/she wants good value for his/her money. Moreover, now-a-days refrigerators are being shifted from the kitchen to the dining cum-clrawing room, the housewife will like it to have an elegant colour, an aesthetic design and finish, etc. These will give her some sort of psychological satisfaction.

Product is the most important variable in the marketing mix of a firm. Since a firm is floated to manufacture and sell a product at a sale price which will yield a reasonable profit for the firm. Product is the center of all marketing decisions. The marketing plan begins with the product and also ends upon the product. So product decisions are the most important decisions.

In other words, the term 'product' may defined as :

"A product is something which is offered to customers to satisfy their needs or wants-physical and/or psychological"

Thus, a product must be able to delivery physical as well as psychological satisfaction and its features, quality, style, brand (name and image), size, packaging, warranties, etc. should be accordingly designed. That is a marketer must see a product as something which the customer would want to buy and satisfy his/her wants or needs with it.

In general usage, product is any object which has an identifiable physical existence. According to this concept, "a product has some physical chemical properties." But in production and operations context the meaning of product is very wide. According to Philip Kotler "A product is a bundle of physical service and symbolic particulars expected to yield satisfaction of benefits to the buyer". Thus, a product incorporates facility, service or an instrument of satisfaction to the buyer who buys it. In the words of W. Anderson "a product is a bundle of utilities consisting of various product features and accompanying services."

TYPES OF PRODUCT

(a) Consumer's Goods

Consumers' goods are meant for final consumption by the ultimate consumers. Bread, butter, Television sets, cosmetics and garments are all consumer goods. On the other hand industrial goods are meant for use in the commercial production of other goods or in connection with carrying out some business activities. Machine tools, iron-ore, and electronic computers are all industrial goods. It should be noted that all goods cannot be classified exclusively as consumers' goods or industrial goods. For example, typing paper is used for both personal and business correspondence and therefore is both a consumer's and an industrial goods. The distinction between consumer's and industrial goods is necessary in order to understand the behaviour of their purchasers. The purchasers of industrial goods have an altogether different approach as compared to the purchasers of consumers' goods.

Consumer's goods can be further classified into convenience goods, shopping goods, and speciality goods. A brief description of these is given below:

(i) Convenience goods are those which the customer usually purchases frequently, immediately and with the minimum of effort in comparison to buying such as cigarettes, newspaper, many food products etc.

(ii) Shopping goods are those which the customer in the process of selection and purchase characteristically compares on such bases as suitability, quality, price and style: such as furniture, shoes, major appliances and ready-made garments.

(iii) Speciality goods are those with unique characteristic and/or brand specification for which a significant group of buyers are habitually willing to make a special purchase efforts: such as specific brands of fancy goods, camera, new automobile etc.

(b) Industrial Goods

Industrial goods are goods which are destined to be sold primarily for producing other goods or rendering services as contrasted with goods destined to be sold primarily to the ultimate consumer. Raw materials, machine tools, fertilizers, computers, maintenance suppliers and semi finished products are broad examples of industrial products. Some goods have common features of being consumer goods as well as industrial goods such as tyres, cement etc. Tyres when sold to motor vehicle company are by our classification industrial goods but when sold to an owner of a private car become consumer goods.

Industrial goods are classified according to the uses they are put into.

(i) Production facilities and equipments. These include Installations, minor equipments and plants and building.

(ii) Installations are those goods which are major items of capital equipment and are necessary for the user's operations. Such items involve large investments and therefore require approval at various levels of the company's management thereby requiring the sales person to convince various persons before the order is actually placed. Such a process is time-consuming. Some of these are manufactured according to orders placed and salespersons of such items require considerable technical knowledge. Since these products are very costly manufacturers do not involve middlemen. Examples are cooling towers, multipurpose lathes, etc.

(iii) Minor Equipments are those which the industrial users use as accessories in their production processes. The users buy these products frequently but according to required specifications. Due to frequent purchase the salespersons must call on the users very often. The PCB and UPS of a computer are ideal examples of such products.

(iv) Plants and Buildings are those products which are essential for the users operations, involve huge capital investments but cannot be sold as complete units. Usually building construction companies execute such orders.

(c) Production Materials

Production materials are essential for the industrial user's manufacturing of the product. Production materials include raw materials, semi-manufactured goods, and fabricating parts.

(i) Raw Materials are the basic items that enter into the manufacturing or production of the industrial users. For low cost raw materials, *i.e.*, when these items form a small proportion of the production costs, buying procedures are routine. Example of such raw material is sand used in manufacturing Glass. However, if the cost of raw materials is high in relation to the finished products total cost, higher management is involved in the purchase and they purchase from suppliers directly. Routine purchase procedures will be followed if the supply and the price are stable and low level executives will do the job.

(ii) Semi-manufactured goods are those which are the basic production materials of one user but the end product of another company. Examples are steel, glass, etc. The prices of such goods are somewhat stable and the purchase is stable. Companies producing such items are large and sell directly to the industrial users but if they sell to small manufacturers middlemen are involved.

(iii) Fabricating parts are those which without change of form are incorporated as parts of the finished product. The 'spark plug' used in CMS, mobiles, scooters, trucks and all other sorts of automobiles is an ideal example. Users buy such items directly from the manufacturer according to their own specific requirements, the buyer negotiates a single sales contract with the seller and tends to build a long-run relationship.

(d) Production Supplies

These are items that an industrial user usually needs for maintaining the production processes. Examples are, coal, diesel, oil, petrol, etc. When these are used in large quantities, *e.g.*, a thermal power plant buying coal, long-term contracts are generated and the negotiation takes place between top managers of both the buying and the selling concern. However, if these items are bought in small quantities. the purchase is routine and made by purchasing officers or executives through middlemen.

(e) Services

Services are intangible products and do not confer an ownership like a good A service may be tried to a physical product (good) by agreement or not. We have classified services into three types in the preceding table. We will now describe each of them.

(f) Management Materials

Management materials include items like type-writers, typing papers, carbon papers, etc. to mainframe computers. Purchase decision of high value materials like mainframe computers, etc. or the installation of a totally computerised accounting system are taken by high level managers and negotiated with higher officials of the selling company. Materials of low value like typing papers are brought by low level executives.

(g) Services Accompanying Tangible Goods

Tangible goods like refrigerators, motor cars, computers, vacuum cleaners and cooking rangers are accompanied by one or more services. Such services would include operation manuals, after-sales-service agreements etc. These enhance the consumer appeal and become more important with sophisticated products.

(h) Major Services Accompanied by Minor Goods and Services

A major service (such as a travel by the Indian Airlines) is here, accompanied by minor goods (such as food and chocolates in the plane) and services (such as trolling the passengers luggage from the plane to the exist of the airport) at some cost.

(i) Pure Services

The customer is offered a service only. An Ideal example is a free medical checkup in your nearby government health centre accompanied by free-of-cost medicines.

DISTINCTION BETWEEN INTERMITTENT AND CONTINUOUS MANUFACTURING SYSTEM

	Intermitient	*Continuous*
1.	Same product is not produced continuously.	Same product produced continuously.
2.	Items produced for order.	Items produced for stock.
3.	Production process flexible.	Production not flexible.
4.	Equipment used for limited time.	Regular use of equipment.
5.	Wide range of product can be manufactured.	Only particular type of product is produced.
6.	Smaller scale of production.	Larger scale of production.
7.	Planning and control operation complicated and tedious.	Planning and control operation simple and easy.
8.	More detailed and too many instructions are required for operations	Single set of instructions is sufficient for operations.
9.	Capital investment may be low.	Capital investment may be high.
10.	Per unit cost of production is high.	Per unit cost of production is low.

Contd.

Intermitient	*Continuous*
11. Less security of jobs.	More security of jobs.
12. Functional type of organisation.	Divisional type of organisation.
13. Requires staff of high technical skill and ability.	Requires more managerial capability and better co-ordination.
14. Control not in line of production.	Control in line of production.
15. Storage is required at each operation.	Storage required only at limited locations.
16. Change in location easy.	Change in location difficult.
17. Product and the process not standardised.	Product and the process standardised.
18. Accuracy low.	Accuracy high.

There may be organisations which may use a combination of both the system at various stages of the production process.

MANUFACTURING SYSTEM AND PRODUCTION PIANNING AND CONTROL

The following is the comparison of production planning and control operations in Intermittent and continuous manufacturing system:

Intermittent/Custom Type	*Cntinuous/Standard Type*
1. Planning is complex and expensive due to number of factors involved.	Planning is comparatively easy and cheaper due to fewer variables.
2. Effective planning and control important for	Other methods *viz.* product product simplification and

Contd.

Intermittent/Custom Type	*Cntinuous/Standard Type*
profitability and efficient utilisation resources.	work simplification are more effective for profitable and efficient utilisation of resources than planning and control.
3. Inventories are generally highly varied and more difficult to control.	Inventory control is comparative easier.
4. Machine capacities are varied and usually must be estimated.	Machine capacities are less varied and are known in advance from past experience.
5. Routing is to be done afresh for each new order.	Routing is to be done either when plant facilities are initially set up or when modified.
6. Scheduling is complex requiring (a) placing of an order in an appropriate priority category, (b) scheduling within an order and (c) setting up the order of work for machine.	Scheduling is mainly concerned with establishing a rate of output sufficient to meet the sales requirement of the period.
7. Dispatching is elaborate needing detailed regulation and production control meet delivery dates.	Dispatching is simple and control is concerned with maintaining the schedules rate of output.
8. Manufacturing is usually authorised through the release of a specific manufacturing order.	Manufacturing is authorised through the release of schedules to various department.

CAPACITY MANAGEMENT

The capacity management problem, once framed in a long-term perspective, revolves around matching of available capacity to demand or making certain capacity available to meet the demand variation. This is done on both the intermediate and short time horizons. Capacity management is very important for achieving the organisational objectives of efficiency, customer service and overall effectiveness. While lower than needed capacity results in non-fulfillment of some of the customer services and other objectives of the production/operations system, a higher than necessary capacity results in lowered utilisation of the resources or, in other words, lower efficiency of the conversion operations. There could be a 'flexibility' built into the capacity availability, but this depends upon the 'technology' decision to some extent and also on the nature of the production/operations system. While some operations systems can 'flex significantly', some have to use inventories as the flexible joint between the rigidities of a system. The degree of flexibility required depends upon the customer demand fluctuations and thus the demand characteristics of the operations system. Fig. 1.8 illustrates the size, and variability of demand and the corresponding suitable operating system structure.

As the product variety increases, the systems of production/operations changes. In a system characterised by large volume-low variety, one can have capacities of machinery and men which are inflexible while taking advantage of the repetitive nature of activities involved in the system; whereas in a high variety (and low volume) demand situation, the need is for a flexible manufacturing system (not necessarily FMS referred to later in the book) even at some cost to the efficiency. It may be noted that the relationship between the flexibility, capacity and the desired system-type holds goods even for the 'service' industry.

DECISION MAKING IN POM

We defined POM in terms of what operations managers do. They manage all the activities of the production systems, which converts inputs into the organisation's products and services. This definition states in very general terms what POM does, but how operations managers manage may be more import to an understanding of POM. Perhaps no other approach helps us understand how operations managers manage than the examination of the decisions in POM, because, in large part, operations managers manage by making decisions about all the activities of production systems.

(i) Strategic, Operating, and Control Decisions

Classifying POM decisions is difficult, but in my experience as an operations manager, decisions tended to fall Into three general categories:

(i) **Strategies Decisions.** Decisions about products processes, and facilities. These decisions are of strategi importance and have long term significance for th organisation.

(ii) **Operating Decisions.** Decisions about planning productio to meet demand. These decisions are necessary if th ongoing production of goods and services is to satisfy th demands of the market and provide profits for the compan

(iii) **Control Decisions.** Decisions about planning ar controlling operations. These decisions concern the da to-day activities of workers, quality of products ar services, production and overhead costs, and maintenan of machines.

Strategic decisions concern operations strategies and the lon range game plan for the firm. These decisions are so important tl typically people from production, personnel, engineering, marketi and finance get together to study the business opportunities carefu and to arrive at a decision that puts the organisation in the b position for achieving its long-term goals. Examples of this type planning decisions are:

(a) Deciding whether to launch a new-product developm project.

(b) Deciding on the design for a production process for a new product.

(c) Deciding how to allocate scarce raw materials, utilities, production capacity, and personnel among new and existing business opportunities

(d) Deciding what new factories are needed and where to locate them.

Operating decisions must resolve all the issues concerning planning production to meet customer's demands for products and services. The principal responsibility of operations is to take the orders for products and services from customers, which the marketing function has generated, and deliver products and services in such a way that there are satisfied customers at reasonable costs. In canying out this responsibility, numerous decisions are made. Examples of this type of decisions are:

(a) Deciding how much finished-goods inventory to carry for each product.

(b) Deciding what products and how much of each to include in next month's production schedule.

(c) Deciding whether to increase production capacity next month by having the foundry department work overtime or to subcontract part of the production to suppliers.

(d) Deciding the details of a plan for purchasing raw materials to support next month's production schedule.

Such decisions are fundamental to the success of the production function and the entire organisation.

Control decisions are concerned with a variety of problems in operations. The facts of life for operations managers are that their workers do not always perform as expected, product quality tends to vary, and production machinery tends to break down and usually does so when it is least expected. Operations managers engage in planning, analysing, and controlling activities so that poor worker performance, inferior product quality, and excessive machine breakdowns do not interfere with the profitable operation of the production system. Examples of this type of decision are:

(a) Deciding what to do about a department's failure to meet the planned labour cost target.

(b) Developing labour cost standards for a revised product design that is about to go into production.

(c) Deciding what the new quality control acceptance criteria should be for a product that has had a change in design.

(d) Deciding how often to perform preventive maintenance on a key piece of production machinery.

The day-to-day decisions about workers, product quality, and production machinery, when taken together, may be the most pervasive aspect of an operations manager's job.

ELEMENTS OF PRODUCTION SYSTEM

The production system is composed of the following sub-systems.

(i) Inputs. Inputs are the physical and human resources utilised in the production process. They consist of raw materials, parts, capital equipment, information, human effort, paper etc. Inputs constitute the variable costs of production.

(ii) Conversion Process. Conversion or transformation processes refer to a series of operations which are performed on materials and parts. These operations may be mechanical, chemical, assembly, inspection, receiving, shipping, etc.

(iii) Outputs. Outputs are the products or completed parts resulting from the conversion process. Outputs generate revenue.

(iv) Storage. Storage takes place after the receipt of the inputs, between one operation and the other and after the output.

(v) Transportation. Inputs are transported from one operation to another in the production process.

(vi) Information. The information sub-system of production system interconnects all physical activities and serves as a basis for managerial decision-making. It provides systems control through measurement, comparison, feedback and corrective action.

System Maintenance

The fourth problem are of operations management is regarding safeguards—that only desired outputs will be produced in the 'normal' condition of the physical resources, and that the condition will be maintained normal. This is an important are whereby 'vigilance' is maintained so that all the good work of capacity creation, scheduling, etc. is note negated. Technology selection and management has much to contribute towards this problem. A proper selection and management procedure would give rise to few problems. Further, the checks (*e.g.*, quality checks on physical/non-physical output) on the system performance and the corrective action (*e.g.*, repair of an equipment) would enhance the chances of having the desired outputs undiluted by other pollutants. The negative aspects of technology and its proliferating applications are only recently being appreciated.

It may be interesting, at this juncture, to trace the history of production and operations management.

DUTIES OF PRODUCTION MANAGER

The duties of the production manager, in general, can be classified as given below:

(i) Production Manager should concern himself with production planning. In every enterprise, Production Manager is responsible for producing the required quantity of product in time to meet the stipulated delivery date. The quantity to be produced depends on the magnitude of demand whereas the time by which the production should be completed is determined by deliver date. Besides this the production department has to make arrangements for input factors and also to produce in economic lot sizes. To achieve all these objectives proper production planning is necessary. Production planning involves the generation and identification of alternative course of action and to select the optimum alternative. This can be done by *(i)* assessing the requirement of various factor of production on the basis of demand forecasts and *(ii)* formulating demand schedule for factors of production to permit purchased of raw material and the production of product in economic lot sizes.

(ii) **Production Manager should Concern himself with Quality Control.** It is the responsibility of the production manager to manufacture the goods and services of desired specifications. Though the quality of the finished goods can be ensured by the inspection of finished goods but it is better to employ measure which minimise the likelihood of producing defective items.

(iii) **Production Control.** It is the duty of the production manager to use the resources at his disposal in the best possible manner as well as to regulate the operation in such a way that desired delivery schedule is maintained. This is done by routing, scheduling and inspection during the production process.

(iv) **Method of Analysis.** There can be a number of ways in which some operation can be executed. Production manager should select the most efficient and economic method to perform the operation.

(v) **Plant Layout and Material Handling.** The physical arrangement of manufacturing components and the equipment for handling the material during production process has considerable effect on cost of production. The material handling system and the plant layout should be most efficient for the given situation.

(vi) **Proper Inventory Control.** Inventory implies all the materials, parts, supplies, tools, and in process or finished products kept in stock for sometime. The procurement policy of these items requires careful consideration and analysis. The purchases should be planned in economic lot sizes and the time of purchases should be so scheduled that the investment in the inventory is at lowest possible level. This implies determination of economic lot sizes and re-order level.

(vii) **Work Study.** Method study and work measurement techniques are applied to find the relationship between output of goods and services and input of human and material resources. The production manager should try to find the most appropriate method of performing various operations involved in a production process so as to obtain the optimum use of the resource as well as increasing the productively.

(viii) **Production Manager should be able to Generate the Interest of the Workers.** To increase their efforts by providing them wage incentives. This will result, an increase in labour productivity.

(ix) **The Cost of Production varies with Different Methods of Production.** The production manager is responsible to follow a systematic approach to control capital and expenditure designed in a way that desired profit is ensured.

FORECASTING IN PRODUCTION AND OPERATION MANAGEMENT

It is imperative that companies have effective approaches to forecasting and that forecasting be an integral part of business planning. When managers plan, they determine in the present what courses of action they will take in the future. The first step in planning is therefore forecasting, or estimating the future demand for products and services and the resources necessary to produce these outputs. Estimates of the future demand for products and services are commonly called sales forecasts, which are the starting point for all the other forecasts in production and operations management.

Operations managers need long-range forecasts to make strategic decisions about products, processes, and facilities. They also need shortc range forecasts to assist them in making decisions about production issues that span only the next few weeks.

SOME REASONS WHY FORECASTING IS ESSENTIAL IN PRODUCTION AND OPERATIONS MANAGEMENT

(i) **New Facility Planning.** It can take as long as five years to design and build a new factory or design and implement a new production process. Such strategic activities in POM require long-range forecasts of demand for existing and new products so that operations managers can have the necessary lead time to build factories and install processes to produce the products and services when needed.

(ii) **Production Planning.** Demands for products and services vary from month to month. Production rates must be scaled up or down to meet these demands. It can take several months to change the capacities of production processes. Operations managers need medium-range forecasts so that they can have to lead time necessary to provide the production capacity to produce these variable monthly demands.

(iii) **Work Force Scheduling.** Demands for products and services vary from week to week. The work force must be scaled up or down to meet these demands by using reassignment, overtime, layoffs, or hiring. Operations managers need short-range forecasts so that they an have the lead time necessary to provide work force changes to produce the weekly demands.

METHODS OF FORECASTING

(i) **Executive Committee Consensus.** Knowledgeable executives from various departments within the organisation form a committee charged with the responsibility of developing a sales forecast. The committee may use many inputs from all parts of the organisation and may have staff analysts provide analyses as needed. Such forecasts tend to be compromise forecasts, not reflecting the extremes that could be present had they been prepared by individuals. This method is the most common forecasting method.

(ii) **Survey of Sales Force.** Estimates of future regional sales are obtained from individual members of the sales force. These estimates are combined to form an estimate of sales for all regions. Managers must then transform this estimate into a sales forecast to ensure realistic estimates. This is a popular forecasting method for companies that have a good communication system in place and that have salespersons who sell directly to customers.

(iii) **Delphi Method.** This method is used to achieve consensus within a committee. In this method, executives anonymously answer a series of questions on successive rounds. Each response is fed back to all participants on each round, and the process is then repeated. As many as six rounds may be required before consensus is reached on the forecast. This method can result in forecasts that most participants have ultimately agreed to in spite of their initial disagreement.

(iv) **Survey of Customers.** Estimates of future sales are obtained directly from customers. Individual customers are surveyed to determine what quantities of the firm's products they intend to purchase in each future time period. A sales forecast is determined by combining individual customer' responses. This method may be preferred by companies that have relatively few customers.

(v) **Historical Analogy.** This method ties the estimate of future sales of a product to knowledge of a similar product's sales. Knowledge of one product's sales during various stages of its product life cycle is applied to the estimate of sales for a similar product. This method may be particularly useful in forecasting sales of new products.

(vi) **Market Research.** In market surveys, mail questionnaires, telephone interviews, or field interviews form the basis for testing hypotheses about real markets. In market tests, products marketed in target regions or outlets are statistically extrapolated to total markets. These methods are ordinarily preferred for new products or for existing products to be introduced into new market segments.

Factors for a Successful Forecasting System

Several factors should be considered in the selection of a forecasting method:

(i) Cost and Accuracy. In choosing a forecasting method, there may be a trade-off between cost and accuracy; in other words, more forecast accuracy can be obtained at a cost. High-accuracy approaches use more data, the data are ordinarily more difficult to obtain, and the models are more costly to design, implement, and operate. Such methods as statistical models, historical analogies, and executive-committee consensus tend to be of low or moderate cost, whereas complex econometric models, Delphi, and market research tend to be high cost. Each organisation must make the cost and accuracy trade-off that is appropriate to its own situation.

The first describes an expensive and complex forecasting system, the second describes an inexpensive and simple forecasting system, and the third describes a dynamic system for selecting forecasting models. That all three organisations appear to be pleased with the accuracy and cost of their forecasting system demonstrates that there is no single forecasting approach that is appropriate for all situations. In many situations, simple and low-cost forecasting methods tend to provide forecasts that are as accurate as more complex and high-cost forecasting methods.

(ii) Data Available. The data that are available and relevant for forecasts is an important factor in choosing a forecasting method. For example, if the attitudes and intentions of customers are a relevant factor in forecasts and if the data can be economically obtained from customers about their attitudes and intentions, then a survey of customers may be an appropriate method for developing demand estimates. On the other hand, if the requirement is to forecast sales of a new product, then a survey of customers may not be a practical way to develop a forecast; historical analogy, market research, executive-committee consensus, or some other method may have to be used.

(iii) Time Span. The choice of an appropriate forecasting method is affected by the nature of the production resource that is to be forecasted. Workers, cash, inventories, and machine schedules are short-range in nature and can be forecasted with moving average or exponential smoothing models. Longrange production resource needs such as factory capacities and capital funds can be estimated by regression, executive-committee consensus, market research, or other methods that are appropriated for long-range forecasts.

(iv) Nature of Products and Services. Managers are advised to use different forecasting methods for different products. Such factors as whether a product is high volume and high cost, whether the product is a manufactured good or a service, and where the product is in its life cycle all affect the choice of a forecasting method.

(v) Impulse Response and Noise Dampening. How responsive we want the forecasting model to be to changes in the actual demand data must be balanced against our desire to suppress undesirable chance variation or noise in the data. Each forecasting model differs in its impulse response and noise-dampening abilities, and the model selected must fit the forecasting situation. For example, let us say that we would like to keep the size of our work force reasonably stable. In this case we might want a forecasting model that has high noise dampening ability, because a forecasting model that has low noise dampening ability would also have a high impulse response, which would result in forecasts that are too erratic for a planned stable work force.

Once managers have selected the forecasting model to use, the performance of the model must be tracked.

❐

2

Faculty Location and Layout Planning

The location of an industry is as important as the choice is for the location of a business or a shop in a city or a locality. Unscientific and unplanned industrialisation is harmful not only to the industrial unit but also to the social and economic structure of the country as a whole.

The degree of significance for the selection of location for any enterprise mainly depends on its size and nature. Sometimes, the nature of the product itself suggest some suitable location. A small scale industry mainly selects the site where in accordance with its capacity the local market for the product is available. It can easily shift to other place when there is any change in the market. But for large scales industries requiring huge amount of investment there are many considerations other than the local demand in the selection of proper plant location. These plants can not be easily shifted to other place and an error of judgement in the selection of site can be very expensive to the organisation.

IMPORTANCE OF PLANT-LOCATION

The selection of location is an important phenomenon for the success of an enterprise and requires through analysis. The selection of location is of paramount importance both for new and already established enterprises. The location choice is vital for any new firm for its success. Because fundamental objective of an enterprise is to maximise its profits which can be done either by increasing sales or by decreasing cost of production. If the enterprise is located near its potential market then the organisation can have better and up to date understanding of the market and thus can formulate more effective production and marketing strategies to increase sales. The reduction in cost of production is possible when a firm is located at a place where all kinds of production economies *i.e.* input factors are available. The relocation of already existing enterprises may be necessary due to dynamic nature of plant location. Selection of appropriate location is important due to the following reasons.

(i) Location of plant partially determines operating and capital costs. It determines the nature of investment costs to be incurred and also the level of many operating costs.

(ii) Each prospective location implies a new location of capacity to respective market area.

(iii) Location fixes some of the physical factors of the overall plant design *e.g.* heating and ventilation requirements, storage capacity for raw material taking into consideration their availability, transportation need for raw materials and finished goods; power needs; costs of labour; taxes, land, construction, fuel etc.

(iv) Government some times plays an important role in the choice of the location keeping view the national benefits.

FACTORS RESPONSIBLE FOR PLANT LOCATION CHOICES

The physical factors associated with location of an enterprise can have a significant impact on the operations of an enterprise and its costs structure. These factors can be qualitative as well as quantitative. Qualitative factors can be measured in terms of some qualitative criteria namely adequate, good, significant etc. Quantitative factors can be measured on cost or some other quantitative basis *viz.* labour, material, housing, land, transport etc.

Certain factors are of great importance in the case of smaller establishments, whereas, others require careful consideration for larger establishment.

According to Dr. Visvesvariaya the decision of plant location should be based on nine M's namely Money, material, manpower, market, motive power, management, machinery, means of communication and momentum to an early start. In general, "a plant should be located at a place where the inhabitants are interested in its success, the product can be sold profitable and the production cost in minimum". In particular, the choice of plant location should be based on following considerations:

(1) Availability of Raw-Material. An ideal location is one where the main raw-material required to manufacture the product is adequately available. This will ensure regular supply of the material and will also reduce the transportation costs. The technical and delivery problems associated with raw-material can be reviewed and discussed from time to time. Alternately, the per unit cost of raw-material should come out to be minimum at the ideal plant location *e.g.* locations of textile mills in Mumbai and Ahmedabad, iron and steel industry at Jamshedpur and Jute mills in Kolkata are guided by this consideration.

(2) Nearness to the Potential Market. Marketing of its goods efficiently is also an important function of an enterprise. If the plant is located near the market then the management can keep close touch with the changes in market environment and formulate its production policies accordingly. But with expansion of markets both at national and international levels this aspect is now of secondary importance. The reduction in marketing costs still remains an important consideration for location to be near the market. The transportation and other overheads are likely to increase with distance between plant and the market. Also in case of factory located near to the market the risk of damage in transportation, loss of demand due to change in fashions etc. is also reduced. Glass, chemical and drug factories are mainly affected by this consideration.

(3) Location should be Near to the Source of Operating Power. In some industries continuous and adequate supply of power is of great significance *e.g.* nylon fibre plant. There are some industries for which cheap electricity may be more important. In such situation location of the plant near to hydel-power stations will provide cheap electricity *e.g.* paper and pulp mills, flour mills etc.

(4) Supply of Labour. Labour is one of the most important inputs in an industrial enterprise. There should be regular and cheap supply of labour, specifically for unskilled labour. In modern times with brisk movement of labour force from one place to other this factor is also of secondary importance. But if there is adequate supply of local labour near the plant then naturally it will be available at cheaper rates *e.g.* Lal Bangles industry in Jodhpur.

(5) Transport and Communication Facilities. Transport is very important for bringing raw-materials fuel from different places marketing of finished product etc. the region well connected with Rail, Road, Water and Air transport system is considered to be more appropriate for the location of plants.

If ratio of product weight to its value is high then more emphasis should be given to transportation cost. In such cases location should be nearer to the source of raw material *e.g.* brick, cement, glass, steel and wood industries. Similarly good communication facilities *viz.* Postal and Tele communication links are of great significance towards the success of an enterprise. Regions with good communication system should be given priority for the selection of sites.

Industries producing goods for export may be located near ports or airports.

(6) Integration with Other Group of Companies. New enterprise owned or operated by a single group of companies should be so located that its work can be integrated with the work of the associated establishments.

(7) Suitability of Land and Climate. Sub-soil of the location should be able to support the load likely to be placed on it.

Similarly, the climatic conditions *viz.* humidity, temperature and other atmospheric conditions should be favourable for the plant *e.g.* damp climate is favourable for textile and cotton industries. These conditions also determine heating and ventilating requirements.

(8) Availability of Housing, Other Amenities and Services. Good housing facility, adequate number of shops, theatres, cinemas, restaurants, local passenger transport and rail services and sufficient availability of gas, water supply, drainage, disposal of waste, fire fighting services can easily attract good staff.

(9) Safety Requirements. Industries like nuclear power stations, processes explosive in nature, chemical process likely to pollute the atmosphere should be located in remote areas.

(10) Local Building and Planning Regulations. Proposed location should not infringe local regulations and bye-laws. A discussion with the survey department of the local authority is most desirable. Laws for the construction of buildings, local taxes etc. should be taken into consideration for the selection of site.

(11) Other Consideration. For the choice of location can below interest on loans, special grants, political situation, low rentals, other benefits to encourage investment, attitude of residents towards the industry, living standards etc.

Besides these considerations, decision regarding the choice of location should be based on the future requirements of the organisation, *e.g.*

(i) Availability of raw material in future when local supply is exhausted or due to technical advancements some other kind of raw material may be required,

(ii) The market may expand due to increase in local population or due to change in habits and tastes of consumers. The possibility of all these alternatives should be properly analysed for the selection of appropriate plant location. In short "the guiding principle in determination of an optimum location of a plant is that per unit output cost should be minimum for the production and marketing of the product:

According to A. Beacham, " if however the entrepreneur acts rationally (in the economic sense) and if he has necessary knowledge he will choose the location which offers the lowest cost per unit of output."

LOCATON OF INDUSTRIES IN INDIA

There is unbalanced distribution of Industries in India. Mumbai and Bengal enjoys about 50% of the factory workers population. The concentration of industries in few selected regions in India has created uneven distribution of population and wealth. In many areas problems of unemployment and poverty are predominant.

Many areas are underdeveloped and backward. Now the government is giving priorities and preferences for establishment of industries in underdeveloped areas. Various incentives and subsidies are provided to entrepreneurs for the purpose.

While granting the industrial licence to any party the government ascertains that the new unit should not disturb the regional balance. The industrial policy resolution of 1956 states that positive facilities should be provided to industrially backward areas. The importance of balanced regional development has been regularly recognised in various five year plans.

MEANING OF PLANT LAYOUT

Plant layout is related to a number of aspects of production and operation management.

Layout problems are fundamental to every type of organisation/ enterprise and are experienced in all kinds of undertakings. Housewife must arrange her kitchen, retailer must arrange his counters and display the items in such a manner which facilities movement and attract the attention of customers, office management position the desks, tables and other equipment in such a way that it facilitates the flow of work. The manufacturing organisation must arrange their facilities, not only the departments within the factory but also the plant, stores and services so as to achieve smooth flow of products.

The adequacy of layout affects the efficiency of subsequent operations. It is an important perquisite for efficient operations and also has a great deal in common with many of the problems.

According to Riggs, the overall objective of plant layout is "to design a physical arrangement that most economically meet the required output quantity and quality". An optimum layout would permit an uninterrupted flow of work through the factory. It ensures best possible utilisation of machines, workers and space. A plant layout study is required to create an arrangement that will minimise unit production costs. Such a study involves a careful analysis of all factors affecting layout. Plant layout is an important decision as it represents a long-term commitment. It is also important because it affects the flow of materials and processes, labour efficiency, supervision and control, use of equipment, use of space, expansion possibilities, etc. Plant layout covers not only the initial layout of machines and other facilities but encompasses revision or improvements in existing layout in the light of changes in the methods and techniques pf production.

The disposition of the various parts of a plant alongwith all the equipment used is known as Plant Layout. It should be so designed that the plant functions most effectively.

Layout problems are common to all kinds of organisations. A retailer must arrange his counter, display of items etc., office management must position desks, tables etc. in such a way that it facilities the flow of work. A manufacturing organisation must position its machinery and other equipment so as to achieve smooth flow of products through their factories.

Objectives of Plant Layout

Layout planning is multi-dimensional in that it must satisfy various and often conflicting objectives. Some of the objectives of plant layout are:

(a) To maintain high turnover of work-in-progress.

(b) To reduce congestion of personnel and material.

(c) To maintain flexibility of arrangement and of operation.

(d) To hold down investment in equipment.

(e) To make economical use of building.

(f) To increase safety of personnel.

(g) To facilitate communication and coordination as required.

(h) To increase quality of work like through better physical (light, temperature, noise) and psychological (possibly of socialising and communicating) conditions.

(i) To provide operations flexibility.

(j) To minimise materials handling costs among different functions.

(k) To facilitate the manufacturing process.

(l) To promote affective utilisation of human resources.

(m) To imprqve morale and labour efficiency.

Advantages of a Good Layout

A good layout can provide a number of advantages to workers and management. Some of these are listed below:

1. To the Worker:

(i) Lesser number of operations and material handling.

(ii) Reduction in length of hauls and motions between operations minimises production time as well as the activities of workers.

(iii) More labour productivity *i.e.* more output per man hour *i.e.* low work in progress and high turnover.

(iv) More safety and security to workers from accidents.

(v) Better working conditions resulting improved efficiency.

II. In Manufacturing Costs :

(i) Maintenance and replacement costs are reduced.

(ii) Loss due to waste and spoilage is minimised.

(iii) Improved quality of product with reduction in handling w.r.t. movement, time and cost.

(iv) Better cost control.

III. In Production Control and Supervision:

(i) Provides more space for production operations.

(ii) Control and supervision operation are provided at appropriate points.

(iii) Better and convenient storage facilities.

(iv) Efficient arrangement for receipt, transportation and delivery of raw material and finished goods.

(v) Result in less inspection activity.

(vi) Cost and efforts in the supervision of production process are minimised.

IV. A good layout leads to efficient and optimum use of machines, labour and capital by minimising per unit production time and maintaining a proper balance between various production departments. This leads to reduction in capital investments. There is effective utilisation of floor space facilities operations, maintenance, service and supervision.

Features of Good Plant Layout

(i) Ease of Working, Greater Safety, and Reduced Health Hazards for Workers. This will go a long way in increasing worker satisfaction and, therefore, labour productivity, Plant layout has much to do with productivity techniques such as work study, job evaluation, incentives and ergonomics; one cannot speak of these productivity related techniques/concepts without relating them to the design of the physical working environment, that is, plant layout. In fact, physical plant layout is one component of the integrated picture for labour productivity improvement, and has to fit properly in relation to the other components of the picture.

This is emphasised here because plant layout theories in their quest for mathematical optimisation tend to overlook the human aspects and treat the subject as one dealing purely with the arrangement of physical spaces. As mentioned elsewhere in this book, user-orientation is an important consideration in management decision-making; and ultimately, the arrangement of the work areas is for the users of the work areas.

(ii) Reduced Handling of Materials. A good plant layout takes into consideration the various flows of materials inside the plant thus reducing the handling of materials.

The choice of the material handling equipment and the systems of storage of materials, have a lot to do with the way the plant facilities are laid out. The decision as to whether one should employ an overhead crane or fort-lift trucks depends much upon how the different departments in the plant are located spatially with respect to each other. Conversely, the choice of whether the material is to be stored in the production areas or in the store determines the physical plant layout. So, the decisions of movement and storage of materials and that of plant layout have mutual feedback. A good physical plant layout should produce economies in the storage and movement of materials.

(iii) Reduced Damage and Spoilage of Materials. If adequate consideration regarding the handling and storage of materials is given, it automatically reduced damage and spoilage of materials.

(iv) Reduced Congestion of Materials, Machinery and Men. A good physical layout should eliminate confusion in the plant. By doing so, it not only makes the life of the supervisor easier but also contributes towards overall improvements in the productivity of the shop.

A good plant layout means a good spatial system. This should make production scheduling and control easier and should consequently reduce the delays in production and increase utilisation of the available plant capacity. In the unnecessary search for materials, in the difficult handlings of materials due to the unnecessary zig-zag movement of materials, and due to the general confusion and wrong information regarding their availability, many production hours have been lost in practice; many unnecessary change-overs of production have occurred. All these can be avoided by a systematic arrangement of the non-living and living entitles that comprise a production plant.

(v) Flexibility with Regard to Changing Production Conditions. A good layout, that is a good spatial system, should be one that is adaptable or Flexible enough to take care of probable future changes in the volume of production, in the range of products manufactured, and changes in the methods/processes of production.

TYPES OF PLANT LAYOUT

There are five broad categories of plant layout:

(a) Product or Line Layout. Product or line layout means the arrangement of the machines in a line (not necessarily straight) in the order in which they would be used in the process of manufacture of the product. It is suitable for the continuous mass production of goods as it makes it possible for the raw materials to be fed into the plant at one end and taken out as finished products on the other.

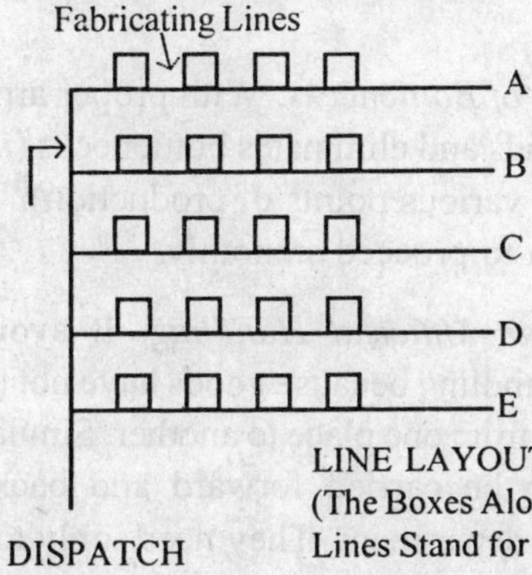

LINE LAYOUT
(The Boxes Along Fabricating
Lines Stand for Machine

In the line type of layout, there will be a separate production line for each type of product. Each line may have the same machines though these may be arranged differently or the machines for each line may be different. The illustration given on the right shows the line layout in a plant.

Product layouts typically use specialised machines that are set up once to perform a specific operation for a long period of time on one product. To change over these machines to a new product design requires great expense and long down times. The machines are usually arranged into product departments. Within one product department several processes, such as forming, machining, and assembly, could be performed.

Workers in product layouts repeatedly perform a narrow range of activities on only a few product designs. The amount of skill, training, and supervision required is small. Although the planning and scheduling activities associated with these layouts are complex, they are not ongoing. Rather, planning and scheduling tend to be done intermittently as product changeovers occur.

Advantages of Product Layout

(i) *Mechanisation of Material Handling.* Since the type of layout ensures continuous flow of materials in a line through various machines, it is easy to use the mechanical devices of material handling like conveyors. In this way, the materials can move quickly and economically under this type of layout.

(ii) *Avoidance of Bottlenecks.* With proper arrangements such layout avoids and eliminates bottlenecks (*i.e.*, the stoppage of work at various points of production). This enables the production to proceed smoothly.

(iii) *Economy in Material Handling.* It avoids unnecessary material handling because goods have not to be transported frequently from one place to another. Similarly, the material has not to be carried forward and backward from the respective department. They need .only to be fed into the

receiving end of the machine; after that no transportation or movement of the materials of the materials is needed till the finished product is manufactured.

Disadvantages of Product Layout

(i) *Product Layout is of Inflexible Nature.* The facilities are designed to perform special operations. The machines cannot be interchanged either in capacity or with regard to any other operation. This results in frequent interruption, expensive change over and move chances of technological obsolescence. In other words the system cannot easily adjust to some modifications in the production process.

(ii) *Venerability to Production Line Shut Down.* If any machine or equipment in production line breaks down the whole production line is immobilised. The reason is that various operations in this system are integrated and co-ordinated to such a fine degree that considerable machine idleness results if one or more machines in the system is behind schedule. Such interruption can be due to absenteeism, poor production scheduling etc.

(iii) *Supervision is more Difficult.* The system requires more specialised and skilled supervision. The supervisor/foreman has to supervise wide range of diversified activities for which they should have thorough knowledge of various machines set-ups, kinds of work done, operating speeds, and feeds, maintenance, loading and scheduling requirement etc. A supervisor under product layout is more prone to neglect one or other of the responsibilities.

(iv) *Requires Heavy Capital Investment.* In this system there is unavoidable duplication of facilities, which increases the capita investment and risks. A product layout is generally characterised by the combination of high proportion of capital investment relative to labour. High capital investment leads to high overhead charges which may be a burden on the faring in lean periods.

(b) Process or Functional Layout. Process layout means the arrangement of similarly machines in a group in one department according to the functions they perform in the plant. Thus, welding equipment may be placed in a separate welding department for the benefit of all lines of department. All lathe machines may similarly be placed at one place in the lathe department.

Process layouts typically use general-purpose machines that can be changed over rapidly to new operations for different product designs. These machines are usually arranged according to the type of process being performed. For example, all machining would be in one department, all assembly in another department, and all painting in another department. The materials-handling equipment generally consists of forklift trucks and other mobile vehicles that allow for the variety of paths followed through the facility by the products produced. The workers in process layouts must change and adapt quickly to the multitude of operations to be performed on each unique batch of products being produced. These workers must be highly skilled and require intensive job instructions and technical supervision. Process layouts require ongoing planning, scheduling, and controlling functions to ensure an optimum amount of work in each department and each work station. The products are in the production system for relatively long periods of time, and large in-process inventories usually are present.

Advantages of Process Layout

(i) In the case of output of smaller quantities and with varying specifications this type of layout is most appropriate.

(ii) In each specialised section, workers expert in the specific operation can be used *i.e.*, scope for more skilled labour leads to better quality in production.

(iii) Each production unit of the system works independently and is not affected by the happenings in another section of the plant. Provides cohesiveness and enables-individual bonus schemes.

(iv) *Effective Supervision.* Supervision and inspection work can be independently and efficiently carried out by each department. The worker in each section frequently becomes very adept and specialised in the maintenance and repair of equipment specification and inspection requirements. There is also saving of time in inspection and control operations.

(v) *Wide Flexibility in Production Facilities.* The system is more flexible to adjust modifications and changes in production strategies. Each machine/equipment can perform a wide range of similar operations. Work can be dope on a short notice with much time spent on production planning and scheduling.

(vi) *Lower Capital Investment.* The production facilities can be utilised to greater capacity with less duplication of machines. The equipment is highly productive and profitable. Overloading of any department can be done by increasing the working hours, routing the work to other machine or by sub-contracting.

(vii) *Machine Breakdown does not Disrupt Production Schedules.* In this layout, machine breakdown does not immobilise the entire production process. If there is a breakdown of any machine in a department the work can be easily transferred to another machine in the same section. In case the department is already working at high capacity, minor modifications in scheduling can readily be made to perform more urgent jobs.

(viii) *Lower Proportion of Fixed Costs to Total Costs.* A peak production level the amount of labour utilised in proportion to capital utilised is high in comparison to product layout. When the decline in demand and plant operation is at a low capacity then smaller labour force can keep the system running full time. Low capital investment makes smaller overhead charges for idle plant. Also the risk on investment is reduced as the facilities are more flexible and are less subject to obsolescence.

Disadvantages of Process Layout

(i) *Difficulty in the Use of Mechanical.* The machines devices for material handling cannot be conveniently employed,

(ii) *Diseconomy of Floor Space.* This type of layout requires more floor space than the product layout.

(iii) *Difficulty of Production Control.* Production control is difficult to enforce under such layout and is both costly and complex.

(iv) *Wasteful Hauling of Materials.* The materials have to be carried forward and backward quite frequently. This means both delay and waste.

(v) *Uneconomical Inspection.* Inspection under this layout is more frequent and costlier because work has to be checked after each operation.

(vi) *Accumulation of Work in Progress.* The work in progress or the stocks of semi-finished products may accumulate.

(vii) *Longer Period of Manufacture.* The manufacturing operations take a longer period than under the product layout.

COMPARISON OF PRODUCT AND PROCESS LAYOUT

Product Layout	*Process Layout*
1. Investment	
Needs high investment in machines/equipment	Comparatively low investment needed.
2. Duration of Production	
Needs less manufacturing time as the economy in time can be planned in the beginning.	Production time can not be economised due to frequent movement of men and material.

Contd.

Product Layout	*Process Layout*
3. Immobilisation Due to Breakdown	
Breakdown of any unit/ component immobilises the whole system.	Breakdown of any machine does not immobilise the whole system.
4. Adjustability to Changes	
Inflexible as each machine can perform pre-designed operation only.	Fexible as different sections can adjust the operations according to changes in operations.
5. Floor Space	
Requires less space.	Requires more space.
6. Men / Equipment Utilisation	
Not to full capacity.	Comparatively better utilisation.
7. Material Handling	
Lesser amount of material handling and comparatively lesser time, money and efforts.	Involves greater handling of material requiring more time, money and effort.
8. Demand and Supply Relationship	
Proper co-ordination between demand and as there are made to stock.	Co-ordination between demand and supply is likely to be difficult as these are made to order.
9. Control and Inspection	
Specialised and expertise control is required thus increasing supervision costs.	Comparatively lesser efforts on control are needed.

Thus both the layouts have their own advantages and disadvantages. In fact merits of one are demerits of the other. The choice and suitability of the layout mainly depends on the nature of the manufacturing system and type of the product to be produced. In general process layout is suitable for intermittent systems and Product layout is appropriate for continuous system.

(c) Group or Combined Layout. In practice plants are generally laid out neither on the pure line pattern nor on the pure functional basis. The basic features of these two types of layout are combined to derive the maximum advantage from them without incurring their disadvantages. It is usual for industries engaged in repetitive certain type for intensive use. Machine groupings of this type are than integrated into the 'line'. Likewise special service facilities like heavy cranes and fabrication stages calling for flexibility (say, welding) may be grouped for use on a number of different parts of a standard product.

In most industrial establishments, plants are rarely laid out in either pure form and a combination of product or process layout is used. It is possible to have both types of layout in an efficiently combined form if the products manufactured are somewhat similar and not complex. Group layout is a combined form of product layout and process layout. In certain batch production industries a variety of products are assembled. Product layout is employed for mass production of common components. In addition, process layout is used for assembling the standard components in batches of products. For example, in soap manufacturing plants, the machinery for manufacturing soaps is laid out in a straight line. But ancillary facilities like heating, power house, glycerine plant and water treatment plant are arranged on a functional basis. Thus, it is a blending of product based and process-oriented layouts. There are departments like grinding and welding for certain processes. However, there is a continuous flow of the product in the process departments. Thus, a combination that produces the desired volume of products at the minimum cost per unit is selected.

(d) Hybrid Layouts. Most manufacturing facilities use a combination of layout types. Following Fig. Shows one such hybrid layout where the departments are arranged according to the types of processes but the products flow through on a product layout. Although hybrids make the identification of layout types fuzzy, it is important to understand the characteristics, advantages, and disadvantages of each type of layout.

(e) Fixed Position Layout. In this type of layout, the major product being produced is fixed at a location. Equipment, labour and components are moved to that location. This layout is used when the materials being processed are large, very heavy and difficult to move. Ship building, locomotive manufacturing, wagon building, aircraft manufacturing, etc., employ fixed position layout. All facilities are brought and arranged around one work centre.

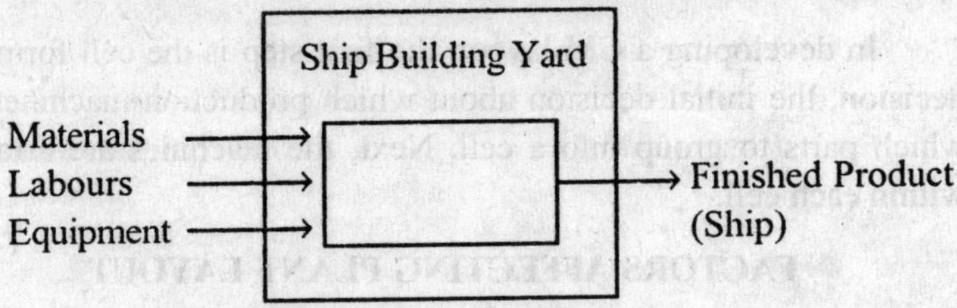

Fig. Fixed Position Layout

Some manufacturing and construction firms use a layout for arranging work that locates the product in a fixed position and transports workers, materials, machines, and sub-contractors to and from the product. Missile assembly, large aircraft assembly, ship construction, and bridge construction are examples of fixed-position layouts. Fixed-position layouts are used when a product is very bulky, large, heavy, or fragile. The fixed-position nature of the layout minimises the amount of product movement required.

(f) Cellular Manufacturing (CM) Layouts. In cellular manufacturing (CM), machines are grouped into cells, and the cells function somewhat like a product layout island within a larger job shop or process layout. Each cell in a CM layout is formed to produce a single parts family—a few parts all with common characteristics, which usually means that they require the same machines and have similar machine settings.

Although the layout of a cell can take on many different forms, the flow of parts tends to be more like a product layout than a job shop. The reasons why a CM layout would be attempted are :

(i) Machine changeovers are simplified.

(ii) Training periods for workers are shortened.

(iii) Materials-handling costs are reduced.

(iv) Parts can be made faster and shipped more quickly.

(v) Less in-process inventory is required.

(vi) Production is easier to automate.

In developing a CM layout, the first step is the cell formation decision, the initial decision about which production machines and which parts to group into a cell. Next, the machines are arranged within each cell.

FACTORS AFFECTING PLANT LAYOUT

The following factors should be considered while planning the layout of a plant:

(1) Plant Location. Plant layout is intimately connected with plant location. As a matter of fact the size and shape of the site and its topography influence the general pattern of layout. Plant site also influences the type of building, mode of transport and the scope of expansion which in turn influences layout. Plant layout is generally a compromise between the ideal layout and the limitations of plant site and building. A decision to relocate offers an opportunity to improve it the arrangement of facilities and services. Thus, plant layout is considerably affected by both the specific site and the general location.

(2) Nature of Product. Standardised products require a product layout whereas custom-made products may need process layout. A fixed position layout would be required for heavy and bulky products. Products involving hazardous and dangerous operations would require isolation of processes. Similarly, value, fragility, volume and quality of product are important consideration in plant layout.

(3) Type of Industry. The nature and type of production process exerts considerable influence on plant layout. Generally, product layout is more appropriate in continuous process industry, whereas intermittent production requires process layout. The sequence of operations should also be taken into consideration. Perhaps no one factor influences plant layout as much as the nature of the productive process involved. A synthetic process requires a line layout so that various materials and parts merge into the completed assembly in a flow. On the other hand, an analytic process takes the form of a tree as it starts out with a single material and spreads out into a variety of resultant materials. A conditioning process requires a layout to accommodate lot or batch manufacture. In such a layout the material undergoes no merging or separation but it is simply subjected to physical conditioning as it flows in separate lots through the variety of operations and processes.

Thus, the layout designer should keep in mind the type of industry and the nature of the manufacturing process while planning a layout.

(4) Spatial Requirements. The spatial needs for machines, material handling equipment and available floor space are important influences on plant location. Spatial requirements also depend upon the position and needs of workers. Employee facilities and safety should be duly considered.

(5) Plant Environment. In planning factory layout, heat, light, noise, ventilation and other aspects of plant climate should be given due consideration. For example, paint shops and plating sections should be located on an outside wall so that dangerous fumes may be removed through proper ventilation. Type of machines, materials and equipment used also exercise considerable influence on plant location.

(6) Repairs and Maintenance. Machines and equipment should not be fixed so close to each other that it may create problems in repairs, maintenance and replacement. Access to machine parts for repairs and maintenance should be provided.

(vii) Balance. Proper balance between processes helps to avoid bottlenecks. The arrangement of machine capacity should be such as to ensure a uniform flow of work. At the same time the layout should be designed in such a manner that there is minimum possible movement of materials and men.

(viii) Management Policy. Management policies regarding size, quality, employee facilities and delivery schedules should be considered while deciding plant layout. For example, size (demand forecast) will determine the size of work stations. Need for flexibility should also be considered: The layout designer must have a complete understanding of management policies that have a bearing on plant layout.

PRINCIPLES OF PLANT LAYOUT

(1) Plan for a Minimum of Materials Handling. The materials handling system must be efficient. In fact, the effectiveness of plant layout will make a major contribution to the efficiency of materials handling system.

(2) Permit All Flexibility Possible. As the change in the law of life, plant layout should have in built flexibility. The equipment and materials so be so arranged that changes can be made at a minimum of cost or disturbance of the manufacturing process. Especially, in automotive industries, where models are constantly changing, the plant layout should be as flexible as possible.

(3) Move the Materials Minimum Distances. This principle brings out the concept of 'straight line' production under the straight line method of production. The movement of materials is minimum. However, in many instances, it is more practical to take a circular paths such as found in 'merry go rounds' used in production foundries.

(4) Avoid or Minimise the Back Tracking of Materials. Back tracking increases the distance of movement and result in congestion of the channels of materials handling. In some industries there are some 'rules of thumb' that have been established by experience in plantlayout. For instance, it is not considered good practice to place large and expensive installations such as heat treating equipment or drying oven for finishes centrally, the preferred practice being to locate them along an outerwall. It should be pointed out that such practices are not yet generally accepted as fundamentals of plant layout.

(5) Allow for Plant Expansion. The plant layout engineer should consider the increase in production when planning the internal arrangements in his factory. It is better for him to make some provision for expansion of the factory.

(6) Principle of Interdependence. Interdependent operations and processes should be located in close proximity to each other. For example, materials should be stored near the area of requirement, transport, etc. This will minimise product travel.

(7) Principle of Flow. The work areas should be arranged according to the sequence of operations so that there is a continuous flow of materials without backtracking or congestion. The layout should allow for easy movement of materials without interruptions or delays. As far as possible movement of materials should be continuous.

(8) Principle of Minimum Investment. The layout should yield savings in fixed capital investment through optimum utilisation of available facilities.

Layout of a Plant is an Expensive Affair

Due care is required in the installation of plant and equipment. Management must remember that plant layout is not an end in itself but is a means top achieves a smooth flow of materials. A sound layout must ensure.

(a) steady and uninterrupted flow of work;

(b) absence of congested traffic;

(c) full utilisation of capacity;

(d) flexibility to meet technological changes and increase in production requirements;

(e) easy control of production;

(f) effective supervision;

(g) low cost of manufacturing.

In addition to the location of production equipment and work centers, the location of plant services (receiving, shipping, warehousing, maintenance, tool cribs) and employee services (parking, cafeteria, locker rooms, toilets, medical, recreation, facilities, etc.) The main consideration in locating plant services is the overall material How patterns. In locating employee facilities the guiding factor is convenience and accessibility to employees.

COMPUTERISED TECHNIQUES FOR LAYOUT

Over the years, computer programmes have been developed to guide the layout engineer in planning the best possible layout. In the past two decades, three well-known computer analyses have been developed—ALDEP, CORELAP, and CRAFT. Some of the widely used programmes in plant layout are given below:

(1) ALDEP (Automated Layout Design Programme). This programme selects at random and locates the first activity. Subsequent activities-facilities, in required size, are selected and placed according to closeness desired or at random if no significant relationships are found. Alternative layouts are generated and compared.

ALDEP—automated layout design programmes—and CORELAP computerised relationship layout planning are similar in that they use essentially the same procedures and logic. Rather than considering the number of products flowing among departments, these programmes use closeness ratings, a relative measure of how desirable it is for departments to be close together. These programmes maximise the total closeness rating for all the departments while complying with the required building characteristics. Very large and complex layout problems are feasible, and each analysis outputs a plotted floor-plan block layout.

(2) CRAFT (Computerised Relative Allocation of Facilities Technique). This technique is used to determine desirable spatial arrangement of production departments in order to minimise the total materials handling cost. Data relating to inter-departmental flow per unit of time, unit load, material handling cost per unit distance, initial block programme are fed into CRAFT. The computer processes these date until it can find no improvements in location and then prints out a block type layout of the location of each of the activities or departments.

CRAFT can handle 40 departments or activity centers and can consider the exchange in location of three departments simultaneously. It is applicable for overall location of major activities as well as more detailed departmental locations within activities. The CRAFT programme is also applicable to a wide variety of non-manufacturing situations, *e.g.*, hospital design, warehouse layout, etc. It can also be applied to equipment design problems where manufacturing costs may with the location of components.

CRAFT—computerised relative allocation of facilities—uses the same procedure and logic as operations sequence and block diagram analyses. CRAFT minimises the total materials—handling cost per time period for the layout. The material movements per time period are converted to cost per time period for movements of each material between departments. Analysts input an initial block layout, and CRAFT modifies the initial layout until no cost improvements are possible. New initial layouts yield different CRAFT layouts, so some experimentation is advised. The program also can handle complex, large layout problems while adhering to complex building characteristics. The outputs of the program are a plotted floor-plan block layout and the cost of the layouts.

(3) CORELAP (Computerised Relationship Layout Planning). In this technique the most related departments are located close to each other. Then other activities are added progressively on the basis of related closeness desired and in required size until all facilities/activities are arranged. It is used to perfect the layollt design.

(4) PLANET (Computerised Plant Layout and Evaluation Technique). Under this programme the "penalty" cost associated with separating departments are computed on the basis of interdepartment flow data. Three heuristic algorithms are used for generating alternative configurations to be manually evaluated and adjusted.

(5) COFAD (Computerised Facilities Design). This technique combines CRAIT-based layout with materials handling selection based on various criteria.

(6) CAN-Q (Computer Analysis of Network of Queses). This programme is designed for analysing the work flow in a production system. It is said to be quite easy to use, very efficient and sufficiently versatile to handle virtually any kind of production system.

These and other computer programmes can save time and effort in large and complex layout problems, but their outputs are only the beginning of a finished layout. Their layouts must be fine-tuned by hand and checked for logic, and machines and other elements of the layout must usually be hand-fitted with templates and cutouts.

TYPES OF PLANT LAYOUT EQUIPMENTS

1. Process Charts

A process chart is a classification and graphic representation of production activities in a plant. Through these charts the whole process can be systematically analysed by sub-dividing the various operations and material moments constituting the production process and then their effectiveness. The study of these charts can reveal the operations that can be eliminated, re-arranged or simplified to achieve economy in production. These charts can be divided in two categories:

(i) ***Operations Process Charts.*** These charts divide the whole manufacturing process into operations and inspections. It indicates the points at which materials are introduced into the process and exhibits the sequence of all operations and inspection except those involved in material handling. This chart represents the basic activities required to manufacture a product.

(ii) ***Flow Process Chart.*** It is a graphic representation of all production activities occurring on the floor of the plant. This chart accumulates and classifies the complete information necessary for the analysis and improvement of plant operations as a whole or of anyone phase. The study of this chart can reveal the operations that can be eliminated, rearranged or simplified to achieve economy in production *e.g.* work stations, storage areas and inspection cribs may be relocated to reduce travel distance and labour time. The inflexibility of the layout can also be ascertained from this chart. The data for constructing flow process charts are collected by tracing the actual' flow of work occurring in the plant from the receipt of the raw material to the completeness of the product. The data includes the distance travelled and the time required for the operations.

2. Process Flow Diagrams

It is both a supplement and substitute of flow charts. It is an aid to visualise the movement of material on an existing floor layout. A single line is drawn to scale on the floor plan to represent the physical movement of material through the entire plant. These show backtracking and excessive movement of material and helps in relocations plant activities to reduce travel distance.

3. Machine Data Cards

This is an effective method to provide necessary information for placement or layout of the equipment. These cards are prepared for each machine showing its capacity, spaces and power requirements, handling needs and the corresponding dimensions.

4. Visualisation of Layout

This is the most common method of planning a layout by making replicas of machines, racks, benches and the equipment and then arranging these an a two or three dimensional plant the floor space.

(i) Two-dimensional Plan or Templates. In practice templates are used to develop layout. The area required by machine/equipment may be cut to scale from a sheet of heavy paper; bristol board or plywood. Then colours may be used to show areas for production machines, benches, racks and other equipments for material handling and storage space. The method consists of following steps:

(a) Scale drawing of the available floor space is drawn showing the positions of columns, electrical fittings, power, water, gas, elevators, rest rooms and other significant features.

(b) A layout plan is chalked out by positioning the machine replicas on the drawing.

(c) Plan is then critically examined with respect to work flow, utilisation of floor space, availability of service facilities like tool sheds, stock rooms etc.

(d) Alternative plans are drawn by re-arranging the replicas and comparative evaluation is made to select the best layout.

The layout selected at this stage can be the basis for replanning the layout when some expansion or modernisation is contemplated.

(ii) Three-dimensional Plan or Scale Models. To have a better understanding about the depth, height etc. of machines, scales or miniature models are constructed in place of templates. Here one uses tiny figures of men and machines like pawns in the game of chess. The three-dimensional models are expensive but provides clarity and vividness.

Three dimensional models provide full visualisation of equipment and processes. In it one can easily detect the weakness of the layout if any. For more exact presentation sometimes a combination of two dimensional and three dimensional models can be used.

The model of a layout can be made by studying the operations involved in the production process:

(i) Key operation are located.

(ii) Locate main and minor gangways. These should be preferred near the walls and not across the floor.

(iii) Locate the subsidiary equipments *viz.* rubbish bins, telephones etc.

In a good layout packing department should be near to despatching point whereas inspection place should be located near the windows for proper daylight.

In addition to this the following specific points should be kept in mind for the layout of machines:

(i) Space occupied by a machines must include some overhang space for the travel of any part or for the movement of material.

(ii) Gangways must be adequate for the collection and delivery of material.

(iii) Floors must be strong enough not only to carry the machine load but also to bear the load of semi-finished and finished goods.

(iv) Servicing facilities and safety devices must be easily accessible.

(v) Sufficient space around the machine must be provided so that operator can move freely to do his work.

It should be observed that the layout of an organisation has an impact on other functional areas. There is a strong interaction between layout planning and other decision areas such as work measurement and method study.

❐

3

Materials Handling

Materials handling is the art and science of moving, packing and storing of materials in any form. It involves the preparation, placing and positioning of materials to facilitate their movement and storage. In other words, materials handling is a system comprising the transfer, movement, warehousing, inprocess handling and shipping operations. It is an interdependent cycle wherein materials are handled several times.

Significance. Materials handling is an essential part of every manufacturing operation. It consumes the major share of the time involved in an operation. The cost of materials handling generally accounts for 20 to 50 per cent of the total cost of converting the raw materials into the finished product. The cost of materials handling consist of *(a)* the cost of owning and maintaining equipment, and *(b)* the cost of operating the system.

The handling of materials influences the efficiency and cost of manufacturing. Materials handling is an important area for reducing costs, increasing productivity and improving cash flow. Manufacturing is largely the story of 'materials in motion'.

Materials handling adds to the cost of the product. Therefore, reduction in materials handling costs will make the product more competitive. The materials handling system should be so designed as to maximise efficiency and minimise cost. Every movement of materials adds to cost and, therefore, materials handling strategy should be to eliminate as much movement as possible. In addition to the elimination of unnecessary movement, the essential movements should be mechanised so as to increase efficiency.

Efficient handling of materials results in several tangible, and in tangible benefits. According to H.A. Harding, "improvements in handling can mean faster production, higher plant capacity, lower stock in process, and less damage to product in all stages. It can force other improvements in production methods and materials".

Objectives. The design, cost and operation of material handling system depend largely upon the objectives for materials handling. The mam objectives of materials handling system are as follows:

(i) Reduction in manufacturing time

(ii) Reduction in the labour cost of handling materials

(iii) Better utilisation of shopfloor and warehouse

(vi) Improvement in the quality of product

(v) Reduction in breakdowns and work stoppages

(vi) Increase in employee safety and comfort

(vii) Better control of flow of materials.

MATERIALS HANDLING AND PLANT LAYOUT

Materials handling and plant layout are complementary to each other. Materials handling system helps to determine storage areas, production flows, aisle widths, space between equipments, in-process materials handling. At the same time, plant layout determines the speed and efficiency of movements of materials from one operation to another. The pattern or flow of materials in a plant influences material handling costs and it should be planned for the layout as a whole.

Principles of Material Handling

The following principles should be followed in the development and operation of an effective materials handling system:

(1) The number and frequency of movements should be minimised. The best handling is 'no handling'. As this is not possible the objective should be 'minimum handling'. All types of handling and rehandling should be minimised.

(2) The time and distance involved in handling should be minimised wherever possible.

(3) Whenever possible flow line and gravity should be used to move materials.

(4) The handling should as far as possible be combined with the production equipment.

(5) Materials should be deposited as near to the point of use as possible.

(6) Continuous and straight line movement is more efficient than irregular movement.

(7) Materials handling equipment should be simple and consistent with the nature of materials and speed of movement. For example; for moving materials over inclined planes, gravity rollers are more appropriate than powered conveyers.

(8) Fixed routes should be established for all handling devices.

(9) Utilisation of handling equipment should be kept as high as possible.

(10) Materials handling system should be flexible so as to accommodate changes in products, plant layout, volume of output, etc.

Efficiency in Handling Materials

The efficiency of the materials handling system is judged by the costs of handling materials. Materials handling costs can be classified into the following categories :

1. Labour Cost. *(a)* direct labour, *(b)* purchasing, *(c)* maintenance.

2. Space Cost. *(a)* Storage, *(b)* production, *(c)* offices, *(d)* gangways.

3. Handling Equipment. *(a)* interest on capital, *(b)* depreciation, *(c)* maintenance.

4. Storage Equipment. *(a)* bins, *(b)* racks, *(c)* pallets, etc.

Reduction in these costs (increase in efficiency) of materials handling is the primary objective of management. Efficiency in materials handling also means minimisation of:

(i) Bottlenecks and breakdowns

(ii) Misuse of space

(iii) Underutilisation of labour

(iv) Poor customer service

(v) Breakage and spoilage of materials.

There is tremendous scope for cost savings in materials handling. Efficient handling also helps to increase production, reduction in fatigue, better employee safety and improvment in working conditions. The following steps may be taken to improve efficiency in matetials handling.

1. Mechanisation. Use of mechanical devices helps to reduce costs of handling materials. But cost savings should be large enough to cover the cost of owning and maintaining the handling equipment. Careful assessment of return is necessary as the investment may be high.

2. Better Systems Design. Methods study is helpful in improving plant layout and materials handling system. Proper selection and arrangement of physical facilities reduces the number and frequency of movements.

3. Effective Organisation Structure. An efficient organisational setup facilitates coordination between production people, materials staff and controller sections.

Careful and mechanical handling of materials, use of existing handling facilities and faster picking up of materials also help to improve efficiency.

Choice of Materials Handling Equipment

The choice of materials handling equipment involves proper balancing of production problems, the capabilities of equipment available and the human factor involved. Production problems consist of the desired volume of production, the type of material to be handled, and the nature of plant layout. The skill, safety and attitudes of employees are important human factors which should be considered in selecting materials handling equipment.

Within these considerations, the following factors should be kept in view while selecting materials handling equipment.

1. Cost. The purchase price: installation costs, labour costs, salvage value and depreciation charges affect the cost of equipment. Operating costs should not be high.

2. Load Capacity. Equipment selected should have the adequate capacity to carry the required load of materials.

3. Space Requirements. The space required to install and operate the equipment is an important factor in selection.

4. Power Requirements. The equipment should be such that it can be operated with the available power.

5. Supervision Required. Automatic equipment requires less supervision than non-automatic equipment.

6. Ease of Maintenance. Equipment should be such that maintenance is easy and can be done at reasonable cost.

7. Speed. Rapidity of materials movement should be considered subject to limits of the production process or plant safety.

8. Flexibility. As far as possible, the equipment should have the flexibilIty to handle more than one class of material. It should be adaptable enough to meet the material handling requirements in terms of load, movement, etc.

❑

4

Production Planning and Control Techniques

When a product is to be manufactured, the production must be carefully planned to ensure the proper method are used and every work centre is assigned the amount of work according to its capacity. While the product is being manufactured, the production must be controlled to ensure that the planned output is constantly maintained. These functions are known as production planning and production control respectively. Although planning and control of production are two different kinds of activity but they are normally the responsibility of the same department.

Production Planning

Planning is the function of looking ahead, anticipating difficulties and taking steps to remove the causes before they materialise. Production planning may be defined as a technique of foreseeing or picturing ahead every step in a long series of separate operations, each step is to be taken in the right place, of the right degree and at the right time and each operation is to be done at a maximum efficiency. Production planning covers a careful and exhaustive study and pre-arranging of the technique involving a long and complicated series of separate organisations so that the required product of the right quality and quantity may be manufactured at the right time and at the most economic cost. It seeks to determine ahead as to what work shall be done within what time it shall be done, where work shall be done and devises the ways and means of doing it in the most efficient and cheapest method.

Production Control

The other important aspect is control of production. Only planning does not ensure that the production is highlighted by planned activities. It is production control that guides and directs the flow of production so that products are manufactured in the best and the cheapest method, that they confirm to the desired quality and that they are ready for sale at the right time. For this purpose, the management marks out a definite course of production, fixed up the time schedule within which production is to be completed and preserves the production line.

According to Fayol "control consists in verifying whether everything occurs in conformity with the adopted plan and established principles. The objectives of control is to point out weakness and shortcomings, if any, in order to rectify them and prevent reoccurrence. It operates on everything *viz.* material, equipment, men operations etc. For control to be effective it must be applied within reasonable time and be followed up by sanctions".

Production planning involves management decision relating to how much to produce, what materials, part and tools will be needed. what step should be followed in the production process, within what time limit the production is to be completed and how much work is to be done by each work station. Production planning is a pre-production activity involving arranging facilities and designing the production system. It is based on sales commitment as to quantity, delivery dates, price, quality, etc.

Production control involves implementation of production plans or schedules by coordinating different activities. It seek to ensure that production operations and actual performance occur according to planned operations and performance. Production operations are constantly evaluated, guided and directed along the plans formulated by the planning department. Production control endeavours to give the best possible service, consistent with available capacities, and at the same time to secure the lowest possible cost.

Definition of Production Planning and Control

Planning and Control are the two important components of the management process. Planning involves the consideration of all input variables to achieve defined output goals. Control involves the corrective actions taken when the actual output varies from the desired one by bringing the actual output in line with the planned output.

Production Planning, in particular, would therefore consist mainly of the evaluation and determination of production-inputs such as labour (manpower), machinery and equipment, materials, and utilities to achieve the desired goals. The definition of the goals is also, of course, a part of the production planning process.

Basically, it is defined as an assemblance of all the factors of production men, materials, machines, technological know how, working capital-well ties together by an intelligent management group with access to an information system. It is therefore, necessary to use proper planning techniques and co-ordinates all the activities.

Objectives of Production Planning and Control

(i) Determining the nature and magnitude of various input factors to manufacture the desired output.

(ii) To co-ordinate labour, machines and equipment in the most effective and economic manner.

(iii) Establishing targets and checking. these against performance.

(iv) Ensuring smooth flow of material by eliminating bottlenecks, if any, in production.

(v) Utilisation of under employed resources.

(vi) To manufacture the desired output of right quality and quantity at right time.

Techniques/Elements/Functions of Production Planning and Control

Following are the production planning and control elements or techniques or functions:

(1) Routing. Routing is the first but the most important and difficult task of the production control. Routing means determination of path or route on which manufacturing operation to be followed in manufacturing a particular product. This route is determined in advance.

Kimball and Kimball has defined the routing as "the selection of path of route over which each piece is to travel in being transformed from raw material into finished product". The routing may involves the following activities:

(i) Determining the volume of production.

(ii) Determining the men, machines and materials to be used in its production.

(iii) Determining the type, number and sequence of production operations.

(iv) Determining the place where production is to be carried on.

In short, routing determines what, how much, when, how and with which to produce.

(2) Dispatching. Routing and scheduling are preparatory steps. Actual production states when permission is granted to commence operations according to plans already laid down. In dispatching orders are issued in terms of their priority and work is assigned to operations. Dispatching in effect determines by whom the work shall be done. Dispatching involves giving the necessary authority to start the work as per the schedule. Work orders and authorisations are issued to the production department to perform the work according to planned sequence, using prescribed tools and predetermined schedules. The dispatching department issues requisitions for materials and tools on the production order and checks to see that the materials, parts and tools are available in time. Adequate instructions are given and work schedules are released to the production department in a coordinate manner. Dispatching is the initiating phase of production planning and control. It translates production plans into output. Orders are issues for the movement of materials, parts and tools to work centres as well as for inspection and recording of work done.

The dispatch section of the production planning and control department is responsible for the following:

(a) Collecting and then issuing to supervisors the drawings, specifications, materials lists, job tickents, route card, requisitions, etc.

(b) Ensuring that materials, parts, tools and other aids are made available to the manufacturing departments at the right time.

(c) Obtaining inspection schedules and issuing them to the inspection section.

(d) Informing the progress section that production is commencing.

(e) Releasing work orders for the start of manufacturing operations.

(f) At the end of manufacture, ensuring that all the drawings, layouts and tools are returned to their appropriate places.

(3) Loading. In planning the production process the management must know when a particular equipment/machine will be available for work on each order or item. For this information a list of the number of machines capable of performing similar operation is prepared. Knowing the number of machine shifts available for each kind of operation and number of shifts required for such operation in the production process to complete the schedule, the planning staff can evaluate whether the work load is greater or less than the capacity of the equipment. This is done by Loading.

Loading can be defined as the study of the relationship between load and capacity at the places where work is done. Loading and scheduling are designed to assist in the efficient and systematic planning of work. Loading provides a complete and correct information about the number of machines available and their operating characteristics such as speed, capacity, capability etc. This information can be used to calculate the difference between work load and actual capacity and then to determine whether customer's order can be completed on due date or not.

(a) Objectives of Loading

The following are some of the main objectives of Loading:

(i) To plan new work orders on the basis of spare capacity available.

(ii) To balance the work load in plant.

(iii) To maintain the delivery promises.

(iv) To check the feasibility of production programmes.

(b) Loading Devices

There are two main approaches for loading *viz.* loading step by step, and machine loading and load charts.

(i) Loading Step by Step. Sometimes an individual production order may require a finite number of operations and the order of these operations may vary too much from item to item. In such cases overloads are scheduled to account for interaction among various operation by identifying the operation which imposes maximum delay on the order. Following are the steps in this approach:

— Find the earliest date and the hours required that can be scheduled onto each operation.

— Determine the hours required at each operation and the time thereafter to complete the job if no loading delay occurs.

— Schedule the bottleneck operation as early as possible.

— Schedule subsequent operation as early as possible.

(ii) Machine Loading. Using information from schedules, weekly/periodic load in hours is determined for each machine and is then recorded on machine load chart. The chart also gives the time for which the machine is busy for parts pertaining to different work orders. A machine load chart for all the machines in a production department shows the future spare capacity of machines. The machines should be loaded to full capacities as idle capacities of machines are sources of loss to the organisation and also increase the cost of production.

(iii) Load Charts. Load charts shows the work assigned to various departments, machines or components of an organisation. During periods of peak/heavy loads information from load charts can be used to determine:

— Priorities to future orders and to decide whether to sub-contract or refuse new orders.

— Provision of overtime or multishift operations.

— Acquisition of extra men or equipment for additional capacity.

One common procedure for Loading is to maintain a register at each machine centre. When any order is loaded on a machine a entry is made in the register showing the estimated time, the order is likely to devote on the machine and the estimated time off. The information can also be presented with the help of Gantt Chart.

(4) Scheduling. One of the important steps in the planning and control of manufacturing operations is the scheduling of output and production stages. Scheduling involves fixing priorities for different items and operations. It establishes the time sequence of operations and indicates the time required for each job operation. Scheduling develops a time table for manufacturing. A schedule is a programme showing list of items to be produced in a given period of time. It determines when an operation is to be performed or when work is to be completed.

(v) Expediting of Follow Up

Expediting or follow up activity of Production control is the last in the series of functions but is the most important step in the production control. Follow up means to see whether the work is being carried on according to the planning and orders and instructions issued to shop under dispatching. It ensures that the materials and tools and equipments are supplied at the job at the right time, to the right person or job and to see where the communication is not clear. In other words, follow up is the means by which the progress and execution of plan is evaluated from time to time and finds out any variations from the plan. The reason for such variations are found out and efforts are, as far as possible, made to eliminate them or minimise them from the plan.

(6) Estimating. Estimating involves deciding the quantity of output to be produced and the cost involved in it on the basis of sales forecast. Manpower, machinery, material requirements to meet the anticipated targets of production are determined. In other words, a production programme is prepared. A bill of materials is prepared listing all the items needed to manufacture the desired output. Time of supply of materials and inventory level are also determined.

Factors Affecting Production Planning and Control

The following factors should be considered in production planning and control:

(1) Type of Product. Complex and seasonal products require much greater care and problems in production planning and control as compared to simple and regular products.

(2) Type of Manufacturing. Continuous manufacturing system involves the problem of line balancing so that no shutdown occurs. In intermittent system, on the other hand, problems of effective use of facilities are important.

(3) Market Forecast. Market forecast determines the volume and rate of production.

(4) Customer Orders. These serve as the basis of production scheduling.

Advantages of Better Planning and Control

(1) Benefits to Consumer

(a) Increased Productivity.

(b) Better values.

(c) Deliveries at proper time.

(2) Benefits to Producers, Community and Financiers

(a) Company can earn more money and can pay better wages.

(b) There will not be any interrupted employment as it was in old days, because at that time there was no planning and hence at the time of rush orders the owners used to empty more persons.

(c) Job security.

(d) Improved working conditions and thus increase satisfaction.

(e) To the investors there is a security of money and adequate returns.

(f) Under such circumstances, the community gets the economic and social stability.

(3) Benefits to the Nation

(a) Security.

(b) Prosperity.

Structure of Production Planning and Control Department

The nature of production and control department can be divided in the three broad categories *viz.* centralised, decentralised and through progress men.

A centralised production planning and control department is headed by the manager who is responsible to the works manager.

(a) To determine manufacturing methods

(b) Prepares operation sheets and instruction cards

(c) Determines time standards

Such system provides better co-ordination of production and service activities with a better basis of taking corrective action. But a centralised production planning and control department cannot have direct knowledge about the actual conditions in the production system and may not be able to adapt quickly to changing local conditions. There is also a possibility of clash with areas of line authority.

Under decentralised production planning and control system each foreman has his own group functioning under his authority. In such set up the foreman is well used with local conditions of the environment and can have complete control over work assignments and various operations. But there may not be any co-ordination over the planning and control activities among different departments which may adversely effect the fulfilment of overall objective.

Control through progress men consists in placing a number of work orders under the responsibility of a progress man who chases each order through the various departments till it is ready for delivery. In such system the progress man can assign priority to an order to expedite urgent orders. But there is limited scope for overall planning and co-ordination and when work load approaches plant capacity, system suffers from extreme stresses.

Scope of Production Planning and Control

(1) Liaison with purchase department for efficient and effective procurement of inputs.

(2) Liaison with marketing department to determine the nature and magnitude of the output.

(3) To plan the layout of the operations indicating in detail the places/points in the system where various production activities/operations are to be performed.

(4) Establishment of time schedules for various stages/levels of production by setting up necessary standards.

(5) Ensuring continuous inspection over the quality of goods manufactured.

(6) Instituting necessary controls to complete the work according to schedule.

Levels of Production Planning

Production Planning can be done at three levels namely Factory Planning, Process Planning and Operation Planning.

(1) Factory Planning

At this level of planning, the sequence of work tasks is planned in terms of building, machines and equipment required for manufacturing the desired goods and services. The relationship of workplaces in terms of departments is also planned at this stage taking into consideration the space available for the purpose. This stage deals with Plant location and layout.

(2) Process Planning

There are many operations involved in factory planning for transforming the inputs into some desired end product. In process planning these operations are located and the sequence of these operations in the production process is determined. Plans are also made for the layout of work centres in each process.

(3) Operation Planning

It is concerned with planning. The details of the methods required to perform each operation *viz.* selection of work centres, designing of tools required for various operations. Then the sequences of work elements involved in each operation are planned. Specifications about each transfer, work centres, nature of tools required and the time necessary for the completion of each operation are prescribed.

THE NEED FOR PRODUCTION PLANNING AND CONTROL

Our customer is our king. It is the customers' order which sets the wheel of our production rolling. Customers' orders give us work. Customers' order give jobs to our workmen. And customer's orders give dividents to our shareholders. Customers therefore, must be kept satisfied. Only satisfied customers give us new orders. Only satisfied customers give us repeat orders. Only satisfied customers get us orders from new customers. A firm which aims at customer's satisfaction is never short of business.

How to keep a customer satisfied?

What does a new customer expect from us?

What does an old customer expect from us?

A customer whether, new or old, expects five things from us:

— Reliable yet reasonable delivery commitment.

— To be advised in case of delay.

— To be helped when he is in difficulty.

— Consistent good quality of products.

— Competitive rates.

How does production planning and control enable the firm to achieve these objectives?

(1) Reliable Yet Reasonable Delivery Commitment. The first thing that a customer expects from his supplier is to make reliable yet reasonable delivery commitment and then to stick to it. To give a delivery commitment is not an easy task. It requires analysis of many a factor. The vendor must check as to what is the load on hand and how early the job can be started for the first operation, second operation, and subsequent operations. He must plan well the requirements of various factors of production. He must ascertain what materials are available, what materials need to be procured, how much time it will take to procure materials (if not available). He must check as to what cutting tools are available and what tools and guages shall have to be purchased; what jigs and fixtures shall have to be made and what time shall be required to make them; what daywise uncommitted capacity is available on company's different production facilities. Only after considering all the above aspects a delivery commitment should be made failing which the commitment is unlikely to be kept up.

To perform the above functions efficiently, production planning is a must.

Once a delivery commitment is made, the vendor must strive hard to meet the delivery commitment. To do that, he must ensure that proper instructions are given to each concerned department. He must follow up with purchase to ensure that materials are received on time and are allocated as per requirement. He must plan the activities of the tool room and do sufficient follow up to ensure that jigs and fixtures are made available to production on time. Also production aids—blue prints, materials, jigs and fixtures, measuring instruments, cutting tools etc. must be issued at the right time and in the right quantities. Lastly, he must see that jobs are started and completed as per plan. Action on these lines, which forms control aspect of production, planning and control, therefore, is necessary to meet delivery commmitments. Many a buyers periodically mail revised "delivery schedules" to their vendors wherein they revise the quantities of some of the items ordered on the vendor. Such amendments will require reallocation of factors of production, procurement of additional materials, splitting up of planned batches, over time working, subcontracting of some of the items currently being made at the home plant and vise a versa. The buyer does not bother what his vendor does to adjust his new schedules. He wants his items regularly and as per dates promised. The vendor's success at such a juncture will mean a satisfied customer who is sure to stick to the company for a long time.

It can therefore be concluded that a good production, planning and control system is a must for a firm to enable it to make reliable promises and then to achieve them.

(2) To be Advised In Case of Delay. Manufacturing is never a smooth sailing. Some delays and interruptions do crop up and tend to hold the timely completion of the jobs. Some sort of reporting system is required to identify presence of the delays and interruptions. A rational approach will be to check up the progress of work, record the progress of work, compare progress against plan, identify deviations from plans, and expedite. wherever necessary to bring the progress of work in line! with the plan. This important function which is called "Progressing" is the backbone of PPC.

However, situations may arise when things are extremely beyond the control of the supplier and no amount of exertion on his part will enable him to stick to the promised date. Some of the events which are likely to upset his plans are :

* Materials required for the item(s) is (are) not received on time.
* One or more machines, required for manufacture, break down.
* Heavy process rejection due to errors in drawings and others.
* Occurence of some act(s) of God such as flood, fire, etc.
* Absence of key operator(s).
* Major accident in the factory.
* Go slow, tool down strike or similar other labour problems, and
* The like.

What should the supplier do under such a situation? He just can't supply according to the schedule. One way to get a customer really mad is first not to supply on time and then not to communicate with him. And this is the second thing which the customer expect from a supplier. He excepts to be advised when the supplier cannot supply as per promise.

Will not the buyer go wild on receiving the supplier's letter ? Yes he will ! He is sure to explode and use all the filthy language on the earth. And then next perhaps the customer will like to know when the supplier is going to ship next. And this date - second date - the supplier just can't afford to miss unless he wants his customer to break away from him. To ensure that the second date is kept up, the supplier should knwo how far the things have gone bad and how much time it will take to bring them back to normal once again. This requires reporting mechanism, the control aspect of Production, Planning and Control.

(3) To Be Helped When in Difficulties. Thirdly, a customer wants occassional special favours. He wants his supplier to entertain his occassional rush orders when he (the customer) is in difficulty. A rush order, however, should not be accomodated at the cost of regular orders. Some rush orders could to taken up, but too many rush orders on the other hand may upset the whole plan and result in broken deliveries of others. Here also the supplier requires planning. At the first instant he should keep his planning little flexible so as to be able to accomodate certain number of rush orders, and at the second instant he must know how many such rush orders can be accomodated without disturbing the basic plan. This is what good production, planning and control aims at.

(4) Consistent Good Quality. Quality control is said to be an integrated function. Quality of end product depends on the quality of its inputs which may be either in the form of quality of purchased items, or quality of items manufactured at the home plant. Quality Control department no doubt has the over all responsibility of quality of raw materials, bought out components, tools, gauges and supplies of purchased items, but the responsibility of quality of items manufactured at the home plant also lies on that department who lays down the manufacturing process. The quality of piece parts depends on how a "process man" does the quality planning in his manufacturing plans:

Undoubtedly, the quality of the job depends on:

(a) proper operations and their sequence. Only proper operations and their logical sequence can keep the defectives at its minimum.

(b) the right selection of the machine. Good quality can be achieved only on machines which have the right process capability.

(c) right selection of cutting tools, jigs and fixtures etc. Good quality jobs cannot be made with unsatisfactory tools.

(d) proper location of inspection stages. Quality manufacture demands that defectives are removed and unnecessary costs are prevented from being expended in further operations.

(e) revisions in the manufacturing process based on the results of the pilot lot. Revisions in the process is made with the object of learning from our mistakes and avoiding the faults in future.

Production Planning and Control is essential methods which will ensure selection of right equipment right tooling and enable the shop to make the simplest but in the fool proof way.

(5) Competitive Rates. The vendor share of buyer's total requirements also depends on the former's price. The lower the vendor's rates, the higher is his share of the buyer's total requirements.

There have been numerous cases where good orders were lost because of rate differences. Vendor should not take up order which does not give him reasonable profit but at the same time he should realise that he cannot be paid higher to compensate for the inefficiencies of his operations. To be on sound footing, such vendor must keep its costs at their minimum so that desired profit can be achieved.

We, as vendors, must cast off the age old concept of treating profit as a surplus arising out of the deduction of cost from price. Competition is growing fast. Quite a few vendors have already started competing with each other to retain maximum business. Time has changed and therefore we must change our concept of cost. A rational approach is that each vendor must work out his own allowable cost or the desired profit considering the price as fixed (maximum price that the customer is willing to pay).

Price – Desired Profit = Allowable cost

Having known the allowable cost, the supplier must evolve the manufacturing process to contain his costs within the allowable limits. To do that, waste of time in its various forms must be reduced to their minimum. The following seven costs can be cut through better Production, Planning & Control.

(a) Waiting Time. "Time waste is the easiest of all wastes and yet the hardest to correct because it does not litter the floor" remarked Henry Ford once. This statement is as true as death. Excessive waiting time is really a big hazard - a big expense.

A closer look around the department can enable us to spot some of these time leaks. We will find some of our operatives waiting at the tool crib. Some may be waiting for raw materials. Other may be waiting for the tools to be sharpened. Yet there may be some waiting for prints and instructions for the next job. These little time leaks, if considered in isolation, do not mean much but too many of these can certainly add to a large amount, may be larger than few big ones. To reduce waiting time, each operative and each supervisor must know what the next job is. Necessary tools, gauges prints, materials etc. must be kept ready well in advance.

(b) Hunting Time. "An operative in an engineering concern spends more than 2% of his time in wandering or looking for the things he needs to do the jobs." We will find them sharing their tools with other operators. Lot of operatives's time is wasted in searching for straps, clamps, bolts, nuts and washers. We can reduce this ineffective time by fixing right place for everything and providing our men a set of everything they need well in advance of starting of the job. Good production planning and control can convert some of these time leaks into useful production hours.

(c) Stalling. "Workers usually try to coincide the end of their jobs with the end of the day by stretching the jobs in hand." A worker usually tends to delay the completion of job so that he does not need to start fresh job towards the end of the day. Why start now, I won't be able to finish it in my shift" is the commonest attitude among our workmen. We can somewhat avoid this by setting the system where by each workman knows when he is expected to complete the job-in-hand and what is his next work assignment. Scientific scheduling can do this!

(d) Interrupted Workloads. "Unplanned over lapping of operations lead to idle machines and job split-ups."

Interrupted work from the previous operation not only results in partial utilisation of the next machine but also seriously undermine morale of the shop. Careful production planning can prevent such unnecessary losses of time.

(e) Costly Overtime. "Poor planning is the common cause of overtime." Prolonged overtime is not merely the extra strain on the finance of the company but means much more. Excessive overtime and hence extra time earnings make the workers accustomed to a new standard of living and any action on the part of the management to reduce or discontinue overtime is disliked by the workers. It is just not palatable to them. The mere knowledge that the company intends to do away with the overtime make the workers slow their pace and in general waste time. The jobs under such situations start falling behind the schedule and thus the company is forced to overtime working. It then becomes a vicious circle and once caught in it the company cannot come out of it. The result is of anybody's guess. The workers go on getting overtime day after day and month after month and thus worsening the already worsened situations. The overall effect is thus the lowering of efficiency-first because of accumulation of fatigue and secondly because of slackening of pace to get overtime. The need for overtime arises due to.

* Unrealistic delivery dates without there being any leeway for unforeseeables.
* Acceptance of too many rush orders.
* frequent delays in receipt of materials.
* Excessive machine breakdowns.
* Lack of qualified workers.
* Insufficient manpower or machines.

The majority of the causes cited above can be avoided by proper planning.

(f) Unproductive Time of the Machines. "Productivity of factors of production to a large extent depends on the quality of supervision". The prime responsibility of the supervisory staff is to ensure that the company's machines work for maximum time and the loss of time due to different reasons is kept at minimum. The productive time of the machines is lost due to weaknesses in one or more of the following supervisory functions:

* Operators' unauthorised absenteeism and the failure of the supervisor to make substitute arrangement.
* Enforced idle time of the machine for want of smooth movement of materials on the shop floor.
* Lack of effective supervision which cause idle time of the machines since operators merely shop around, visit unnecessarily places of personal needs, steal longer tea breaks, resume work 5-10 minutes late in the beginning of the shift and after lunch break and close work 10-15 minutes prior to lunch break and the end of the shift.

Wastage in factors of production enumerated above occurs not only because of poor quality of supervision but also when the supervisory staff gets burdened with routine functions namely materials planning, tools planning, movement of materials on the shop floor, machine loading, expediting etc. PPC relieves supervisory staff from clerical functions, and thereby enable them to spend more time for training of workmen, proper allocation of work to workmen, trouble shooting, and maintaining shop discipline.

(g) Higher Overhead Costs. Production planning and control, as concluded in the preceeding paragraph, relieves supervisory staff from a number of clerical responsibilities. Supervisory staff, therefore, gets more time for training of workmen, trouble shooting, maintaining shop discipline and improvising methods of work. At the same time they can handle more workmen and more machines, which reduces supervisory overheads.

(h) Poor Labour Efficiency. "Workmen who get accustomed to working intermittently never work continuously".

This is no exaggeration. It is a fact based on human physchology and it holds good not only for workmen but also for supervisory personnel. Many a times in large companies, jobs get delayed due to irregular deliveries of materials, interruptions at the preceeding operations, lack of smooth flow of materials, delayed instructions from. the supervisors improper loading and scheduling, lack of sufficient volume of work etc. and as a result workmen are either rendered idle or are utilised for part of the time. And if such delays are frequent, workmen get accustomed to partial working and thus the efficiency on the shop floor suffers a set back. They even do not work continuously when sufficient work is available.

PPC can prevent such a situation by exercising better control on availability of tools and materials, monitoring a close control on work-in-progress on the shop floor, re-allocating jobs from other machines by shifting idle operator to other machine, changing the route, ensuring smooth movement of materials from and into the different shops, and reporting cases of idle time of men and machines to enable the scheduler to release new jobs.

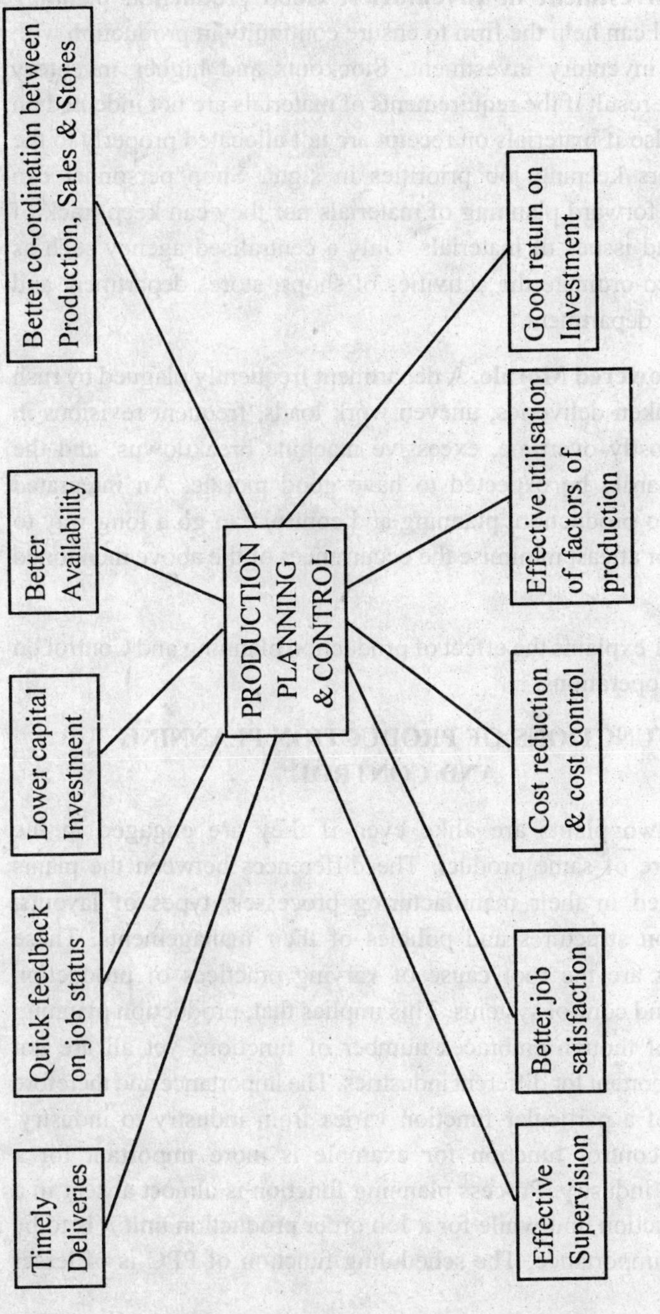

Fig. 1 : Effect of Production Planning & Control

(i) Investment in Inventories. Good production planning and control can help the firm to ensure continuity in production with minimum inventory investment. Stockouts and higher inventory investment result if the requirements of materials are not indented on time and also if materials on receipt are not allocated properly to the work orders keeping job priorities in sight. Shop personnel can neither do forward planning of materials nor they can keep track of receipts and issues of materials. Only a centralised agency such as PPC can co-ordinate the activities of shops, stores department and the buying department.

(j) Lowered Morale. A department frequently plagued by rush orders, broken deliveries, uneven work loads, frequent revisions in process, costly overtime, excessive machine breakdowns, and the like can hardly be expected to have good morale. An integrated approach to production, planning and control can go a long way to eliminate or atleast minimise the occurrences of the above mentioned losses.

Fig. 1 explains the effect of production planning and Control on the firm's operations.

FUNCTIONS OF PRODUCTION PLANNING AND CONTROL

No two plants are alike even if they are engaged in the manufacture of same product. The differences between the plants are reflected in their manufacturing processes, types of layouts, organisation structures and policies of their managements. These differences are the root cause of varying practices of production planning and control systems. This implies that, production planning and control though embraces number of functions yet all are not equally important for different industries. The importance and therefore the need of a particular function varies from industry to industry. Materials control function for example is more important for a processing industry. Process planning function is almost absent in a flow production unit while for a Job order production unit it is to be of crucial importance. The scheduling function of PPC is of lesser importance for a mass production unit while it is very important in a intermittent manufacture. The allotment of function to the PPC department therefore, depends on the type of industry. It can, nowever, be concluded without exaggeration that it is the job shop company which requires the most detailed and the most sophisticated system of PPC. It is this type of industry which requires almost every function of PPC. To highlight the areas of responsibilities of PPC, we must consider a job order production unit and analyse in general the various activities that are performed from the receipt of an enquiry until the despatch of goods to the customers. Such a detailed listing of activities will enable us to pinpoint the areas of responsibilities of the PPC department.

(1) The Sales Enquiry. The production procedure starts with the receipt of a sales enquiry in the sales department. The enquiry may be accompanied by a sample or a blue print, or any other suitable quality description so as to give an idea of what is required by the buyer. The sales enquiry may be received either,

* due to the efforts of the company's salesmen or agents, or
* in response to the company's advertisements, or
* from an old customer for new items, or
* from a new customer when directed by the old customer, or
* as a result of company's own reputation for doing a particular type of work.

(2) Technical Feasibility. The original sales enquiry or its copy together with the attachments is forwarded to Engineering Department or Product Development or to a senior technical person in the company in the absence of any formal department to check on its technical feasibility.

The enquiry is studied for materials, limiting dimensions, heat treatment details and accuracies to establish whether or not the enquiry is for one of standard items of the company or it is for the one which shall require to be manufactured. For the items to be manufactured to customer's design, the enquiry is further studied to establish whether or not:

* the company's facilities have spare capacity.
* the company's available facilities are capable of doing the job within the desired accuracies.
* the materials required for the items are available/can be procured within the reasonable period/special materials which can not be procured.
* The special tooling (if any) required to manufacture the job is available.
* The quantity required by the customer is of interest to us.

The enquiry which is found infeasible is returned with a relevant remark back to sales department who in turn informs the customer accordingly.

The enquiry that is found feasible is translated into the rough design by the Engineering or Product Development Department. Only rough design is prepared at this stage since no actual order has yet been received. The order may or may not materialise and hence it is advisable to limit the expenses to the minimum.

(3) Routing and Tentative Delivery Period. The Routing section of PPC translates the rough design into rough manufacturing plan. It prepares the bills of materials, performs make-or-buy analysis, determines the operations necessary for each part to be made at the company's own plant; decides the machine tool for each operation; and estimates time (set-up as well as processing time) for each operation.

The scheduling section of PPC then decides on the tentative delivery period after checking its load charts.

(4) Cost Estimates. The costing department works out the requirements of raw materials for each part. Machining cost is determined based on estimates of operation wise timings and machine hour rates. Tooling cost is estimated for both standard as well as special tools. Packaging and packing charges are also computed and added separately.

(5) Quotation. The information from costing group is passed on to the sales department to prepare quotation after adding necessary profit. This quotation is sent to the buyer either through post or is handed over personally.

(6) Receipt of Purchase Order. If the company's quotation is approved of, the potential buyer sends his purchase order. The purchase order is received by the sales department. The sales department scrutinises the contents of the purchase order so as to ensure that the rate and other terms and conditions are in accordance with those stated in the quotation. Once the purchase order is in order, the sales department raises a document called SALES ORDER or ORDER ACCEPTANCE. One copy of the order acceptance is forwarded to the Production, Planning and Control Department and another copy to the Engineering Department.

(7) Engineering Drawings. The Engineering Department on receipt of the copy of the order acceptance transposes the rough design into manufacturing drawings. The preparation of the manufacturing drawings involves making drawings for every part. The engineering department also prepares part lists.

(8) Materials Control. All the information developed by the engineering department is sent to PPC department. The PPC department then works on the part-lists supplied by the Engineering Department and establishes the requirements of stock items (standard items) and raw materials. The stores is then informed of the requirement of raw materials and parts and on the dates on which they are required. The dates are determined by the PPC after refering to the delivery commitments (if already made). The stores in turns checks on the availability of the required items, reserves their quantities against work-orders (wherever they are available), and raises purchase indents for the items that are out of stock.

(9) Routing. The routing section of Production, Planning and Control next determines the proper routing the sequence of operations and the machines to be used.

(10) Scheduling. The scheduling section of PPC refers to its load and schedule chart and fixes up the start and completion dates of each part and each operation keeping promised delivery date in mind.

(11) Dispatching. The order and instructions prepared by the department are released to the concerned supervisors as their authority to perform the work according to the method outlined in the route sheet and to a predetermined schedule.

(12) Progressing. The progressing cell of PPC collects manufacturing shops, records progress of compares progress against the plan.

(13) Expediting or Follow-up. Manufacturing activity is not a smooth activity. Unexpected delays and interruptions crop up. Special efforts are required to eliminate these delays and keep the rate of production upto the schedule.

DIMENSIONS OF PRODUCTION CAPACITY

An essential part of aggregate planning is a comprehensive understanding of each production system's capacities. Of particular importance are the answers to the following questions:

(i) How Much of Each Production Resource is Available? Production capacity in each time period may be constrained by factors such as the number of workers or the number of machines.

(ii) How Much Capacity is Provided by Each Type of Resource? The amount of resources required to produce a single product allows the translation of demand into production capacity needs. Labour standards (labour-hours per product) and machine standards (machine-hours per product) are commonly used to translate demand into the number of workers and machines needed.

(iii) At What Step in Production do We Determine Capacity? In product-focused production, capacity may be determined by the gateway operation, or the first operation in a production line. In process\focused production, capacity may be determined by a bottleneck operation, or an operation with the least capacity for a product. In other types of production, capacity may be determined by the number of labour-hours or machine-hours in a particular production department or an entire factory.

(iv) How Much does it Cost to Scale Capacities Up or Down? The cost of hiring, laying off, and recalling employees, for example, can affect plans for providing production capacity.

TOOL ENGINEERING JIG AND FIXTURE DESIGN

Tool design is the designing of tools for the most effective and economical operation. Although it is one of the most important areas of production manufacturing engineering. Tool design is overlooked by almost all the industrial curricula because it is so large and complex (and often an art as opposed to a science) that it would be very difficult to cover this subject adequately.

Similarly, jig and fixture design is an important phases of production manufacturing engineering passed by in many industrial engineering curricula for the same reasons. A fixture is a design used to hold and locate a workpiece. The vice found in home workshops is a simple example of a fixture. In highly repetitive and exacting work, fixture design can be very important. A jig is similar to a fixture except that it also guides the tool into the work piece. Jig and fixture must be designed for each unique application. Consequently, 'the designer must be highly creative and knowledgeable in the area.

PROGRAMME ENGINEERING

Programme engineering is synonymous with production planning and control. The output of methods planning are process sheets, route cards and jig and tool orders. Taking into account the expected date of availability of tools as advised by tool planning and material control, programme engineering releases job cards. Programme engineering comprises production control shop progress, material control and programme evaluation.

IMPORTANCE OF PRODUCTION PLANNING

The success and growth of any organisation mainly depends on planning. In present world there is tough competition, rapid development technology and quick changes in human behaviour and daily requirements. Due to these factors there is lot of uncertainty associated with every system and to counterbalance it, production planning becomes a valuable phenomenon.

Koontz and O'Donnel have emphasised that "Planning may be likened to navigation. The navigator lays out a plan and sets a course towards an objective. But his job is not completed by doing so. Instead, he constantly reaches his position as he proceeds towards his goal, modifying his plan as errors or unforeseen circumstances prove that his course is leading to some point other than the goal sought".

Through production planning most appropriate objectives for an enterprise can be determined. There can be a number of alternative choices for the enterprise and production planning measures can be applied to select the most appropriate set of alternatives taking into consideration the resources of the enterprise. Mathematical techniques can be used to determine the optimum choice when the situation is normal and certain, but in the case of uncertainties associated with the phenomenon planning should be done with provision of modification to meet out the risks.

Planning ensures most efficient resources *viz.* material, capital, and labour. It tries to distribute the work load in such a manner that there is uniform use of resources during peak as well as dull periods of demand for goods and services. Planning provides basis for effective production control. Planning formulates the production schedule and fixes the targets in terms of time and effort for each operation *i.e.* the work standards are formulated. The control operations can be applied to measure the planned performance of the operations. Thus it is evident that planning occupies an important place in management of production process. The level of performance as well as the success of an enterprises depends on effective planning. Following are the main characteristics of a good planning procedure :

(i) It should have a well-defined objective.

(ii) It should be simple and easy to apply in practice with flexibility to adjust in changing situations.

(iii) Reliable and up-to-date information should be available for planning the process.

(iv) It should be capable of laying down appropriate standards and targets for effective control of the operations.

(v) It should be based on sound decision making principles.

LINE BALANCE (BALANCING)

The balancing of operations in terms of equal times and in terms of the time required to meet the desired rate of production is the problem of line balance. It is the part and parcel of line production. The desired rate of production is converted to a time per work station, that is called by various engineers the balancing factor, balancing time, cycle time or station time. This balancing factor or station time is equal to the reciprocal of the rate of production that is it equals one divided by the rate of production.

Perfect balance is rarely achieved, there is always some extra time in atleast one operation. However, an operator with idle time to balance may often be assigned additional work not necessary to his operation, such as handling material to the line, extra inspection of his work, applying lubricants, label or tag. Because of the difficulty of dividing machine operations, it is far harder to balance forming or fabrication lines than assembly lines, were the assembly time can be split at many places and the workers more readily.

To balance lines effectively, good, reliable, pre-determined time data should be available. A great deal of line balancing has been done without this very valuable and flexible aid, using direct time studies. The problem however, with using some direct studies is that when making changes and testing different line balances, one does not always have the time study element for the particular configuration desired. Therefore, the method must be actually performed by someone, and time studies must be made to develop the correct standard time.

Mechanics of Balancing

Balancing a line involves establishing a relationship among:

(i) The rate of production.

(ii) The operations necessary and their required sequence.

(iii) The time necessary to perform each operation and preferably each element of operation.

These become prerequisites for the line to be set up, it must be designed for a given rate of production; for it to operate as a unit, the operation time must be such as under as methods time measurement, standard data and machine capacity come into their own here. They are fundamental to establishing a balance line, except in those cases where an overall time is estimated and the workers are left to balance out the operations themselves.

Steps in Balancing

The steps in balancing involves the following:

(i) Lists the required operations or elements there of.

(ii) List them in sequence.

(iii) Show the operation or elemental time for each, indicating which is the controlling or bottleneck operation.

(iv) Adjust operation by combining or dividing operations or changing the methods indicated above so as to get a total time for each operation that is equal to the balancing factor or station time.

(v) Draw diagram, or otherwise put down on paper the operations times and manpower of the balanced line, and be sure it is understood by operating foremen or leadmen.

This is called 'paper balance' and should be worked out before the line is laid out. After the line is installed, rebalancing or readjusting the balancing is common, the extent of this being directly related to how accurately the original balancing was done.

ASSEMBLY PROGRESS

This sub section receives the job cards from assembly scheduling. In order to make an assembly, the concerned jig should be free and all the parts should be available in the kit store. Assembly progress checks the availability of parts well in advance of loading an assembly in order to identify the shortage of parts, complies a shortage list and sends it to manufacturing progress. Assembly progress performs the following tasks:

(i) Loads the Jigs.

(ii) Moves assemblies from jig to jig.

(iii) Arranges for inspection.

(iv) Credits completed items to stores.

(v) Prepares a list of assemblies-behind-schedule.

(vi) Dispatches spares to the customer through shipping department.

CAPACITY PLANNING

Capacity Planning is the process of estimating requirements of machines and men to meet targets of production. Capacity planning considers for each machine standard labour hours, labour efficiency to compensate for sub-standard performances, plant efficiency factor to compensate for the time that may be lost due to unavoidable delays and interruptions (*e.g.* scheduling delays, machine break-downs, preventive maintenance, operator's unauthorised obsenteeism, power failure, manufacturing difficulties, etc. converting requirements of machine hours into "equivalent number of machines", evolving decisions as to what proportion of the total requirement is to be sub-contracted and finally taking decisions to meet short term and long term requirement of machines.

INPUTS OF "MACHINE CAPACITY" PLANNING

(a) Items to be Manufactured. The list of the jobs currently being processed and the jobs proposed to be added into the near future. The most common source of this information is the company's "bill of material" of each product.

(b) Standard Output for Each Job and Each Operation. The second important information is the output standard for each operation to be performed on each job. The accuracy of the output standard is equally important. The most common source of this information is the "route-sheet" or "process-sheet". It not only gives the list of operations to be performed but also the machine tool(s) to be employed and the standard time for each indicated operation.

(c) Quantity to be Processed of Each Job. The quantity to be manufactured of each item on the list is equally important.

(d) Labour Efficiency Against Output Standards. Output standards are set by the industrial engineering department considering normal operators and normal pace of working. All workers do not meet these standards even if the standards are equitable. Apprentices and old workmen simply are not able to attain them. Over and above these, there is generally a group of "deliberate slackers", "bossy", "organised class" of workmen who set their own standards. And in lieu of substandard performance, requirements of men and machine hours should be corrected by dividing the standard hours by labour efficiency. This implies that if in total 400 standard milling hours are required per month, then we need equivalent of 400/0.80 = 500 hours if the labour efficiency in our milling section is 80%.

The labour efficiency figure changes from machine to machine and from company to company. Actual figure of labour efficiency must be considered to compute capacity requirements. Colourful figures may please the management but will reflect ultimately in broken deliveries, frequent job split ups, over time working, nervous breakdowns of the senior staff, and lower morale on the shop.

(e) Plant Efficiency. Plant efficiency factor considers enforced idle time of the machines because of scheduling deleys, machine breakdowns, preventive maintenance etc. Plant efficiency factor varies from equipment to equipment and company to company. These range generally from 0.50 to 0.95. For example, if total 600 grinding machine hours are required per month, then we need equivalent of 600/0.80 = 750 hours if our plant efficiency factor is 0.80.

The plant efficiency factor can be established by PPC either by estimation or by conducting work sampling studies.

(f) Multiplicity of the Shifts. Multiplicity of the shifts implies the number of shifts that the firm should run on each working day. Single shifts increase investment while multiple shifts increase labour costs and supervision costs. Wage premium equivalent to 20 to 25% is common for third shifts. Ordinarily the productivity is low in the second shift and much lower in third shift while losses due to defectives are higher in multiple shifts.

The decisions concerning multiple shifts, therefore, is not a simple question. Much depends on the relative importence of the building and equipment investment costs and labour costs which varies from industry to industry.

In general, multiple shifts, are economical for industries such as steel, chemicals, oil refineries, and other having large investments in buildings and equipment per workman while single or double shifts are desirable for those industries which have low capital investment per workman. The right approach, however, is to conduct economic analysis for each situation.

(g) Sub-contracting. Sub-contracting is the process of off-loading some of the firm's manufacturing requirements to outside vendors to design peculiar to the firm for economic reasons to angument existing manufacturing facilities. Sub-contracting undoubtedly is the most convenient and the fastest method of meeting the firm's investment and labour costs at minimum. The decisions to subcontract however, must be backed by the systematic and careful cost analysis: cost comparison between the costs to make and the costs to buy. Such an analysis is specially significant where new capital equipment is involved.

(h) Management Policies. Some typical management policies that influence capacity planning are the decisions :

(i) not to invest in machines where sub-contracting is possible.

(ii) to perform critical operations which are liable for rejections at the home plant.

(iii) to restrict multiple shifts to two except for the equipments which involve heavy capital investments.

(iv) to run semi-automatic, automatic and other equipments deviod of possibility of rejection on 3 shifts basis.

(v) to buy another machine as soon as the utilisation of the existing machine(s) exceeds the pre-fixed figure (say 80%) on two shift basis.

(vi) not to consider for availability those machines which have functionally degraded.

(vii) to maintain sufficient inventory of consumable as well as replacement spares for the machines to which no substitutes are available.

PROCEDURE TO ESTIMATION OF REQUIREMENTS OF MACHINES

The basic procedure is as under:

(a) Collect bill of materials and route sheets of the items to be processed at the company's own plant.

(b) Prepare work load data sheet for each work centre (machine tool group). The work load data sheet should give the list of jobs to be processed on machine tool, operations to be performed for each job and the standard time for each indicated operation. For accurate estimates standard time may be entered for 100 nos.

(c) Estimate and record average requirements per period (per month) of each job listed on the load data sheet.

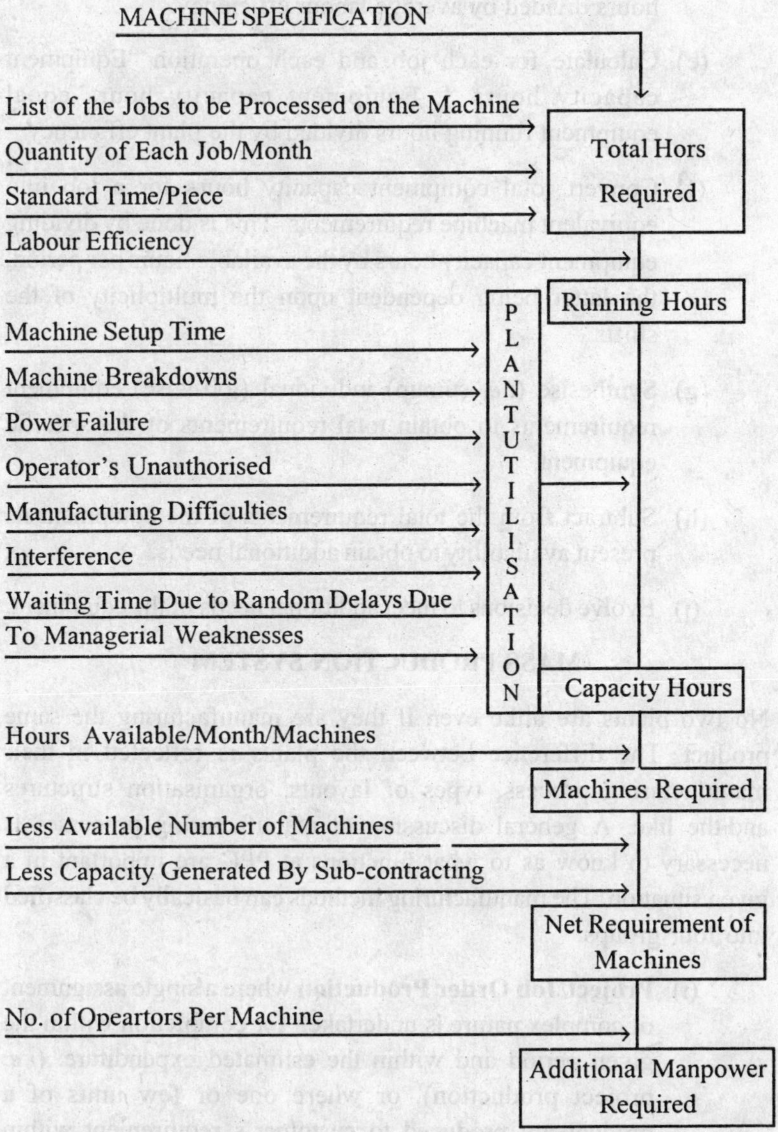

Fig. The block diagram of the steps to the determination of capacity needs.

(d) Calculate for each job and for each operation " Equipment Running Hours". Equipment running hours equal standard hours divided by average labour efficiency.

(e) Calculate for each job and each operation "Equipment capacity hours ". Equipment capacity hours equal equipment running hours divided by the plant efficiency.

(f) Convert total equipment capacity hours for a job into equivalent machine requirements. This is done by dividing equipment capacity hours by the available hours per period, the latter being dependent upon the multiplicity of the shifts.

(g) Synthesise (*i.e.* sumup) individual (job-wise) equipment requirements to obtain total requirements of the specific equipment.

(h) Subtract from the total requirements of the equipment its present availability to obtain additional needs.

(i) Evolve decisions to meet additional needs of the equipment.

MASS PRODUCTION SYSTEM

No two plants are alike even if they are manufacturing the same product. The difference between the plants is reflected in their manufacturing process, types of layouts, organisation structures and the like. A general discussion of manufacturing processes is necessary to know as to what functions at PPC are important in a given situation. The manufacturing methods can basically be classified into four groups.

(i) **Project/Job Order Production** where a single assignment of complex nature is undertaken for completion within the given period and within the estimated expenditure. (*i.e.* project production), or where one or few units of a product are produced to customer's requirement within the given date and within the price fixed prior to the contract. (*i.e.* Jobbing production)

(ii) **Batch Production** where limited quantity of each type of product is authorised for manufacture at a time.

(iii) **Mass and Flow Production** where a production run is conducted either on a single machine or on a number of machines, arranged according to the sequence of operations and several number of a product are manufactured at a time and stocked in warehouse awaiting sales.

(iv) **Continuous or Process Production** where production run is conducted for an infinite period.

The above mentioned manufacturing methods are now detailed below :

JOB ORDER PRODUCTION

Job order production is characterised by the manufacture of one or few numbers of a single product designed and manufactured strictly to customer's specifications, within the given period and within the price fixed prior to the contract. Some typical examples of industries engaged in jobbing production are; general repair shops; fabricators; special purpose machine tool manufacturers; workshop to manufacture jigs and fixtures for other units; building contractors; tailoring shops manufacturing made-to-measure suite of clothes; manufacturers of ships, cranes, furnaces, turbo-generators, pressure vessels; and others manufacturing articles made to customers orders.

Characteristics of Job Order Production

(1) Small Production Runs. Jobbing production is characterised by the manufacture of one or few pieces of a product at a time under a separate contract. The production is made strictly to customers' specifications.

(2) Flow of Materials. The flow of materials and components between different stages of manufacture is highly discontinuous due to imbalance operation wise work content.

(3) Manufacturing Cycle Time. A considerable amount of pre-planning and organisation is necessary in such a venture. Relatively long delays occur at the assembly as well as at the materials processing stages due to lack of materials or components, imbalanced work flow, design changes, design errors detected during manufacture, inaccurate work measurements, etc. which tend to lengthen the manufacturing cycle time. At times, the time needed to design the product exceeds its manufacturing time.

(4) Layout of Plant & Equipment. Plant and equipment is designed or procured and arranged to obtain maximum flexibility. General purpose machines and handling equipments capable of performing variety of operations with minimum set-up times are installed in lieu of variety in products. The machines are arranged to give process layout—layout by function. Similar machines capable of doing similar type of operations, are grouped together and kept at one place; milling machines are placed at another place; drilling machines are kept at third place, gear cutting machines are located at fourth place; and so on and so forth. Each group of machines is usually designated as a work centre or a section or a shop.

The grouping of machines gives a lot of flexibility in loading and scheduling. Temporary machine breakdowns and operator's absenteeism can be taken care of by shifting jobs to another machine or shifting operators from less important jobs to important jobs.

(5) Skill of Labour. The labour force is usually very skilled-highly qualified trade apprentices who are expected to work from minimum instructions. Instructions regarding "what to make" are issued in the form of specifications while instructions as to "how to manufacture" are usually oral. The workmen being highly skilled are expected to work independently and display a great deal of initiative and judgement. They are required to set up their own machines and prepare their own special tools or production aids in order to further the manufacture of a part or a assembly.

(6) Quality of Supervision. Highly competent general engineers are engaged as foremen in the base workshop and a group of site engineers, practical men, with thorough training, capable of taking independent charge of each contract are employed to work at site.

Therefore, these engineers (supervisors) in a jobbing production are the resevoir of job knowledge. The supervisor besides being able administrator is expected to improvise and determine best work methods, determine tool requirements, select the best process and provide management with reliable estimates of labour and materials for specific orders. The span of control the number of workmen to be supervised by a supervisor—is kept low because of technical nature of the job.

(7) Work-In-Progress. The work-in-progress inventory in a jobbing production is generally very large as detailed scheduling and progress control in this type of production is economically infeasible. For various reasons, jobs get delayed causing temporary work shortages. To overcome work shortages and keep men and machines busy, more work is released to the shops which in turn increases work-in-progress.

(8) Functions of Production Planning And Control. The success of jobbing production mainly depends on the ability of the engineer incharge of the contract.

* Materials are indented and purchased on receipt of orders unlike in batch or mass production where material requirements are planned well in advance.
* Tools control function is simple. Standard tools are stocked while special tools are either made on the shop floor by the operators or purchased on request from supervisor.
* Process planning activity is almost absent. Drawings and specifications are directly given to the supervisor who is expected to decide work methods, select optimum process, fix up machine tools to be used and estimate time required to complete an operation.
* The scheduling activity is more or less decentralised. A schedule is prepared to show the start and completion date of each major component of the product. Job tickets giving completion date of each component are raised and

given to the shop. The activity of day to day scheduling is left to the individual shop supervisor.

* Progressing function is relatively very simple. Day to day information on the progress of work on the shop floor is diffcult due to sluggish activity. Production meetings are, therefore, held to improve control. Supervisors attending these meetings are thus expected to account for job progress.

BATCH PRODUCTION

Batch production is characterised by the manufacture of a limilted number of a product (but many such quantities of different products) produced at regular intervals and stocked in warehouses as finished goods (or finished parts) awaiting sales (or withdrawl for assembly). Typical examples of batch production are : process industries such as pharmaceuticals, paints, chemicals; medium and heavy engineering industry engaged in the manufacture of electric motors, switch gears, heavy motor vehicles, internal combustion engines; manufacturers of ready made garments; manufacturing and assembly shops such as machine tools; sub-contractors which take on machining of batches of components to the drawing of a large manufacturer; etc.

The working of batch production can be understood from the following example :

A firm manufacturing tractors require axle shafts. Two axle shafts are required for each tractor. The axle shafts are made from steel forgings. 500 nos. of forgings—500 being the batch size—are faced and centred. The batch is moved from facing and centering machine to the copying lathe were the shafts are copy turned. The copy turned jobs are next moved to gear hobbing machine and then to spline hobbing machine respectively to perform gear cutting and spline cutting operations. The batch similarly undergoes further remaining operations in succession-gear shaving, heat treatment, centre lapping, straightening, cylindrical grinding, spline grinding until the final operation that is inspection.

This is a typical example of batch production. The jobs comprising the batch move from one operation to the next. No subsequent operation is performed until all the jobs have undergone the previous operation. At times, however, the subsequent operation may be started to overlap the previous operation. The items comprising the batch on completion of last operation are usually delivered to the stores. The quantity produced in a batch is usually in excess of immediate demand. More progressive organisations work out economic lot size—the quantity which strikes an optimum balance between the preparation cost and the cost of carrying inventory—for each of their major component/product.

Characteristics of Batch Production

(1) Short Runs. Batch production is also characterised by short production runs and frequent changes of set up. The equipment and the assembly set up is used for a limited number of parts or assemblies and is then changed to make a different product. The production is generally made to stock.

(2) Skill of Labour. The labour force is expected to possess skill in one specific manufacturing process : turning, milling, drilling, welding, grinding, hobbing, fitting etc.

Simpler machine set-ups may be performed by the operator but those involving complex operations are set by the separate machine setter.

(3) Quality of Supervision. The supervisors have considerable knowledge of a specific process. Supervisor in the grinding section for example, may not know about turning and drilling work but is expected to possess a fund of knowledge of different types of grinding operations.

Similarly, a supervisor in the hobbing section is expected to have sound knowledge in working of different types of hobbing machines.

(4) Extent of Supervision. The amount of supervision required in batch production is lower than that of jobbing production and is dependent on the batch size. The ratio of direct workmen to supervisors is more or less a function of batch size. The smaller the batches, the lower is the ratio of direct workers to supervisors, and vicea-versa. This is because smaller lots require the supervisors to spend a great deal of their time in allocating new work, giving instructions, follow up on the shop floor for proper movement of materials from and to the machines, identifying delays and interruptions, and arranging, in consultation with planning, work load in his section to keep his men busy.

(5) Layout of Plant & Equipment. Plant and equipment is designed or procured and arranged to obtain maximum flexibility. General purpose machines and handling equipments capable of performing variety of operations with minimum setup times are installed in lieu of variety of products. The machines are arranged to give process layout layout by function. Similar machines capable of doing similar types of operations are grouped together and kept at one place. Presses for example, are put together and kept at one place, milling machines are placed together at another place, drilling machines are kept at the third place, gear cutting machines are located at the fourth place and so on. Each group of machines is usually designated as a work centre or a section or a shop.

(6) Materials Handling. Materials handling in batch production as compared to jobbing production is small. Individual components and parts are placed in trolleys or in bins and are transported as unit loads. Materials handling may be mechanised by deploying power driven trucks.

(7) Manufacturing Cycle Time. The manufacturing cycle time is comparatively smaller than jobbing production but is much more than mass and flow production. The batches of work tend to queue up at different machines due to differing cycle times, batch sizes and sequence of operations.

(8) Work-in-Progress. Work in progress is comparatively large due to varying work content of different components, imbalances in manufacturing times, formation of queues between the machines.

(9) Flexibility of Production Schedules. Disruptions due to machine breakdowns or absenteeism do not seriously affect production as another machine can be used or another operator from another machine can be shifted.

(10) Functions of Production Planning and Control. Functions of production planning and control in a batch production are more complex than those in jobbing production or mass and flow production:

* Materials control and tools control functions are important. Scientific stock-control system needs to be used to ensure routine replenishment.
* Detailed operational layouts and route sheets are prepared for each part of the product.
* Loading and scheduling needs to be more detailed and more sophisticated since every machine requires to be individually scheduled.
* Progressing function is very important to collect information on progress of work. A separate progress card need to be maintained to record progress of each component.
* Expediting is generally necessary since jobs many a times due to imbalances in work contents tend to lag behind.

MASS AND FLOW PRODUCTION

Mass as well as flow production are characterised by the manufacture of a several number of a standard product produced and stocked in the warehouses as finished goods awaiting sales. The goods under mass production are manufactured either at a single operation or a series of operations on one machine. Typical examples of mass production units are continuous manufacturing industries such as plastic goods, sintered products, hardware; manufacture and assembly shops of automobiles, refrigerators, radios, television sets, electric fans, motors, domestic appliances etc.

Characteristics of Mass & Flow Production

(1) Flow of Material. The flow of materials is continuous and there is little or no queueing at any stage of processing.

(2) Machines and Plant Layout. Special purpose machines are used and the plant assembly stages are laid out on the basis of product layout—the layout-by-sequence.

(3) Materials Handling. Materials handling is comparatively less firstly because materials move through a short distance between stages and secondly the materials handling activity is mostly mechanised by conveyors and transfer machines.

(4) Skill of Labour. Relatively low skilled labour is employed.

(5) Manufacturing Cycle Time. The manufacturing cycle time is very short. The machine capacities are balanced by duplicating machines wherever necessary.

(6) Quality of Supervision. Supervision is relatively easier as only few instructions are necessary and that too at the start of the job.

(7) Work in Progress. Work in progress is comparatively less since the manufacturing line is balanced.

(h) Flexibility in Production Schedules. Interruptions **due to breakdowns and absenteeism seriously affect production as stoppage of one machine usually disturbs the working of other machines. Systematic maintenance and "Provisioning of stand-by-operators" are, therefore, two major management functions.**

CONTINUOUS OR PROCESS PRODUCTION

Continuous or Process production is characterised by the manufacture of a single product produced and stocked in the warehouses awaiting sales. The flexibility of such plants is almost zero as only one type of product can be produced in such plants. Typical examples of such plants are sugar, steel, cement, paper, coke, refineries, etc.

Characteristics of Continuous or Process Production

(1) Layout of Plant & Equipment. The layout of plant, shape and size of its buildings, location of services and storage yards, position of cranes and conveyors is such that material flow is unidirectional and at the steady rate. Special purpose machinery and equipment with built-in controls to measure output and regulate input are employed to suit the need.

(2) Materials Handling. Materials handling is highly machanised. Conveyor system and automatic transfer machines move materials from one stage to another.

(3) Manufacturing Cycle time. The manufacturing cycle time is almost zero. The whole plant is like one large machine wherein raw materials enter at one end and emerge as finished product at the other end.

(4) Skill of Labour. Production labour consists of semi-skilled-workmen and skilled technicians.

(5) Quality of Supervision. The supervisor in continuous production is highly qualified and is expected to possess considerable knowledge of processes involved.

(6) Work-in-Progress. The work-in-progress inventory is very small as material flow is continuous.

(7) Production Planning & Control Functions in Continuous or Process Production

* Materials control function is of crucial importance. Materials need to be planned well in advance. Scientific inventory control system is a must for such plants.
* Tools control function is almost absent because of the nature of the plant.
* Process planning activity is absolutely not required since it is the plant which decides the route.

* Scheduling activity is very simple and is merely restricted to final targets.
* Progressing and expediting functions are extremely simplified and are merely limited to recording of the final production at the end of the shift.

AGGREGATE PLANNING

The aggregate plan is made within the broad frame work of the long-range plan. Usually, the planning horizon for such plans ranges from a month to a year. The physical plant and equipment capacity would be fixed over this planning horizon. Therefore, the sales orders have to be meet by strategies like using overtime, hiring of extra staff (temporary) or layoff of such persons, carrying inventory or giving a subcontract. The intermediate planning time-horizon derives its 'intermediate' character due to the 'type' of decisions that need to be taken, given a certain framework of long-term decisions which have been taken. What the actual time span of such planning should be six months of 24 months or less than six months is dependent upon the business, technology and production system of the particular organisation.

The first step for such planning would be to make a sales forecast of demand for the intermediate range. And based on this sales forecast one has to develop the aggregate production strategy. A production aggregated plan can be developed by the following procedure:

Checking as to whether the total requirements for the forecast period are within the combined equipment and manpower capacity of the plant. If the forecasted sales requirements cannot be met by existing plant capacity including any additional capacity that can be installed within the intermediate planning period, the sales forecast may have to be scaled down to the maximum capacity that is available during the aggregate planning period.

Now the alternative production plans (aggregate) have to be made and the one that is most economical will be selected. We could have a production plan which closely follows peaks and valleys in the production requirements forecast or we could have a steady production rate equalling the average of these peaks and valleys. There could be other plans which could be combinations of these two plans.

STEPS IN AGGREGATE PLANNING

(i) Begin with a sales forecast for each product that indicates the quantities to be sold in each time period (usually weeks, months, or quarters) over the planning horizon (usually 6 months to 18 months).

(ii) Total all the individual product or service forecasts into one aggregate demand. If the products are not additive because of heterogeneous units, a homogeneous unit of measure must be selected that both allows the forecasts to be added and links aggregate outputs to production capacity.

(iii) Transform the aggregate demand for each time period into workers, materials; machines, and other elements of production capacity required to satisfy aggregate demand.

(iv) Develop alternative resource schemes for supplying the necessary production capacity to support the cumulative aggregate demand.

(v) Select the capacity plan from among the alternatives considered that satisfies aggregate demand and best meets the objectives of the organisation.

AGGREGATE PLANNING IN PRODUCTION AND OPERATIONS MANAGEMENT

Aggregate planning is necessary in POM because it provides for:

(i) Fully loaded facilities and minimises overloading and underloading, thus reducing production costs.

(ii) Adequate production capacity to meet expected aggregate demand.

(iii) A plan for the orderly and systematic change of production capacity to meet the peaks and valley of expected customer demand.

(iv) Getting the most output for the amount of resources available, which is important in times of scarce production resources.

Aggregate planning is the key to managing change in POM because the changing patterns of customer demand and the plans for providing production resources that adapt to those changes are fundamental to aggregate planning.

LEVELS OF PRODUCTION PLANNING

Production Planning can be done at three levels namely Factory Planning, Process Planning and Operation Planning.

(i) Factory Planning. At this level of planning, the sequence of work tasks is planned in terms of building, machines and equipment required for manufacturing the desired goods and services. The relationship of workplaces in terms of departments is also planned at this stage taking into consideration the space available for the purpose. This stage deals with Plant location and layout.

(ii) Process Planning. There are many operations involved in factory planning for transforming the inputs into some desired end product. In process planning these operations are located and the sequence of these operations in the production process is determined. Plans are also made for the layout of work centres in each process.

(iii) Operation Planning. It is concerned with planning. The details of the methods required to perform each operation *viz.* selection of work centres, designing of tools required for various operations. Then the sequences of work elements involved in each operation are planned. Specifications about each transfer, work centres, nature of tools required and the time necessary for the completion of each operation are prescribed.

❒

5

Scheduling

Every order whether it is from a customer or from the assembly benches must be completed on or before the contracted date (*i.e.* promised). To ensure that the delivery date is met, each component entering the assembly should be made available on time. Scheduling function of PPC makes it possible by determining starting and completion date of each of the operations listed on the process sheet. Scheduling is the process of fitting a shop order into the uncommitted time available for a machine or a group of machines required for the manufacture of the item and with in the total time which is no greater than the promised delivery period.

Scheduling has yet another objective to fulfil : to confirm or revise the tentative delivery date promised in the original quotation. At times while scheduling a work order, it is discovered that delivery date originally and tentatively promised can not be met. This may be due to materials not being available immediately or due to increased plant loading while the customer was deciding whether or not to award the quoted job to this company. Determination of the realistic delivery date can only be made after detailed and firm scheduling.

Scheduling is not as simple as it appears to be from the foregoing paragraph. The scheduling must:

* ensure maximum utilisation of the plant at minimum cost.
* ensure that requirements of manpower is optimum and is evenly distributed, there being no peaks and valleys.
* keep itself abreast of hiring, dismissals, retrenchment, holidays, leaves, etc. of the work force.

* possess upto date information regarding availability of materials, expected delivery dates, materials rejection, shortages, purchase orders cancelled etc.
* possess upto date data on each machine regarding its breakdown, availability of spares, average frequency of breakdowns, servicing and overhauling schedules, replacement schedules, etc.
* possess complete information on performance standards and their revisions, method improvement, changes in materials and machines etc.
* obtain quick feed back from shops regarding delays and interruptions which may hold up production activity.

INPUTS OF SCHEDULING

The following are the major inputs of the scheduling function:

(a) **Performance Standards.** The first and the foremost requirement of good scheduling is the availability of performance standards. The information on performance standards enables the scheduler to determine the machine capacity in order to assign required machine hours and man-hours for the various operations. Good scheduling is always possible if the time study or industrial engineering department exists in the plant. The performance standards for repetitive jobs in such plants are available and for new jobs they can be estimated from tables of synthetic standards prepared by the department.

Should this not be the case, the approximate time estimates can be prepared by breaking the task into elements and then estimating time for each manual and machine element. Simple arithmatic formulae may be made use of to compute time for each of the machine elements considering tool travel, speed, feed per revolution, number of cuts, etc.

Again if this is not possible, the scheduler can make use of past records of the same or similar jobs.

And even if it is not there, particularly in jobbing production units, cost estimates prepared for the purpose of quotations can be obtained from the sales department to be used as basis of scheduling.

And if neither time study department exists nor historical data is available, the scheduler can consult concerned production supervisors to finalise time estimates.

(b) **Unit of Measurement** refers to the unit in which the loading and scheduling is to be extended. This unit of measurement is usually different for different industries. Industries such as sugar, cement, fertilizers, foundries, steel mill etc. generally use weight (kgs/tonnes) as a unit of measurement while in textile mills, it is in length (meters). The most common unit of measurement in engineering firms is "man-hours" or "machine-hours".

(c) **Unit of loading and Scheduling** refers to the duration for which loading and scheduling should be done. The unit of loading and scheduling—scheduled start and finishing timings—depends on the company's scheduling needs and the operating cycles. This implies that scheduling should be done on daily basis if the company makes promises in days and it should be done on daily or weekly basis if promises are made in weeks.

(d) **Effective Capacity per work centre** implies effective hours available for production on a machine or on a work centre in a week, or in a month. Theoretical capacity equals number of normal working hours of that machine. Usually there are interruptions. A few examples of these interruptions are:

* Power failure
* Preventive Maintenance
* Waiting for inspection
* Operators engaged in other than production activities (functions or celebrations)
* Machine engaged for technical studies

* Tool tryouts, jigs and fixture tryouts
* Operator left work place for official discussion
* Machine breakdown (electrical or Mechanical)
* Operator absence
* Tool breakage
* Defective materials (hard material reduced speeds and feeds) or materials of specification (*e.g.* excess stock removal).
* Operator training time
* Rework
* Late start and early close
* Overtime or incentive payment collection
* Operatives' trade test.

On account of the above mentioned interruptions, the job(s) is (are) sure to fall behind schedule unless the influence of these interruptions is taken into account.

To arrive at realistic machine capacity, the theoretical capacity is multiplied by Utilisation Index. The industrial engineering department of the company can supply PPC department with such indices from their work sampling studies. In the absence of such an information, the scheduler usually assumes utilisation of 75% or 80% or a similar figure when preparing job—schedules. This is not at all a correct approach. Work-sampling studies conducted by the Industrial Engineering department usually provide rational figures of utilisation index over arbitrarily selected figures.

The effective capacity of a work centre is calculated as under :

(i) Calculate theoretical capacity per period. Theoretical capacity is obtained by multiplying number of machines by normal hours available per machine per period.

(ii) Establish utilisation index after allowing time for delays and interruptions which can not be avoided even by scientific production planning and control.

(iii) Calculate net available capacity per period by multiplying theoretical capacity by the average utilisation index.

(iv) Establish average labour performance standards. Calculate effective capacity efficiency against per period by multiplying net capacity per period by the average labour efficiency.

Such a computation may be made machine—wise and kept ready for use at the time of scheduling. The schedule time for the required quantity then can be calculated at the time of scheduling as under:

Schedule time (hrs) for required quantity:	Std. time (hrs.) per unit	×	Required quantity

(e) **Extent of Rush Orders.** Provision of rush orders is another important consideration in scheduling. No machine should be scheduled for its centpercent (100%) effective capacity because if a rush order comes in, scheduling has to be changed to allow rush order to be put through the shops. Such rush orders, if received frequently, are bound to put the company's scheduling out of gear.

The disturbance due to rush orders can be avoided by not scheduling the machine for 100% effective capacity thereby leaving some un-committed capacity per period per machine. This un-committed time is utilised to accomodate rush orders and thereby avoiding the need to alter the remainder of the scheduling.

Time needed for rush orders depends on the frequency of rush orders. Each firm should work out its own average time spent on processing rush orders.

There are different methods of accomodating rush orders:

(i) The easiest method is to leave some capacity (depending upon the average time spent on rush orders per period) unscheduled on each machine per period. This method is useful when semicentralised system of scheduling is adopted.

(ii) Another to leave scheduled method of scheduling of rush orders is un-scheduled capacity between two jobs. This method is useful when centralised system of scheduling is followed.

(f) **Over lapping of operations** is yet another useful consideration in scheduling. Over lapping of operations refers to running of a job simultaneously on more than one machine and it occurs in jobs which involve two or more operations. Over lapping of operations helps to reduce the manufacturing cycle time and hence the delivery period, to the customer.

Decision to overlap operations is a simple affair if the time per piece for the succeeding operation is equal to or more than the time per piece on the preceeding operation. Both the operations can run simultaneously. However, an interruption at the preceeding operation may cause the work of the next operation to stop, hence some time may be allowed to be elapsed between operations from the beginning of the first so that in case of delay there is already accumulation of some units ready for the operation. One or two days may be considered sufficient for the purpose.

Overlapping poses a problem when the time per piece for the succeeding operation is less than the time per piece for the preceeding operation. Elapsed time should be such that till the last piece remains to be processed at the preceeding operation, some work should be available at the next operation. The theoretical elapsed time between two consecutive operations can be worked from the following formula:

$$\begin{array}{l}\text{Theoretical}\\ \text{elapsed time}\\ \text{between two}\\ \text{operations}\\ \text{(hours)}\end{array} = \frac{\left[\begin{array}{l}\text{Std. time/piece}\\ \text{at the first}\\ \text{operation}\\ \text{(mins)}\end{array} - \begin{array}{c}\text{Std. time/Piece}\\ \text{at the next}\\ \text{Operation}\\ \text{(mins)}\end{array}\right] \begin{array}{l}\text{Batch}\\ \text{Quantity}\end{array}}{60}$$

The above relation is purely theoretical because no safety is provided in case of interruption at the first operation. It may be desirable to have 1-2 days safety in the elapsed time. This changes the above relation to:

$$\text{Elapsed time between two operations (hours)} = \frac{\left[\begin{array}{c}\text{Std. time/piece} \\ \text{at the first} \\ \text{operation} \\ \text{(mins)}\end{array} - \begin{array}{c}\text{Std. time/Piece} \\ \text{at the next} \\ \text{Operation} \\ \text{(mins)}\end{array}\right] \text{Batch Quantity}}{60} + 1 - 2 \text{ days}$$

(g) **Individual Job Schedules.** A part or component generally undergoes a number of operations some of which may be carried out simultaneously while others may need to be completed before the next operation is started. The process sheet of the component does not indicate overlapping of operations whereas the job schedule does. The job schedule of the component is generally fixed and does not require to be changed unless there is change in method of manufacture.

How Many Job Schedules?

One job schedule is prepared for each component. A company which manufactures a wide range of products therefore, prepares large number of schedules which are filed to be used as a basis for production control.

Such schedules are not dated but specify the time required for each operation. Once delivery date is fixed, the job schedule is dated and starting and completion dates of each operation are derived considering the load chart.

Main information to be entered ?

A job schedule should contain the following information.

(i) Identification data such as part name, part number etc.

(ii) Batch quantity.

(iii) Variable information in the form of columns to show: .

— operation number

— operation description

— machine/work centre

— effective capacity/day

— set up time

— standard time

(iv) Columns to record the running time for each operation.

How to Draw a Job Schedule ?

(i) The constant information is entered first in the schedule which is followed by batch quantity. The variable information such as operation numbers, operation descriptions, machines and effective capacity/day is then entered in the schedule.

(ii) The time (hrs) is then calculated for each operation as under :

$$\text{Time (hrs for an} = \frac{\text{Std. time / piece} \times \text{Batch quantity}}{60} \text{ operation}$$

From the time figure calculated above, the length of operation run (days) is calculated :

$$\text{Operation run (days)} = \frac{\text{Time (hrs) for an operation}}{\text{Effective capacity / day (hrs / day)}}$$

(iii) Each operation run is shown in the schedule by extending it by the suitable length which equals the time (days) required to complete the batch quantity for that operation.

Overlapping of operations, wherever possible is also considered.

❒

6

Product Design and Development

Product design is concerned with the form and function of a product. Form design involves the determination of what a product would look like, *i.e.*, product's shape and appearance, what it will be made of and how it will be made. Functional design deals with what the product will do and bow it works.

TYPES OF PRODUCT DESIGN

(i) Functional Design

The first requirement of a good product is that it should effectively perform the function for which it is developed. A handsome product which does not function to the satisfaction of the customer is of no use. For example, a ball pen should give smooth and even ink flow in writing. The various parts of a technical product, *e.g.*, an electrical circuit, should be within easy reach (accessible) both during use and servicing. For instance, in modern radio and television sets the removal of the back plate reveals the business side of the circuit, thus avoiding the removal of the many screws and other parts.

(ii) Form Design

Aesthetic considerations are also important particularly in decorative items like ornaments, pictures, etc. But other products should 'also' be so designed as to be attractive and not offensive to the eye.

A product's design must satisfy market requirements and be economical to produce. The designer has to design proper quality at a competitive price. Thus, there are two aspects of product design:

(a) **Design for Selling.** The product should be planned from the customer's point of view as otherwise it will not sell. Use of product, time required to carry out the product function, etc., are important factors.

(b) **Design for Making.** Generally, product design is a function of the engineering department. The final design is the outcome of joint efforts of sales, research and engineering people. Design for making should be such that it can be manufactured at a reasonable cost. This may mean use of sub-assemblies in assembled products. Due consideration should be paid to reliability and serviceability. Accessibility of various parts both during the use and for repair is another aspect which needs careful attention during product designing.

THE PRODUCT LIFE CYCLE

Every product has a certain life and consists of various phases. The sales history of a product shows various phases from introduction through growth, maturity and decline. The sales show distinct stages each being a challenge to the marketer. Profits too rise and fall. It is, therefore, necessary for the company (or the marketer) to devise appropriate marketing, financial, production, purchasing and personnel strategies for each of the phases of the life-cycle. We will briefly describe each stage alongwith the marketing objectives and various strategies to be adopted during each stage.

(i) Introduction. This stage, when the product is first made available for distribution and purchase in the market, is also called the "Market Pioneering" stage. It is characterised by low sales, high cost per customer, low or negative profits, only a few customers (innovators) and few competitors. The Marketer must aim at creating product awareness and enticing trial. The Marketing strategy consists of offering a basic product, a cost plus price, building selective distribution, spending heavily on advertising to build product awareness among the dealers and the innovators and intensive sales promotion efforts to entice trial.

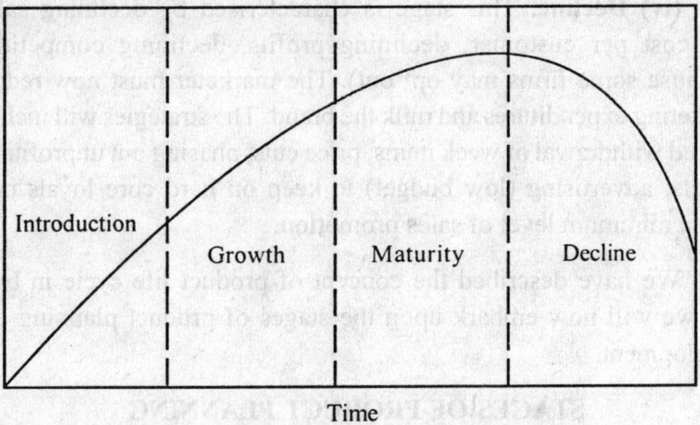

Fig. Various Stages PLC

(ii) Growth. During this stage sales rise rapidly, costs per customer reach a lower (average) level than the introduction stage, profits rise fast, a large n~mber of customers (the early adapters) buy the product and competition increases rapidly. The marketers objective is to gain maximum market share. The marketing strategy in this stage consists of offering an improved product (in terms of quality, features and style), entering new market segments and appropriate prices to penetrate such markets, entering with high intensity new distribution channels, spending same (as that in the introduction stage) or a little more on advertising for building interest among and educating the customers and reduced sales-promotion efforts so as to take advantage of the high demand.

(iii) Maturity. During this stage the sales growth has a decreasing rate and the duration of this stage is somewhat longer than the previous one. Other characteristics include low cost per customet, high profits, stable competition and then declining competition in the later parts of the stage. The marketers objective is to maximise market profits and at the same time defend the market share. Marketing strategies include diversification of brands and models, prices that match or beat competitors, intensive distribution, advertising that stresses brands differences and benefits and sales promotion to encourage brands switching.

(iv) Decline. This stage is characterised by declining sales, low cost per customer, declining profits, declining competition (because some firms may opt out). The marketer must now reduce marketing expenditures and milk the brand. The strategies will include phased withdrawal of week items, price cuts, phasing out unprofitable outlets, advertising (low budget) to keep on hard core loyals only and, a minimum level of sales promotion.

We have described the concept of product life cycle in brief and we will now embark upon the stages of product planning and development.

STAGES OF PRODUCT PLANNING AND DEVELOPMENT

(i) Generating Products Ideas. The initial task of the product planner is to develop product ideas. Some of the chief sources of product ideas are:

(a) Internal programmes that encourage innovation,

(b) Marketing research,

(c) The company's internal R and D activities,

(d) Venture teams,

(e) The products of the competitors, etc.

Briefly put, product idea generation means fusion of a perceived need with the recognition of technical opportunity.

(ii) Screening. The ideas collected are scrutinised to eliminate those in consistent with the product policies and objectives of the firm. Some ideas may already be protected by patents and some others may not be fit for consideration because of the non-availability of raw materials for production. Thus, most of the ideals screened need not essentially be good. They may be further subjected to a more detailed examination. The main intention of this phase is only to eliminate unsuitable ideas as quickly as possible. The procedure adopted includes:

(a) Expanding each idea into full product concept,

(b) Collecting facts and opinion to decide whether the product idea could be converted into a business proposition, and

(c) Assessing each idea for its potential value of the company.

(iii) Developing and Testing Concepts. The attractive ideas obtained after screening must be developed into finer concepts. This means that these ideas have to be elaborated meaningfully in terms of the customers of the product, the primary benefits to be build into the product and the occasion of purchase of the product etc. The planner must also determine what competition the product will face once released into the market—*i.e.*, he/she has to determine the product's position in the market as well as the brand's position in relation to competing brands. All these can be done with the help of a 'product positioning map' and a brand positioning map respectively. Now, the concept has to be evaluated in terms of its market potential. Testing product concepts is the device for such purpose. Concept testing is done through presenting an appropriate group of target customers, questions relating to the credibility of the product attributes, their need level, perceived value of the product, intention of purchase, ultimate users and frequency of purchcse. The planner then summarises the response to find out whether the concept has a broad and strong customer appeal.

The importance of developing and testing concepts can be emphasised in the words of Theodre Levitt as "Everybody sells intangibles in the market place, no matter what is produced in the factory". Thus, concepts—their development and testing are equally important for physical products and services as well.

(iv) Business Analysis. It is a continuation phase of screening. Here creative analysis is applied to the idea finally selected. Product features are analysed and a rough programme for its development is fixed. Here emphasis is on the following:

(a) Further study on each idea in a detailed manner,

(b) Determining the desirable market features for the product and its feasibility, and

(c) Developing specifications and establishing a definite programme for the product.

(v) Developing the Preliminary Marketing Strategy. Having developed the product concept and tested it, the product planner must now develop the marketing strategy appropriate for introducing the product into the market. First, he/she has to establish the size, structure and behaviour of the targeted market, the product positioning and the objectives of sales, market-share (and its growth) and profits for the first few years. Second, he/she must establish the products price, distribution strategy and the overall marketing expenditure for the first year. Third, he/she has to plan the longterm (say, ten years) sales and profit objectives as well as the marketing-mix strategy for that period.

(vi) Commercialisation. Here the product is submitted to the market and thus commences its life-cycle. Commercialisation is also the phase where marketing is most active in connection with the new product. This stage is considered to be a critical one for any new product and should therefore be handled carefully. For instance, it should be checked whether advertising and personal selling have been done effectively and whether proper outlets have been arranged for the distribution. Despite the care with which the previous development stages have been planned, unforeseen events can impair commercialisation seriously. The following activities is usually undertaken during this stage:

(a) Completing final plans for production and marketing.

(b) Initiating coordinated production and selling programmes.

(c) Checking results at regular intervals.

It should be remembered that new products should be launched in the market only stage by stage. In other words introduction may be restricted to a few region in the first instance.

FACTORS AFFECTING PRODUCT DESIGN

The major factors affecting process design decisions are following:

(1) Nature of Product/Service Demand;

(2) Degree of Vertical Integration: forward and backward integration;

(3) Production Aexibility: product and volume flexibility;

(4) Degree of automation;

(5) Product quality.

(1) Nature of Product/Service Demand. First, production processes must have adequate capacity to produce the volume of the products/services that customers want. And provision must be made for expanding or contracting capacity to keep pace with the trends of sales. Some types of processes can be more easily expanded or contracted than others, and the choice of the type of production process will be affected by the forecasted product/service demand.

Business plans set the prices of products and services. Prices affect sales volume, product design, and the required production capacity and costs. Therefore the choice of price and the choice of the design of production process must be synchronised.

(2) Degree of Vertical Integration. One of the first issues to resolve when developing production processing designs is determining how much of the production of products/services a company should bring under its own proof. Vertical integration is the amount of the production and distribution chain, from suppliers of components to the delivery of products/services to customers, that is brought under the ownership of a company. The degree to which a company decides to be vertically integrated determines how many production processes need to be planned and designed.

Because of shortages of both capital and production capacity, small businesses and start-up venture ordinarily choose to have a very low degree of vertical integration. In the beginning, when products or services are being introduced to the market, as much of the production of products as practical will be contracted to suppliers. Likewise, distribution of products will be contracted to shipping and distributor firms. As the businesses grow and products nature, however, more and more of the production and distribution of products typically will be brought back in-house as the companies seek more ways to reduce costs and consolidate their business.

The decision whether to make products or buy them from suppliers is not a simple decision. But the starting point is to determine whether the cost of making components is less than that of buying them from suppliers. Unless there are clear cost advantages to making components in-house, such issues as the following are not likely to be as important: Is enough investment capital available to expand production capacity to make the components? Does the company have the technological capability to make the components? Are there high-quality suppliers available? Is there a risk that suppliers will become competitors?

(3) Production Flexibility. Production flexibility means being able to respond fast to customers' needs. Flexibility is of two forms, product flexibility and volume flexibility, both of which are determined in large part when production processes are designed. Product flexibility means the ability of the production system to quickly change from producing one product/service to producing another. Product flexibility is required when business strategies call for many custom-designed products/services each with rather small volumes or when new products must be introduced quickly. In such cases, production processes must be designed to include general-purpose equipment and cross-trained employees who can be easily changed from one product/service to another. Also, new forms of flexible automation allow great product flexibility.

Volume flexibility means the ability to quickly increase or reduce the volume of products/services produced. Volume flexibility is needed when demand is subject to peaks and valleys and when it is impractical to inventory products in anticipation of customer demand. In these cases, production processes must be designed with production capacities that can be quickly and inexpensively expanded and contracted. Manufacturing operations are ordinarily capital-intensive, which simply means that the predominant resource used is capital rather the labour. Thus, in the presence of variable product demand, capital equipment in production processes must be designed with production capacities that are near the peak levels of demand.

(4) Degree of Automation.

A key issue in designing production processes is determining how much automation to integrate into the production system. Because automated equipment is very expensive and managing the integration of automation into existing of new operations is difficult, automation projects are not undertaken lightly. Automation can reduce labour and related costs, but in many applications the huge investment required by automation projects cannot be justified on labour savings alone. Increasingly, it is the goals of improving product quality and product flexibility that motivate companies to make the huge investments in automation projects. As with other factors affecting the design of production processes, the degree of automation appropriate for production of a product/service must be driven by the operations strategies of the firm: If those strategies call for high product quality and product flexibility, automation can be an important element of operations strategy.

(5) Product/Service Quality. In today's competitive environment, product quality has become an important weapon in the battle for world markets of mass-produced products. In earlier times, it was thought that the only way to produce products of high quality was to produce products in small quantities by expert craftsmen performing painstaking hand work. Mercedes and Rolls Royce are examples of automobiles that were produced with this approach. In recent times, many mass-produced products such as Japan' Toyota automobiles are considered to be of very high quality. The choice of design of production process is certainly affected by the need for superior product quality. At every step of process design, product quality enters into most of the major decisions. For many firms, the issue of how much product quality is required is directly related to the degree of automation integrated into the production processes, for automated machines can produce products of incredible uniformity.

MEANING OF STANDARDISATION

This means fixation of some appropriate size, shape, quality, manufacturing process, weight and other characteristics as standards to manufacture a product of desired variety and utility *e.g.*, manufacture of television sets of standard size of the screen using standard components and technology, having blades are made of standard size and shape to suit every kind of razor. The concept of standardisation is applicable to all factors of production namely men, machines, materials and finished goods. These standards can become the basis to evaluate the performance of various components of production in a manufacturing process. In the words of Behel, Smith and Stackman:

"A standard is essentially a criterion of measurement, quality, performance, practice established by custom, consent or authority and used as a basis for comparison over a period of time. The setting of standards and the co-ordination of the industrial factors to comply with these standards and to maintain them during the periods for which they are effective is known as industrial standardisation."

According to Dexter S. Kimball "Standardisation in the manufacturing sense is the reduction of anyone line to fixed types, sizes and characteristics."

Standardisation becomes the basis of production control operations and works as a catalyst in directing and operating the working of business enterprises. It identifies and compares various products, systems and performances in an enterprise. It is the function of the department responsible for designing the product to provide the guidelines and infrastructure for standardisation of the whole system keeping into consideration the requirements and specific wants of the customers. Any error committed at the designing stage towards standardisation may be too expensive to be rectified.

For an organisation designing of the product without considering standardisation aspect is of no value or significance.

Franklin F. Folts has described the concept of standardisation as, "Simplification of product lines and concentration on a restricted predetermined variety of output is one common application of the principles of standardisation as found in industry. Standardisation may be extended to all factors in the production process."

Standardisation is an instrument to manufacture maximum variety of product out of minimum variety of components by means of a minimum variety of machines and tools. This decreases working capital requirements and reduction in manufacturing costs.

Standardisation also implies that non-standard items are not to be manufacturer except when consumers order them especially.

Some standards are enacted by law *viz.*, automobile windscreen must be made of safety glass. Usually there are institutions, societies and governmental departments that regulate the standards. In a factory, it is best to have standardisation committee drawing its members from sales, engineering, production, purchasing, quality control and inspection. Sales department and engineering department have to work closely in effecting changes towards standardisation because the older products that have been sold are affected for after-sales service spare needs. Within an organisation, it is the engineering department who sets standards for the materials to be procured and specifications of the end products and the mode of testing the products.

Advantages of Standardisation

(i) Standardisation in designing, purchasing of raw material, semifinished and finished goods and of the manufacturing process tries to eliminate wastage and reduce the cost of production. Reduction in varieties of raw materials means reduced investments in stocks and less attention to stock control.

(ii) Standardise product components reduce tool costs, permits larger and more economical lot sizes of production, avoid losses for obsolescence and reduces capital requirements for work in progress.

(iii) Production in larger quantities can be planned which results in less set-up costs.

(iv) By minimising the operations in production process it provides facility to introduced mechahisation and use of more specialised tools and equipments.

(v) Service and maintenance costs as well as marketing expenses are reduced.

(vi) Encourages the manufacturer to products of new style, use and performance with an object to generate more customers.

(vii) The value of the standardised product lying in stocks or in transit can be easily evaluated for the purpose of advancing loans.

Disadvantages of Standardisation

Product standardisation leads to some disadvantages also. These are:

(i) Too much standardisation has an adverse affect on the efficiency and morale of the workers. They in the long run feel bored and fedup in doing the same routine again and again. The spirit of challenge and initiative vanishes with passage of time.

(ii) During the initial process of product development where frequent improvements and changes may be necessary to bring the product and the production process upto the mark, standardisation may create obstacle in innovations.

(iii) For small scale enterprises standardisation may not be advantageous.

Tolerancing

Product specifications lay down precise characteristics of products. Production people are expected to follow and achieve these characteristics in the process of manufacture. In practice variations may arise despite all possible efforts and care. Variations arise'due to the limitations of machines and workers. Therefore, the designer should lay down the extent of variation in any design feature that could be allowed. For example, the outer diameter of a product may be defined as 20 mm ± 0.1. This means that the diameter should not differ 20 mm by more than ten percent. Laying down of such tolerance limits is known as 'tolerancing'. All dimensions must have working limits within which the products must comply. These limits should be a compromise between the maximum the designer can tolerate and the minimum the production can accept consistent with their efficient manufacture. Generally, designers like their designs to be much as accurately as possible. Very often they make their tolerances too tight for efficient manufacture. Too tight limits will result in high levels of rejects, inspection and machine setting. Standard tolerances should not be used indiscriminately without due consideration to the particular situation.

Standards are laid down by engineers, scientists, manufacturers and research organisations. For example, the Bureau of Indian Standard (formerly Indian Standards Institute) lays down standards. Products bearing ISI mark command greater confidence from buyers and the mark is considered a sign of good quality.

Diversification

It implies policy of producing different types of products by an enterprise. Thus it is reverse of simplification. The concepts of diversification and simplification are associated with the nature of the industry *e.g.*, in the case of capital goods industry simplification is more important as the customers give preference to economy, accuracy and performance of the product, whereas in an consumer goods industry diversification leads to produce variety of goods in terms of style, shape, colour, design etc. The establishment facing tough competition are forced to diversify their activities to capture the market. In general diversification can be adopted for the purpose of

(a) utilisation of idle/surplus resources,

(b) stabilisation of sales,

(c) to cope with demand fluctuations, and

(d) for survival of the organisation.

Do care and precautions should be taken in the formulation of diversification policy. Proper and extensive market analysis at different levels of the quality and quantity of the products should be done to determine the levels of profitability. This will help in selecting most appropriate diversification strategy under the prevailing circumstances.

Advantages of diversification are :

(a) Increase in sales due to production of different kinds of products. This also leads to increase in volume of business.

(b) Needs of wider section of consumers are fulfilled.

(c) 'Risk minimisation' in the case of quick and unpredictable demand variations.

(d) Uniform and balanced production programme can be chalked out without any consideration of slack or boom periods.

Disadvantages of diversification are :

(a) Due to increase in number of operations the production process becomes quite complicated and sometimes expensive.

(b) Production planning and control operations becomes complicated and time consuming requiring extra efforts.

(c) The size and the variety of items in the inventory increases with diversification introducing more problems.

(d) Workers of different type of skills and expertise are required.

Product Differentiation

Product differentiation refers to the process of making a product different in some respects from the competitive products. In standardised products, physical differences are in significant and can be copies quickly. Therefore, producers create some psychological differences in their products. Such differences may not be tangible or material but they are significant to the consumers. The strategy of product differentiation is used by a firm to maintain control over the price of the product. Production differentiation is an important decision area of product strategy particularly in competitive economy. It provides the following benefits:

(a) Helps to attract customer's attention in the face of alternative products.

(b) Satisfies the demand of different segments of the market.

(c) Encourages non-price competition.

(d) Assists in facing competition from competitors products.

(e) Provides a measure of control in the matter or pricing.

Product differentiation tend to increase the problem and costs of advertising and sales promotion,firms with limited product line find product differentiation particularly useful.

Simplification

Simplification of product design is the elimination of the complex features so that the intended function is performed but with reduced costs, higher quality, or more customer satisfaction. Customer satisfaction may be increased by making a product easier to recognise, buy, install, maintain, or use. Costs can be reduced through easier assembly, eliminated operations, less expensive substitute materials, and when less material is wasted as scrape.

The concepts of specifications, tolerances, standardisation, and simplification are all important in designing products for ease of production. Of particular importance is that products must be designed to accommodate automated machinery.

Assembly Charts

Assembly charts are typically used to provide an overall macro-view of how materials and sub-assemblies are united to form finished products. These charts list all major materials, components, sub-assembly operations, inspections, and assembly operations. An assembly chart that shows the major steps in assembling an electronic hand-held calculator. Follow through these steps and try to visualise the actual operations for producing this familiar product.

Assembly charts, sometimes called gozinto charts (from the words goes into), are ideal for getting a bird's eye view of the process for producing most assembled products. They are also useful for planning production systems for services when those services involve processing tangible goods, as in fast-food restaurants, dry-cleaning shops, and quick tune-up shops for automobiles.

Production Information System

Production information systems is a network to generate necessary information and process it to make various decision related to some production system. It consists of communication channels and information processing centres collecting information from its sources of origin, storing, updating, collating and processing it and then supplying the processed information to the various users of the system.

A production information system can be viewed as an independent group of sub-systems each related to its successor, each performing a different function though yet united with others for achievement of the overall objective. It interacts with both its internal and external environments.

COMPONENTS OF PRODUCTION INFORMATION SYSTEM

The components of the system can be described as:

(1) Long Term Planning. This implies planning the conversion system specifying the sequence of operations, capacity of the system, plant location and its layout aspects. The decisions derived have long term impact and are difficult to undo once implemented. Information for taking such decisions is complied periodically for determination of appropriate product mix.

(2) Annual Production Plan. These are meant to plan the use of transformation process. These plans are drawn from sales programmes by optimising inventory carrying costs, costs on labour with hiring and firing of personnel etc. These plans are revised periodically.

(3) Inventory Control. It is generally expressed in terms of money and number of units produced. It deals with preparation of laster inventory and production schedules.

(4) Production Scheduling. These decisions are to determine : what to make, when to make, how to make, how much time is required to make it, production plan, bill of materials and operations sheets providing the necessary information for the preparation of production schedules.

(5) Dispatching. Time standards are formulated through operation/route sheets supplied by planning and engineering departments. Cost standards are calculated through cost cards and job tickets and the quality standard are prescribed by design and engineering sections.

Thus production information system is a matter of planning and generate records for decision making. MacNeice has sub-divided these records into three types:

I. Records of Basic Information

(i) Blue Prints,

(ii) Bill of materials,

(iii) Time value of fundamental operations, and

(iv) Production routing.

II. Records Showing What is Available

(i) Raw material records,

(ii) Work in process,

(iii) Semi-processed stock,

(iv) Finished goods stock,

(v) Information about tools, jigs, fixtures, gauges and personnel available.

(vi) Machinery and equipment details.

III. Historical Records

(i) Records of production,

(ii) Records of waste and reject,

(iii) Records of machine performance,

(iv) Records of sales, and

(v) Records of absenteeism.

The nature of these records can vary for different type of plants and production systems as well as according to the situation and needs of the management.

In a small organisation the preparation and maintenance of these records is the job of shop floor. But it becomes an important function in medium and large scale organisations having separate section for collection and preservation of such records. Usually this work is done by dispatchers who continually observe the actual implementation and compare it with the programme previously intimated.

Production Planning and Control Information System

The designing of an effective production planning and control information system for a given plant requires a clear comprehension of the nature of the manufacturing problem and an understanding of the planning and manufacture of standard products. For designing effective production planning and control procedures a materials and tools records and control system must be derived and machine capacity data must be complied.

Information needs for PPC System are:

(i) Full details of forecasted sales by product and actual sales. This will provide necessary inputs to the production managers to modify there plans as and when required. Such data is useful in managing the problems of under and over production.

(ii) The availability on a daily basis of productive details regarding the overtime, working, additional shift arrangement and any subcontracting facility if and when needed.

(iii) Data relating to materials stock, the availability of supplies and the leads times needed for deliveries into the system and distribution from the system.

(iv) Knowledge of company policy relating to work in progress and buffer stock levels.

(v) Details of the factory organisation, layout and maintenance facilities available.

(vi) Human factors which might affect the operation of the plan *e.g.*, absenteeism and industrial unrest if any.

Characteristics of Production Information System

(i) It should always be tailored to the need of a particular organisation. It can never be specific or general.

(ii) The involvement of top management in the formulation of production information system is essential.

(iii) Data base should be wide.

(iv) It must be flexible and should be supplied timely.

(v) Data would be capable of easy interpretating and presentation.

(vi) The cost of procuring the information must not over ride the relative advantages accused.

In production system most of the information needs are in the area of:

(i) Production, Planning and Control.

(ii) Materials management *viz.*, purchase, stores and inventory control etc. with an objective to optimise production by identifying the variance so that these could be closely monitored.

MATERIALS MANAGEMENT INFORMATION SYSTEM

The economic working of business enterprises requires that the available capital resources are used most judiciously. Material costs usually account for well over 50% of the investment in the enterprise. Thus attempt to organise information in materials management *viz.*, purchase, processing, storage and production can help in conserving on the outlay of capital investment on materials *i.e.*, at least by 5% reduction in material costs. In this case the information system must meet needs of the total material planning within the company *e.g.*, to determine the Economic Order Quantity for purchase, monitoring buyers performance, vendor analysis, forecast future needs for ordering materials and to prepare exception report. The system has to cater the needs of material for purchasing department, production objectives and capacity planning.

Objectives of integrated approach in materials management can be:

(i) To minimise investment in inventories.

(ii) To provide material of a specified quality at the lower cost.

(iii) To perform functions of material handling and storage so that storage costs are minimised.

(iv) To cut through standardisation, value analysis, waste control and import substitution.

(v) To improve procedures and to delegate authority and responsibility at various levels of materials management.

(vi) Materials waste must be minimised if not eliminated.

An integrated approach to materials management must look at all the above problem areas in co-ordinated manner.

The information needs for purchase management can be:

I. For Planning Purchases

(i) Details of items to be purchased with specifications.

(ii) Possible sources of supply.

(iii) Prices.

(iv) Delivery time.

(v) Reliability with past performance.

II. For Controlling Purchase

(i) Orders to be placed.

(ii) Orders actually placed.

(iii) Delay in placing orders.

(iv) Materials expected to be received.

(v) Materials actually received.

(vi) Delay in receipt of material, and

(vii) Problems and actions.

OPERATION STRATEGY AND CONTROLS

A corporate mission is a set of long-range goals unique to each organisation and including statements about the kind of business the company wants to be in, who its customers are, its basic beliefs about business, and its goals of survival, growth, and profitability. Fig. shows that operation strategies are derived directly from the corporate Mission and business strategy.

Business strategy is a long-range game plan of an organisation and provides a road map of how to achieve the corporate mission. These strategies are embodied in the company's business plan, which includes a plan for each functional area of the business, including production, marketing, and finance. Business strategy is developed while considering an assessment of global business conditions and the distinctive competencies or weaknesses of the company's business units. Global business conditions include such factors as an analysis of markets, analysis of competition in those markets, and economic, political, technological, and social developments.

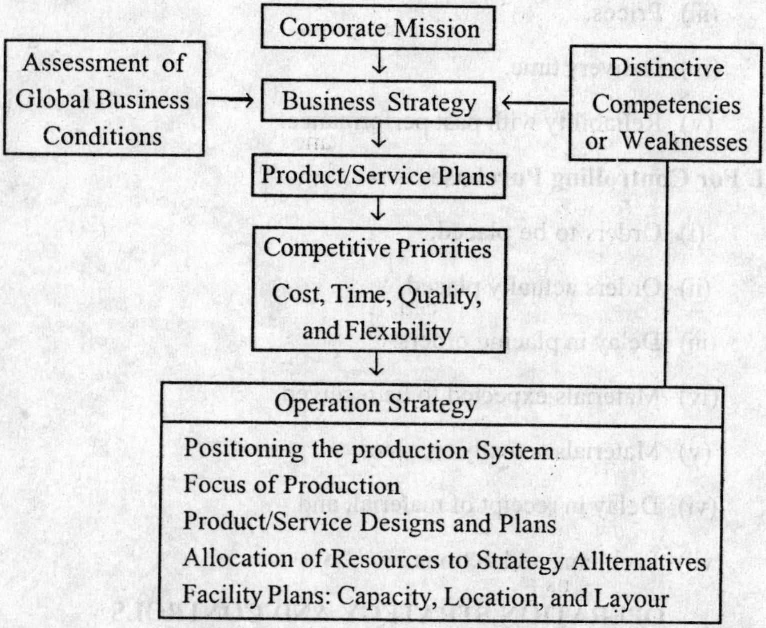

Fig. 2. Developing Operations Strategy

Distinctive competencies or weaknesses represent great competitive advantages or disadvantages in capturing markets. They could things like automated production technology, a skilled and dedicated work force, an ability to quickly bring new products into production, a talented sales force, or worn-out production equipment. The central focus in farming business strategy is finding ways to capitalise on a firm's distinctive competencies and developing new ones so that market shares can be developed or increased.

Operations strategy is a long-range game plan for the production of a company 5 products and services and provides a road map for what the production function must do if business strategies are to be achieved Operations strategies include decisions on such issues as what new products must be developed and when they must be introduced into production, what new production facilities are needed and when they are needed, what new production technologies and processes must be developed and when they are needed, and what production schemes will be followed to produce products/services.

ELEMENTS OF OPERATIONS STRATEGY

Operations strategy is discussed in the following sections:

(1) Positioning the Production System. Positioning the production system in manufacturing means selecting the type of product design, type of production processing system, and type of finished-goods inventory policy for each product group in the business strategy.

There are two basic types of product design, Custom and Standard Custom products are designed according to the needs of individual customers. The choice of this type of product results in many products, each being produced in small batches. Flexibility and on-time delivery are usually needed for this type of product. A magnetic resonance imaging (MRI) system for a large hospital is an example of this type of product. The choice of Standard products results in only a few product models that are produced either continuously or in very large batches. Fast delivery and low production cost are usually needed for this type of product. A television set is an example of a standard product.

There are two classic types of production processes, product-focused and process-focused. Product-focused production is also called line flow production, production lines, and assembly lines. In this approach, the machines and workers needed to produce a product are grouped together. This type of production is usually best if there are only a few standard products, each with a high volume.

Assembly lines such as in auto manufacturing typify these systems. Because such systems are usually difficult and expensive to change to other product designs and production volumes, they are not very flexible. Process-focused production is usually best when producing many unique products, each with a relatively low volume. Each production department ordinarily performs only one type of process, such as painting. All products that need to be painted would be transported to the painting department. Custom products usually require this form of production because process-focused systems are relatively easy and inexpensive to change to other products and volumes, thereby offering great flexibility. If a business strategy calls for custom products whose market strategy requires the competitive priorities of flexibility and on-time delivery, then process-focused production is usually preferred.

There are two types of finished-goods inventory policies: produce-to-stock and prpduce-to-order. In the produce-to-stock policy, products are produced ahead of time and placed in inventory. Then when orders for the products are received, the products are shipped immediately from inventory. In the produce-to-order policy, operations managers wait until they have the customers' orders in hand before they produce the products. If fast delivery of products is important, then produce-to-stock is usually preferred because the products can be shipped directly from finished-goods inventory. McDonald's uses a produce-to-stock policy and Burger King ("Have it your way") uses a produce-to-order policy.

Once the type of product design, production process, and finishedgoods inventory policy have been selected for a product, much of the structure required of a factory has been established. To further explore factory structure, let us consider the scope of a factory's operations.

(2) Focus of Production. An important element of operations strategy is a plan for each production facility to be specialised in some way. Wickham Skinner refers to this idea of specialised factory as the focused factory: "A factory that focuses on a narrow product mix for a particular market niche will out perform the conventional plant which attempts a broader mission. Because its equipment, supporting systems, and procedures can concentrate on a limited task for one set of customers, its costs and especially its overheads are likely to be lower than those of the conventional plant. But, more important, such a plant can become a competitive weapon because its entire apparatus is focused to accompany the particular manufacturing task demanded by the company's overall strategy and marketing objective."

In the 1970s and 1980s, corporate mergers occurred at an unprecedented pace. As Lee lacocca states: "Nobody's building a better mousetrap anymore. They're trying to figure out how to do a leveraged buyout of the mousetrap company." In many of these mergers, operations were consolidated into larger, diverse, and unfocused production facilities, and all too often the result was that they did not do anything particularly well.

In contrast, our foreign competitors from Asia and Europe usually have smaller and more focused production. Many U.S. production facilities have become smaller and more focused. An example of these smaller and more specialised facilities is the emergence of minimills in the U.S. steel-making industry. These mills make a narrow range of steel products, are located near their markets, use significant amounts of scrap metal as base stock, and usually have incentive plans for their employees. These smaller mills have been very profitable and are capturing an increasing share of the U.S. market, even from South Korean and Japanese companies.

Factories and service facilities usually becomes more focused in two ways: specialising in only a few product models or a few production processes. It is desirable for factories and service facilities to be specialised in some way so that they will not be vulnerable to smaller and more specialised competitors that can provide a particular set of customers with a better set of cost, delivery, quality, and customer service performance. Of course, we cannot concluded that smaller facilities are always better. Economies of scale have to be taken into consideration in choice of size of production facilities, Long-Range Capacity Planning and Facility Location. Nevertheless, the tendency for U.S. production facilities to be larger and unwieldy is recognise.

(3) Product/Service Plans. An important part of business strategy is plans for new products and services to be designed, developed, and introduced. Operations strategy is directly influenced by product/service plans because:

(a) As products are designed, all the detailed characteristics of each product are established.

(b) Each product characteristic directly affects how the product can be made or produced.

(c) How the product is made determines the designs of the production system, and the design of the production system is the heart of operations strategy.

As a product is designed and developed, it enters the introduction stage of its life cycle, In this stage, sales begin, production and marketing are developing, and profits are negative. Successful products move on to the growth stage when sales grow dramatically, marketing efforts intensify, production concentrates on expanding capacity fast enough to keep up with demand, and profits begin. Next comes the maturity stage when production concentrates on high-volume production, efficiency, and low costs; marketing shifts to competitive sales promotion aimed at increasing or maintaining market share; and profits are at their peak. Finally, the product enters decline stage of its life cycle, which is characterised by declining profits and sales. Eventually the product may be dropped by the firm or replaced by improved products.

There is a trend toward shortened product life cycles, particularly in industries such as computers and consumer goods. Shortened product life cycles have three important effects:

(a) The amount of spending on product design and development is increased.

(b) Production systems tend to be whipsawed by continuously changing product models. This creates the need for flexible production systems that can be easily changed to other products.

(c) Operations strategies emphasis the ability to bring new product designs on stream quickly. CAD/CAM, is allowing some companies to respond faster to designing and redesigning products and launching them into production quickly.

(4) Production Process and Technology Plans. An essential part of operations strategy is the determination of how products will be produced. This involves planning every detail of production processes and facilities. The range of production technologies available to produce both products and services is great and is continuously increasing. Combining high-technology production equipment with conventional equipment and advising effective overall production schemes are indeed challenges. Automated production technology is an important strength to be used as U.S. companies strive to capture shares of global markets.

(5) Allocation of Resources to Strategic Alternatives. All companies today have limited resources available for production. Cash and capital funds, capacity, research labs, workers, engineers, machines, materials, and other resources are scarce in varying degrees to each firm. Because for most companies the vast majority of the firm's resources are used in production, shortages of these resources impact most severely on their production systems. These resources must be divided among, or allocated to, products, business units, projects, or profit opportunities in ways that maximise the achievement of the objectives of operations. Allocation decisions, which are constrained by the availability of resources, constitute a common type of strategic decision to be made by operations managers today.

(6) Facility Plans: Capacity, Location and Layout. How to provide the long-range production capacity to produce the products/ services for a firm is a critical part of setting operations strategy. Enormous capital investment is required to make production capacity available. Land and production equipment may need to be purchased, specialised production technologies may have to be developed, new production equipment may need to be made or purchased and installed, and new factories may need to be located and built. The decisions involved have long-lasting effects and are subject to great risk. If poor decisions are made or if circumstances change after the company has committed to a choice of alternatives, companies will live with the results of these decisions for many years.

SCARCITY OF PRODUCTION RESOURCES

The scarcity of production resources recently led one marketing executive to comment "Manufacturing personnel used to call me and ask what they should produce. Now I call them and ask them what they can produce ." Certain raw materials like titanium and nickel, personnel skills, coal natural gas, water, petroleum products, and other resources are periodically unavailable or in short supply and probably will become scarcer in thefuture. Giving the finite supply of these scarce resources to firms and give an ever-increasing demand and important issue in the formation of business strategy is how to allocate these resources among business opportunities.

Social-Responsibility Issues

The attitudes in U.S. corporate boardrooms toward social responsibility are evolving from doing what companies have a legal right to do, to doing what is right. While the reasons for this evolution are varied and complex, these factors are thought to be important:

(a) Consumer Attitudes. There is increasing evidence that consumers and consumer groups are influencing companies to act responsibly. This influence is felt through such things as resolutions presented at stockholder meetings, consumer preference for particular socially responsible products/services, and political/lobbying activities.

(b) Government Regulation. Local, state, and federal agencies and laws are a growing force in controlling the behaviour of U.S. businesses. The EPA (Environmental Protection Agency), OSHA (Occupational Safety & Health Act), Clean Air Act of 1990, and the

Family Leave Act of 1993 are only a few of the many societal constraints imposed on businesses.

(c) Self-Interests. Companies are changing the way they behave regarding social issues because they perceive that long-term profits will be greater if they act responsibly.

These categories of social-responsibility issues will be discussed: the environmental, employee, and societal impacts.

(i) Environmental Impacts. Concerns about the global environment abound: ozone layer, rain forests, global warming, and acid rain; petroleum and chemical spills, toxic and radioactive waste disposal, and air, ground, water, light, and sound pollution; and energy conservation, landfill waste reduction, and recycling of paper, glass, aluminium, and steel. Some U.S. companies are doing to protect the global environment and conserve natural resources. Some companies have seen these developments as business opportunities. Entirely new industries have been created in the United States to supply products/services related to the environment. These industries provide products that range from smokestack scrubbers for cleaning polluted air to equipment for cleaning oil spills to consulting services offering advice about the environment.

With the trend toward international firms and production sharing. the need for standardising government regulations of the environment seems obvious; otherwise, firms will tend to gravitate to the less-regulated countries. A case in point exists along the U.S. Maxico border. Unless environmental regulations between the United States and Mexico can be standardised in the NAFTA agreement, the environment is sure to suffer in this region. There has been some progress in multinational agreements, as evidenced by such things as international conferences on protecting the environment, multinational agreements regulating the release of industrial chlorofluorcarbons (CFCs), and multinational agreements on curtailing the catches of whales and dolphins.

(ii) Employee Impacts. Labour shortages, social and consumer pressure, ethics, and local, state, and federal laws all work together to cause companies to develop policies governing the fair treatment of employees. Employee safety and health programmes; fair hiring and promotion practices with regard to age, race, colour, gender, religious preference, and disabilities; benefit programmes including health care for employees' families, day-care programmes for children of working parents, pregnancy leaves, elder-care programmes for dependants of employees, retirement plans, and other policies are provided for by U.S. companies. Some programmes are mandated by law and are supervised and enforced by governmental agencies. Other programmes are undertaken voluntarily. Special-interest groups have lodged boycotts against the products/services of companies believed to be engaged in unfair treatment of employees.

Such programmes are costly. Employee benefit programmes are thought to be one of the largest factors in the cost advantage that Japanese auto plants enjoy here and abroad when compared to U.S. factories. But employee morale and productivity, recruitment and retention of employees, turnover of personnel, consumer demand for a company's products, and cost of defending against lawsuits and boycotts are all affected by employee policies. And ethics, the code of company behaviour that is considered to be morally right or wrong, also plays a part, the package of employee benefits and company employee policies are all of strategic importance because long-term profitability is acutely affected.

(iii) Societal Impact. Gerald Graham, a professor at Wichita State University, thinks that society grants the right for companies to exist. When society suffers because of pollution, unethical practices, inadequate safety and health regulations, discrimination, and crime caused by companies, the companies also suffer. It is morally appropriate for management to get involved in helping society, and it is also a sound, long-term strategy for success. Providing fair value in products/services, providing products/services that ensure customer safety, tamper-proof packaging, production and marketing of products harmful to the health of customers, promoting baby food rather the breast-feeding of babies, and investing in companies operating in South Africa are examples of issues being discussed today.

❒

7

Management Control

According to Schwartz, "a product is something a firm markets that will satisfy a personal want or fill a business or commercial need", and includes, "all the peripheral factors that many contribute to consumer's satisfaction." These factors may include reputation of the manufacturer, the warranty, credit and delivery terms, the brand name, and the courtesy shown by the sales and service personnel. From a perusal of these definitions, it is obvious that a product is not only a tangible entity. The intangible services and psychological attributes such as prestige, image, etc. which consumers look for an marketers provide in these tangible items are also an integral part of the product. For example, Nirlon Synthetic Fibres and Chemicals Ltd., Bombay offers a 3-tier after sales service, called NASA 4, along with its tangible product conveyer belts. The services include a highly qualified Technical Survey Group which studies the customer's needs in depth constructions for the most stringent individual requirements.

Belting recommendation/rationalisation reports are prepared after a complete analysis of the individual conveyor system Then there is a Maintenance Consultancy for the customer's technical experts and engineers arrange courses and seminars on the maintenance and proper usage of conveyor belting. The third service is the on-site Belt-Splicing and Repair Services by the company's skilled supervisor. Thus, when a customer buys a Nirlon conveyor belt, he buys NIRBELT along with all the associated intangible services mentioned above. Likewise, when Hindustan Lever Ltd., Bombay offers Pear's soap, it does not merely offer a bathing soap—a tangible attribute but also 'mother's love for a child'—a psychological attribute.

ESSENTIAL FEATURES OF PRODUCT

Notwithstanding variations in the emphasis and focus in the above definitions, the consensus of opinion about the meaning of the term 'product' converges on some points. These points may be referred to as the 'essential features' or 'ingredients' of 'product' These are briefly described here.

1. Tangible Attributes. To be called a product, an item should have the characteristic of tangibility. It means it may be touched, seen, and its physical presence felt as, for example, an automobile, scooter, pressure cooker, shaving cream, toothpaste, etc.

2. Intangible Attributes. Alternatively, it may be intangible in the form of a service as, for example, repairing, hair-dressing, banking or insurance services. These services may be bought independently/exclusively or may be associated with tangible products. For example, automobile servicing may be exclusive when sought independently after an automobile has been bought, or it may be an associated feature when free-servicing is offered by the seller along with the automobile.

3. Peripheral or Associated Attributes. Product may have peripheral or associated attributes to facilitate its identification and acceptance by buyers. Such attributes may be a brand, package, warranty, credit and delivery terms. By and large, brand and package are such attributes which are common to many products. For example, Hindustan Lever's vanaspati ghee has a brand name DALDA and its package exhibits a conspicuous palm tree with which it has come to be identified by consumers. Its brand name has developed such an image in the market that all kinds of vanaspati ghee that being sold is often referred to as Dalda ghee; it has become a generic name for all types of vanaspati ghee.

4. Exchange Value. For marketing purposes, every product, whether tangible or intangible, should have an exchange value and should be capable of being exchanged between buyer and seller for a mutually agreed or acceptable consideration.

5. Consumer Satisfaction. From the marketing viewpoint, products should have the ability to deliver value satisfaction to consumers for whom these are intended. This satisfaction may be both real and/or psychological. For example when a housewife buys a Lakme lipstick she not only buys a chemical compound having some tangible features but also buys 'beauty'. The former may deliver a real value but the psychological value is delivered by the latter. It is for this reason that product is often referred to as 'bundle of utilities' or 'a bunch of value satisfactions'.

6. Business Need satisfaction. In order to be a product, an item should also have the attribute of satisfying a business need. The basic business need obviously is to earn profit on the product sold. However, it may be to meet a societal need also. For example, cholesterol edible oil product may satisfy a societal need; it may or may not whether it generates profit or not, but whether it has that attribute of generating profit or not.

After having described the essential features of the term 'product', a product may be defined as a set of tangible, intangible and associated attributes capable of being exchanged for a value with ability to satisfy consumer and business need(s).

Analogous Terms. In order to further facilitate understanding, it would be appropriate to know the meaning of some other terms also which often recur in any discussion about product. Some of these terms are discussed here.

1. Product-Mix. Also referred to as product portfolio, product-mix is 'the composite of products offered for sale by a firm or a business unit'.

2. Product-Line. Product-line is a group of closely related products which are able to satisfy a class of need, to be used together, to be sold to the same customer groups, to be moved through the same distribution channels, or fall within given price ranges.

3. Product-Item. Product-item is a specific version of a product that has a separate name or designation in the seller's list.

Classification of Products. Traditional Classification: It has been our premise that production finds its raison detre in consumption. But products are not always bought for end consumption by buyers. They are bought for intermediate uses also; they are bought for intermediate uses also; they are bought for conversion into other kinds of products through a manufacturing process.

Some products, therefore, serve as inputs for other products. Some products survive a number of uses while others do not; survive a number of uses while others do not; some products are bought frequently relative to others. It is because of these differences in the purposes, motives, attitudes, shopping effort and frequency of purchases that in marketing products have been classified differently. Traditionally products have been classified as follows:

1. Consumer and Industrial Products. Consumer products are those products which are destined for use by ultimate consumers or households and in such form that they can be used without further commercial processing. Whereas industrial products, are those products which are destined to be used by buyers as inputs in producing other products and for further commercial processing. In other words, consumer products are meant for personal and non-business use whereas industrial products are meant for non-personal and business use. For example, soap, toothpaste, wrist watch, hair-oil, cigarettes, scooter, etc. are meant for personal use and are, therefore, classified as consumer products while machine tools, computers, trucks, machinery, etc. are meant for non-personal and business use of producing other products. Here are, therefore, classified as industrial products.

2. Durable and Non-durable Products. Products, both consumer and industrial, have also been classified as durable, non-durable and services. Durable products are those tangible products which normally survive many uses like, for example machinery, cars, scooters, furniture, coolers, air-conditioners and refrigerators. Non-durable products, on the other hand, are those tangible products which are normally consumed in one or a few uses like, for example, lubricating oils, soap, toffees and cornflakes. Services are those intangible products like activities, benefits or satisfactions which are offered for sale, for example, hairdressing, banking and insurance, etc.

3. Convenience, Shopping and Speciality Products. Consumer products have further been subclassified on the basis of the degree and natufe of shopping effort put in by consumers. Two attempts in this connection are relevant. The first attempt was made by Melvin. T. Copeland of the Harvard Business School back in 1923 whose classification of consumer products has received wide support. Accordingly, consumer products have been divided into the following three types:

(a) *Convenience Products.* Convenience products are those consumer goods which a customer usually purchases frequently, immediately, and with the minimum of effort in comparison any buying, as for instance, soap toothpaste, bread, chewing tobacco, biscuits, etc.

(b) *Shopping Products.* Shopping products are those consume goods which the customer, in the process of selection and purchase, characteristically compares on such based as suitability, quality, price and style, as for example, refrigerator, cooler, fans, mopeds, sightings, etc.

(c) *Speciality Products.* Specially products are those consumer goods with unique characteristics and/or brand identification for which a significant group of buyers are habitually willing to make a special purchasing effort, as for instance, ice-cream, special eating items, fancy goods, etc.

Modern Classification. Aspinwall Theory: Over the years many refinements in the above product classification have been suggested buy by far the most widely accepted revision and the one that meets the above criticism of the traditional classification has been the one suggested by Aspinwall. This is, in way, a second major attempt at product classification after the one attempted by Copeland. Aspinwall's characteristics of Goods Theory has three brad facets. First, it spots products on a continuum and does not classify them in discrete classes. Second, it takes into account five product characteristics and not tow. And, third, it gives new names to products spotted along the continuum.

1. The Continuum. As opposed to discrete products classes, the modern classification spots all products along a continuum with two basic categories at each end of the continuum, one at each end. Any product falling between these two ends represents some combination of these two basic types. Products may, therefore, be spotted at the centre of the continuum or near one of the ends of the continuum depending on the mix of its characteristics.

Table 1

Modern product classification

	The Continuum		
Product characteristics	*Red*	*Orange*	*Yellow*
Replacement Rate	High	Medium	Low
Gross Margin	Low	Medium	High
Adjustment	Low	Medium	High
Time of Consumption	Low	Medium	High
Searching Time	Low	Medium	High
	Goods	Goods	Goods

2. Product Characteristics. In order to spot products along the continuum, the following five product characteristics have been identified:

* ***Replacement Rate.*** The rate at which a product is purchased and consumed by users in order to provide the satisfaction a consumer expects from the product.

* ***Gross Margin.*** The difference between the paid-in cost and the final realised sale price.

* ***Adjustment.*** The amount of services applied to goods in order to meet the exact needs of the consumer.
* ***Time of Consumption.*** The measured time of consumption during which the goods gives up the utility desired.
* ***Searching Time.*** The measure of average time and distance form the retail store.

To spot any product along the continuum, it may be rated on a scale from zero to hundred on the basis of the aggregate of these product characteristics. At the one end of the continuum, are spotted the products with high replacement rate, low gross margin, low adjustment, low time of consumption and low searching time. On the other hand, products with diametrically opposite characteristics are spotted along the other end of the continuum. At the centre of the continuum are products which have a medium rating on the scale.

3. New Product Names. Products are named by colours so as to facilitate their identification on the continuum. Products spotted at the one end get red colour, those at the other end get yellow colour; while those at the centre get orange colour. Thus in terms of colours, products are classified as Red, Orange and Yellow with scope for an infinite colour combinations on the continuum from red to yellow and orange in between.

Product is an important component of the marketing-mix. "It plays a central role in the activities of all organisations, for it is the medium through which they seek to achieve their dual objectives of maximising both consumer and organizational satisfaction." It is true that when in harmony with other components of the marketing-mix, namely, selling, advertising pricing, and distribution, products develop considerable capacity to satisfy consumer and organisational needs.

Consumers look upon products marketed by business houses as sources through which their varied needs are satisfied and happy living ensured. Unless there are products with all their associated attributes, no consumer can expect to gather need satisfaction.

Similarly, the basic corporate need for profit is also satisfied by products. It is the product through which a company exploits market opportunities and generates sales volume and revenue. Adequate sales volume and revenue ensure corporate profitability essential for business survival and growth. One of the recent Indian example of the difference a product can make is provided by the product-video tape- manufactured and exported by M/s Esquire Video Films Services (P) Ltd. Bombay. The company intends to exploit the vast market potential among the immigrants, estimated to be 32 million of the Indian sub-continent in different parts of the world who were being supplied video cassettes by clandestine manufacturers hitherto. The importance of this product may be gauzed by the potential threat it poses to the export of Indian films, and subsequent withdrawal of support to the company by Indian Film Exporters' Association.

Besides, operationally, product is a competitive weapon of very great potential. Whenever, competitive pressures develop in the market, consumer preferences change or otherwise there emerges a need for more approximate product-market integration, product as a component of the marketing-mix may be differentiated, modified or innovated.

Significantly, this change in product need not always in terms of tangible attributes which is relatively difficult; it may be in terms of intangible or assocated attributes also. For example, competitive advantage may be gained by changing the package, colour, or trading terms ever. Thus, there is enough scope for management to manoeuver this component of the marketing-mix to bring about greater product-market integration. It is its flexibility and effectiveness as a competitive weapon that enhances product's significance in the marketing—mix of a company.

Notwithstanding top managerial awareness about the profit—contributing potential of products, it is not uncommon to find prominent companies confronted with product failures. For example, when Hindustan Lever introduced Signal toothpaste with Hexachlorophene, till then considered an important ingredient of dental care, it suddenly found itself exposed to adverse medical opinion regarding the use of Hexacholorphene. The kind of setback its new red and white striped toothpaste received in the market was unparalleled relative to the number of products successes to its credit. Shield, and antiseptic cream marketed by M/ s Smith, Kline and French failed in spite of its repeated repositioning in the market. Similarly, Alkali and Chemical Corporation of India Ltd's Savlon antiseptic cream and liquid failed in the fifties; it has recently been relaunched.

Although many cases of product failure have come to light no data about product failures are nationally available in India. An indication of product failure phenomenon may, therefore, be gathered from the product failure estimates developed abroad.

The facts regarding product failure given above are startling and are sufficient to make any marketing manger nervous. But product failure has not been identically defined by all. There have been varied concepts of product failure to some, product failure means no or abysmally low sales volume or losses and no-profit situation.

To some others it means disappearance of product from shelves or abandonment/ withdrawal of product from the market by marketer. However, from the managerial viewpoint, a product may be deemed to have failed when it fails to achieve product objectives set out buy a company. When this indicator of product failure is accepted, a product may fail to achieve product objectives and yet continue to be on the product-line.

An analysis of different studies beings out eight major reasons for product failures. These include, lack of meaningful product uniqueness, poor planning, wrong timing, enthusiasm crowded on facts, product failed to perform, company politics and unexpected high product cost. An analysis of 18 of Cadbury's product failures reveals the following major reasons:

— Recipe 7

— Conceptual shortcomings 4

— Price 3

— Package 2

— Low volume 2

Product planning is the process of determining that line of products which can secure maximum net realization form the intended markets. It is an "act of marking to and supervising the search, screening, development, and commercialization of new products; the modification of existing lines; and the discontinuance of marginal or unprofitable items" The managerial decision making in this area centres around deciding the type of products company should develop and sell so that products serves as an instrument of achieving marketing objectives. It also involves surveillance of product behaviour and deciding whether it deserves to be on the product-line, abandoned, or repositioned.

The aim of this managerial activity is to ensure that product-line of the company is confined to logical, well designed, and individually justified product items so that company is placed in strong competitive position. Product planning then would ensure that products do not work at cross purposes, are designed on the basis of research inputs provided by marketing research, and contribute to the fulfillment of consumer and business needs.

It is therefore, suggested that in a company every new product formulation should undergo a customer-oriented product planning process before it is introduced in the market reveals that the process of product planning starts with the conception of product ideas. The ideas so generated are screened for their commercial and technical merits by the marketing department.

When the ideas appear to have both types of merits, marketing research to acitivised so as to probe their market potentialities with regard to consumer acceptance, to scan market segments, and to identify possible price ranges. The favourable marketing research findings lead management to reappraise these ideas from the viewpoint of company facilities and constraints in the fields of finance, production, raw materials and state regulations.

Reappraised product ideas are then turned over to marketing executive for approval. Marketing executive for approval. Marketing executive passes them on to the business analysis group for their appraisal in terms of economic viability. The economically viable product ideas so approved and received back from the marketing executive are transmitted along with consumer specifications, to engineering people for developing product prototype(s). The prototype(s) so developed is evaluated and approved for test-product runs on a small scale so as to test-market it and gather market reaction and response. The results of the market testing are analysed and necessary changes, if needed, are made in the prototype(s) before full-scale production runs are undertaken and product delivered to consumer.

The above described customer-oriented product planning process reveals that it is composed of a sequence of six activities, namely:

1. Idea generation
2. Screening
3. Business analysis
4. Product development
5. Test marketing
6. Commercialisation.

The product planning process starts with the generation of product ideas. Product idea generation means "fusion of a perceived need with the recognition of a technical opportunity" The perceived need may be new or old, apparent or latent, or may be currently unfulfilled or inadequately/inefficiently fulfilled. When a technical opportunity is recognised to satisfy this need, a product idea is generated. For example, when T.I. Cycles of India Ltd., Madras developed a weighing scale-cum-stand for liquefied petroleums gas, it perceived Indian housewife's need to avoid an uniformed exhaustion of gas from cylinder and consequent embarrassment and kitchen problems. It then fused this need with available technology to generate a product idea about such a weighing device. The product idea may, however, result in both a new product or an improved product depending on the consumer need.

Creativity cannot be ordered. But such unorganised and haphazard product ideas generation depends heavily upon the chance factor. When a company badly needs a product idea to meet a consumer need or sustain company growth and idea generation is not organised, the only alternative is to wait infinitely for some genius to generate an idea. But then it may be too late. No business organisation can possibly subsist with such a situation. Besides, "when there is no formal management responsible for gathering ideas, many useful ideas are lost for ever to the company." Organised Sources As such, it is always profitable to organise a product ideas structured in the manner best suited to company needs, for example, there may be a product planning committee, Think Tank or some such kind of structure whose task may be to scan the internal and external environment, stimulate relevant thinking and procure ideas.

The product ideas may be procured form a variety of sources both from internal and external environment. Some of such sources are described below:

1. Consumers. In any business organisation, consumers are a veritable source of product ideas. These my relate to new product or may suggest improvements in the existing products of such product ideas by consumers may be in the form of an expression of need through company's marketing research agencies or may be in the form of a an expression of dissatisfaction with the current product performance through company's complaint-registering system. Whatever may be the mode of idea submission, the idea originating from consumers have better potential for success because of consumer's proximity to the product-use situation the studies conducted by Meadows and Peplow also show that idea from customers have higher probability of commercial success than do idea from laboratory. In case of industrial products, it is hypothesised by Hippel that consumer-active idea generation is more relevant and useful.

2. Scientists and technologists: Scientists and technologists working in different scientific activities are also a very important source of new product ideas. Their continuous search for new scientific knowledge may provide important clues for meaningful product development. These scientific of a company by establishment of a Research & Development division, Or, alternatively, the scientific research output may be gathered from the external environment of the company and sifted for product ideas. Such sources in the external environment may include state and industry's research institutions and universities.

Many companies have started their own R & D operations so as to generate product ideas and develop them. For example, Hindustan Lever's research centre is the largest of its kind in the private sector of India where over 250 scientists work. The company has invested nearly Rs. 3 crores in it and the recurring expenditure per year comes to rupees one and half crore.

The R & D organisation of Asian paints Ltd., Bombay is one of the largest in Asia in the paints industry with over 50-scientists and technologists working in a wellequipped laboratory. It is one account of these efforts that the company currently has over 3000 active formulations to meet diverse consumer requirements. Similarly, a small pharmaceutical company, Neivedita Chemicals Ltd. Bombay has developed vitamin B2-5 phosphate sodium, a basic drug required for Vitamin B complex formulation, by its own R & D efforts.

Many research scientists are also working in a large number of research institutions established by the government and industries. Their output has resulted in important product ideas. For example, the Central Food Technology Research Institute has provided ideas and devploped the famous Coca Cola substitute "77" Similarly, the product idea generation and development of 'Miltton'—a vegetable toned milk which is a blend of groundnut protein, glucose, vitamins, minerals, and standard milk also goes to the credit of CFTRI scientists. The ideas and technology to manufacture ductile iron spun pipes was developed by the scientists at the Torsteel Research Foundation in India which is currently manufactured by Indian Iron and Steel Co. Ltd.

In more than 100 Indian universities and other academic institutions, scientists are incessantly working on both basic and applied research. Careful and systematic management contracts with such scientists can help cull out thousands of important product ideas which normally remain unapplied in scientific journals.

3. Competitors, Salesmen and Distributors. These three are also important sources of product ideas. Competitors often prepare themselves to out-manoeuvre their peers in the market by surprising new product introductions. By a carefully planned marketing intelligence system, in which sales men and distributors may also be roped-in, a company many procure these product ideas and neutralise the competitive advantage planned by competitors. Sales men and distributors are otherwise also very important sources of product ideas because of their proximity to market and interaction with consumers.

4. Consultants. The consultants engaged by a company to advise on company problems is a good source of product ideas. On account of their dealing with different kinds of clients they come across a variety of product-lines and product problems. Without in any way compromising their professional integrity they can pass on some very useful product ideas while suggesting solutions to company problems.

5. Bankers. Development and commercial bankers in India like the industrial Development Bank, Industrial Finance Corporation, State Finance Corporations, and public and private sector commercial banks, may also provide useful product ideas. They gather these ideas from the project and feasibility reports received by them as also from the interaction with their borrowers. During the course of their dealings with such, bankers, company executives may obtain important lead about product ideas.

6. Patents' Office. New discoveries and inventions are often patented by their owners with the Registrar of Patents. A company may get valuable product ideas from the information sought from the Registrar's office. This information may relate to the new patents registered and those which have expired. In case of the former, company may attempt to secure manufacturing licence from the patent owners whereas in the latter case, it may think of going for production of a new product without in any way infringing the Patent Act.

7. Foreign Sources. Foreign sources of new product ideas are generally international trade fairs and exhibitions and technical collaborators. Fairs and exhibitions visited by company executives and scientists expose them to the new ideas. Foreign technical collaborators provide both the product idea and the necessary know-how to convert is into a product. In India, many manufacturing companies have received important product ideas from their collaborators.

It is not uncommon that many a times companies receive unsolicited product ideas. Such ideas should be handled with care because entertaining and use of such ideas may lend a company into legal battles in respect of patent right violations. It is for this reason that many companies absolutely refuse to even entertain such ideas unless they are patented. Such policy though full of caution may deprive a company of many valuable product ideas. In such cases, therefore, the reasonable course would be to seek an undertaking from the idea sender than it is original, has not been sent elsewhere, and that it does not violate anybody's patent rights.

While looking for new product ideas, marketing management must understand that there is nothing like any best source. Each source may be important. Therefore, executives should always be open minded for the receipt of product ideas. Nonetheless, in the executives' search for new product ideas, the following guidelines may be relevant:

* Establish new product goals.

* Organise the search for sources; do not depend on chance. A network must be established carefully and nurtured lovingly.

* Keep alert to what is 'new' by industry, by materials, and by geographical location.

* Use many sources on an imaginative, open minded basis. Do not be limited to anyone source.

* When a good source of product ideas is found, keep at it. there are very few highly creative 'corners' within people's minds and its business organisations, and they will be responsible for most of your company's good ideas.

Idea Generating Methods. It has been suggested that product idea generation should be an organised idea generating system has been highlighted previously. In such system, companies may make use of many useful idea generating methods. For example, in a company people associated with idea generating task may list the attributes of an object, say fountain pen, and then modify different attributes, say, nib, tongue, cap, size, colour, etc. in search for a new combination that may possibly improve the object. This method has been called the Attribute listing method.

Morphological analysis may also be undertaken by isolating the most significant dimension of a consumer product problem and then examining all the relationships, among them. People knowledgeable in consumer problems and technological opportunities, called experts, may be asked to participate in the brainstorming sessions in which they put forward an infinite number and variety of ideas in the context of a specific consume problem without bothering about criticism. Or alternatively, operational creativity may be generated by not defining the consumer problem specifically and keeping it as broad as possible so that participants in the session put forward as many ideas as possible without getting tied down to specifics.

Instead of such brainstorming sessions, the Delphi Method may be used wherein experts may be asked to analyze, suggest, comment and recommend on a problem the alternative solutions till a consensus of opinion is built-up regarding product idea. Likewise, instead of asking experts to think over consumer problems regarding a product, a Problem Inventory analysis may be undertaken wherein a consumer group may be selected and interviewed or asked to deliberate and discus about product problem and prepare an inventory of product problem points and their alternative solutions.

After product ideas have been generated from different sources, including marketing research, the next step in the sequence of product planning activities is screening of these ideas. Screening means critical evaluation of product ideas generated by a company. The purpose of screening is to abandon from further consideration those product ideas that are incompatible with objectives and constraints. Every product idea should, therefore, conform to objectives both company and marketing and constraints to which company is exposed in order to successfully come out of the screening process. The objectives to which product ideas are usually expected to confirm include, namely, consumer need satisfaction ales volume, profitability, market share, company image, etc. In the context of these objectives, the relevant questions to be asked include; is idea capable of meeting consumer need in a specific market segment? It is capable of generating sale volume and profits? It is compatible with company images?

The constraints to which product ideas are expected to conform, include, technological know how, state regulations, operational scope as enshrined in the object clause of company's memorandum of association, and company strengths and weaknesses in the area of manufacturing, finance, marketing personnel, purchasing etc. It is one thing to have a fantastic product idea and quite another to have a relevant, practical, down-to-earth idea capable of being executed by a company.

It is important because in real life situations companies always operate in the background of constraints. In India, for example, a company in the large industrial sector cannot execute a promising product idea if its development and commercialisation is statutorily reserved for small and/or cottage sectors of industry. A cotton textile company cannot manufacture dhotis, which is reserved for handloom and powerloom sectors even if it holds great promise.

The single largest benefit of screening process for any company is that it saves company of the involvement in the subsequent expensive activities in the product planning process. For the purpose of screening product ideas many methods have been suggested. However, two methods have received wide support from marketing managements. These include, check-listing and idea rating. These are briefly described hereunder.

Checklists are widely used by marketers in the screening process. A checklist enumerates desirable product 'characteristics on a scale providing guidance to the screener. A model checklist for screening product ideas. To facilitate idea elimination, each point on the scale may be assigned a value. For example, in the given figure 5, value is assigned to Excellent and value very poor.

Thus each idea has a potential to attain maximum 45 value points and minimum 9 value points. The experience of the screener may, however, indicate the optimum point level which may be used to pass on ideas to the next stage for further consideration, the ideas which do not reach this optimum point level will be eliminated from further consideration. The number of desired product characteristics or only indicative; many more may be added to the list depending on the company requirements.

As an improvement over the checklist method, idea rating as a viable screening methods has also received wide support from the marketing people. Whereas in the checklist methods, factors were evaluated on the basis of their quality in terms of 'excellent' or 'very poor', in the rating method, these qualitative values are given quantitative ratings. Also each product characteristic/ factor is assigned a weight on the basis of their relative importances as judged by the screener. In this case, the screener attempts to evaluate product idea against the sphere of performance and arrives at his best estimate in terms of value points and puts 'x' below the value point chosen. Subsequently the factor value is multiplied by factor weight so as to arrive at a product. The products of all the factors as shown in 'e' column when totaled indicate the relative worth of the idea. The screener may arrive at a minimum acceptable rating for ideas to be worthy of being passed on to the next stage. The hypothetical product idea has a rating of .720 which exceeds the minimum acceptable rating of .70 and as such is worthy of being passed on to the next stage.

In another rating method, O'Meara expresses value points not as single scores but as a probability distribution. As such under the sub-element 'relation to prespnt distribution channel' the score shows a .9 probability for very good value that is a score of .9 x 10; and a .1 probability for good value that is, a score of.1 x 8. The composite score for the product under this subelement is accordingly .9 × 10 + .1 × 8 = 9.8.

This composite score is then multiplied by the factor weight given in then multiplies by the factor weight give in column, that is 5 to impart a total contribution to over all screen rating of 9.8 x 5 = 49.0. the contribution be each subelement to the total expected utility is likewise computed so as to arrive at Total Expected Utility of Product Idea. Besides these two types of screening methods, attempts are continuously being made to refine screening methods, so as to approximate idea assessment to reality. For example, the Multi-state Sequential Screening process has been developed by the famous American Consultancy firm of Booz, Allen and Hamilton.

Nonetheless, the refinement of the screening method should always be moderated with the cost and time involved in the screening of product ideas. Also, every screener must limit the selection of product ideas to those that can be translated into necessary competitive advantage Likewise, it is always appropriate to select products that do not divert company attention from the structure of its overall success pattern.

Once product ideas successfully come out of the screening tests they are passed on to the next state of Business Analysis.

Business analysis may be defined as an evaluation of product idea in depth with a view to determining its financial, competitive, manufacturing, and markting viability in a given set of business environment. It is relatively a more expensive exercise carried out at the brass-tacks level and is aimed at sifting out those ideas which promise profits and an early investment payback.

The exercise involves projections of future demand, sales, costs, investments, and return there on. It helps management to have a preview of the product's complete profile before it can make any firm financial commitments. After having arrived at these projections, the information may be plotted on a rating scale on the pattern. Subsequently, the total score on the scale may be matched with the minimum acceptable rating to arrive at a decision to either drop the product idea or to pass it on to the Product Development Stage. However, before the idea is passed on to the state, usually it is appropriate to develop product specifications so that product development is always consumer oriented.

Since a company is required to make financial commitments as soon as the idea passes out to the next state, the analytical exercise is usually undertaken by specialists in the areas of finance and accounting who employ a variety of tools to arrive at different kinds of projections. Some of the important analytical devices used by these specialists include Breakeven Analysis, Earnings flow Discounting, Marketing-Mix Model, Bayesian Decision Theory, and Risk Analysis.

The product idea after having been thoroughly screened and analysed in the preceding stages of product planning is received in this stage for conversion into 'product'. It is in this stage that an idea gets the shape of a concrete product associated with all the necessary attributes on the basis of consumer specifications received from the preceding stage. The purpose of this stage is to attempt to develop product prototype so as to certain whether the idea has the technical potential and the company has the necessary technology, whether existing, developed or procured, to manufacture product that will satisfy consumer and business need.

By and large, it is a 'techno-commercial' job done by the engineering or research and development personnel of the company in close association with the product planing people. The whole product development task may be divided into six broad jobs, namely, engineering, consumer preference testing, branding, packaging, patenting and developing a communication programme. However "these jobs are not performed in a sequential manner. Rather these are performed simultaneously and synchronise so that by the time the product is fully developed it has all the attributes—tangible, intangible and associated and imparts a synergic impact on the market.

Engineering. The engineering aspect of the product development task involves, first, development of appropriate product drawings and designs/laboratory compounds, second, checking and rechecking them with the consumer specifications and, third, building up a prototype that will work economically and efficiently. This is basically a technical job and is carried out in company workshop or laboratory. The focus of the whole job is to build up such a product prototype that approximates closely to the consumer product specifications.

Consumer Preference Testing. However, where such engineering jobs are not so extensive, for example, in consumer products like food items, tolietaries, cotton textile, etc., consumer preference testing assume importance. Consumer preference testing various combinations of product attributes developed by the company are tested on consume groups so as to determine as to which combination of product attributes is perceived by consumers as having the desired attributes the one which approximates closely to the perceived attributes is finally chosen for production.

The products are broadly administrated tow types of consumer preference tests. These are, namely, the blind and Identified Tests and the Single and Comparative Tests. In the former, new products may be tested blindly meaning thereby without any brand or company identification or may be identified with the proposed brand name and package. Or alternatively, blind and identified test may be combined by using separate and comparable consumer samples. Properly controlled evaluation may then be attributed to the brand and package. In the latter type of tests, the product may be tested independently or relative to other competitive products. Three major testing alternative are available to marketers.

1. Monadic Test. Respondents use product in an environment as close to real life as possible, evaluate the product and transmit their reactions to the company through a questionnaire and/or a rating device.

2. Direct Comparison Test. Respondents use the new product as also other products, may be competing ones, evaluate all of them concurrently by using them at a given point of time and feed their reactions to the company.

3. Staggered Test. Respondents use the new product as also other products, may be competing ones, evaluate all of them independently by using them at different points in time and feed their reactions to the company.

Branding and Packaging. Along with the engineering and preference testing goes the job of developing appropriate brands and packages the associated product attributes. Brand, package, style and colour are such attributes which help consumers in identifying and distinguishing company's product. These jobs are very relevant and have to be done with meticulous care. Exclusive legal rights for the use of brand name may be obtained under the Trademarks Act, 1958 for a maximum period of 16 years subject to further renewals. Multiple branding and packaging alternatives are available to marketers, the details of which may be found in the subsequent pages.

Patenting and Formulating Communication Programme. While the above referred to jobs are in progress, marketing management of a company formulates an initial communications programme and completes formalities to obtain patents/copyrights of the products developed. Patenting confers exclusive legal rights on the company for a period of time to make use of the technology developed so as to manufacture products. In India, the maximum patent life for a product is 16 years and this right has to be Law in

India may be found. The formulation of the communication programme involves identification of sales force, advertising and sales promotion needs in relation to the new product and resources requirements to meet these needs.

Prpolem. The time log: Nonetheless, one of the major problems confronting marketers in this stage is the time lag between idea conception and product development. Documents the elapsed time between the start of the development and large scale and national distribution in respect of some products in the USA. It shows that the time lag may vary from 1 to 80 years. Although, it is very difficult to prescribe any time horizon for product development, it is the experience of the marketers world over that products lose market opportunity when time lag is excessive. When time lag is excessive, it is possible that the competitors snatch away the opportunity or / and consumer needs, preferences and behaviour change rendering the product unprofitable or even irrelevant.

But more than the undue of time, an undue haste in product development is hazardous. "The insufficient time allowed for proper development is then expressed in other ways in accounting for the high rate of product failures". The fact is that it takes much longer to develop new products than usually is thought to be the case. It is, therefore, essential that management provides for product development that time period which my be said to be reasonable in a given competitive setting and consumer behaviour backdrop so that there is neither loss of market opportunity nor consumer rejections.

Test—Marketing Defined. Test-marketing has been defined as a "research technique in which take product under study is placed on sale in one or more selected localities or areas, and its reception by consumer and trade is observed, recorded and analysed". In this stage the new product and relevant marketing programme is tried out for the first time in well selected market segments under representative marketing environments.

This stage of product planning process is more relevant to consumer products relative to industrial products. On account of small number of customers, in case of industrial products marketers are able to make personalised efforts to secure customer reactions, but in respect of consumer products, however, it is not possible. Markets for consumer products are composed of a large number of consumers with a wide range of behaviour patterns. As such, these markets are required to be reached in a formal organised and systematic manner so as to test the product.

Rationale. The rationale of test-marketing a new product and the associated marketing programme lies in a number of trade-offs a company experiences on account of it. These may be broadly summarised into three.

1. By test-marketing a product, marketing management is better place to evaluate its effectiveness in terms of sales volume and profitability. Although, volume and profits are not the objectives of test-marketing, they undoubtedly serve as valuable indicators of the effectiveness of product and the marketing programme. Test-marketing provides important dues about the product weakness and deficiencies which escape the attention during the development stage. It provides an opportunity to understand the working and relative importance of the different components of the marketing-mix in making the new product a success. It also awakens marketers to the existence of potential financial and environmental hazards of the new product which is otherwise difficult to assess. In sum, it may be said that the wisdom gained by spending a small amount on a small-scale operation considerably helps management in augmenting the profit potential of a new product and also in averting a major marketing failure which may lend a company in a financial lurch.

2. In test-marketing, marketers also get an opportunity to ascertain the nature and dimensions of consumer reactions to the new product and the marketing programme. Although, the new product development is based on the consumer research findings, the final product that emerges is always a blend of what consumer expects and what company can produce. It is possible that the consumer profile may change by the time product is introduced by the time product is introduced it is not uncommon that consumers

develop some such notions about Product which act as a barrier against product-acceptance. For example, consumers developed a notion about Mother Dairy's milk that it is not pure milk and it is blended with some kind of power which gets granulated after boiling. Mother Dairy had to take a lot of pains through advertising to counter this 'rumour'; whether it succeeded or not is anybody's guess as no empirical evidence is available. Nevertheless, it highlights the importance of test marketing which offers "an opportunity to obtain from consumers a wide variety of information relevant to the test operation, including fact, opinions and attitudes concerning the test product and competitive products."

3. One of the important trade-off provided by test marketing is that it triggers off market and competitive reactions. When a new product is introduced it is not unnatural for competitors to think of it as a potential danger to their market share. As a consequence, they reformulate their marketing strategy and attempt to reposition their product so as to counter the impact of new product launch. Nonetheless, these reaction of competitors may very well be exploited by gathering, through marketing intelligence network, the foreknowledge of the way competitors propose to react. Thus, the company may neutralise competitive assault or make it counterproductive. The credit for building up this trap goes to the test marketing.

Subject Matter of Test-Marketing. The type of information to be gathered from test marketing usually depends on the objectives of testing laid down by management. For example, if the objective is to find out the consumer reaction to the taste/colour of the product or price competitiveness of the product, the information to be sought would naturally be to attain these objectives. Nevertheless, there are some information points which are usually checked in test marketing. These include, namely.

* Potential sales volume generation
* Identification of innovative buyers
* Comparison of target and actual number/types of buyers

* Recognition of strong points of product by buyers
* Ability of advertising message to transmit products' strong points
* Competence to attain planned distribution
* Potential for repeat purchases.

For example, Government Soap Factory, Banglore carried out test marketing of its new detergent power POINT to assess the consumer's opinion of washing effectiveness, quantity required, soaking time and effect on hands. The test sample comprised 400 housewives representing a cross-section on the city's population.

Agencies for test-Marketing. The test-marketing exercise is usually carried out by the company itself. It is based on the premise that the marketing team charged with products; commercialisation is best suited for testing it. However, testing by company's team is not without pressures and hazards the impatience to commercialise the product often lead to premature interpretation of test data. Also, there is usually an element of unwillingness on the part of company's team to accept negative test results. There are strong possibilities of company's dealers pressurising company for an early commercialisation of the product owing to lurking profit potential. The way to overcome these pressures is to have a rugged objective attitude and an awareness of the penalties of product failure after commercialisation. Still another way is to entrust the testing job to an outside agency. However, while engaging an agency, care should be very explicitly laid down. Also, an assurance should be sought as regards the ability of the agency to carry out the test meticulously.

Other factors in test-marketing are the following:

(1) Selection of Test Market. The test market to be selected should be a restricted geographical area which represents the national market. In India, cities like Bangalore, Bombay, Chandigarh, Delhi and Calcutta are usually selected by companies to test market their products. There should not be fewer than two markets for each variation to be tested. However, where the purpose of the test is to estimate the sales potential of a product to be nationally marketed, markets in, at least, four geographic areas should be used. As the significance of the variables to be tested decreases, the number of markets necessary to reflect the effect of these variables increases.

(2) Projection. Marketing achievements in the test market should be recorded and then projected nationwide. For example, if monthly volume in 2 per cent of the country is Rs. 3.500. then the total volume projected would be Rs. 3500/0.02—Rs, 1,75,000.

(3) Demographic Validity. All available data should be carefully reviewed to make sure that the test market is by and large representative of the whole market in terms of social class, caste, age and other demographic variable.

(4) Behavioural Validity: All available data should be reviewed also to make sure that the test market is representative in terms of consumption of similar or substitute products.

(5) Competitive Validity. It is also advisable to be assured that competitive strength in the test market is approximate the those in the whole market. Also, a check should be made to ensure that 'jamming' resulting from competitors' promotional programme does not invalidate test results.

(6) Strategy Validity. After having considered the above factors in test-marketing, it is also advisable to check up different components of the marketing-mix to be employed in the test-marketing and their probable future relationships. It is important because distortion in nay one components at the commercialisation stage would bring about distortion in the rest results and the actual product performance. For example, if testing is accompanied by an aggressive sales promotion campaign/penetration price but not so in commercialisation stage then subsequent results would be different.

Post Tests-marketing Options. Nevertheless, when test market results are available to the marketing management of the company, usually three broad options are available. These include, namely,

* abandonment of the product,
* additional testing, and
* commercialisation.

It is possible that the test results are not encouraging in terms of the objectives to be attained; possibly they demand revision of the objectives and strategies set out by the company. Alternatively, these may not be so discouraging but sill indicate the need for further testing in order to gather more information to make an appropriate decision with regard to commercialisation. Alternatively, the results may be encouraging and signal commercialisation of the product.

The decision to commercialise a product idea is the end result of the whole process of product planning. However, not all ideas that qualify for being processed successfully reach through to this state; in fact, a large number of product ideas die out in one or the other stages of the product planning process. Only those ideas which can sustain the rigours of various tests administered during the process, really reach the stage of commercialisation.

Commercialisation of product idea may be defined as the process of finally deciding the product profile, building up requisite manufacturing an ancillary facilities and appropriate marketing programme in the background of the test marketing results, and introducing the product in market for sale. Thus, the process of commercialisation involves some of the following activities:

* Deciding product characteristics and package
* Branding and trade-marking
* Building-up/procuring manufacturing facilities.
* Building up an appropriate marketing-mix
* Introducing product in the market.

The activities named above involve enormous managerial time and corporate money. The corporate experience and research studies indicate that the time an money spent in this stage exceed even the cumulative cost of the preceding stages of the product planning process. It is therefore, essential that the whole job is managed well. There has to be meticulous planning of product launching and all operations preceding it. There has to be an effective coordination and control of the operation before product enters the market.

When a product idea is commercialised by a company, the product enters the market and competes with the existing products to secure maximum share of consumer income. It brings in sales and generates profits. However, like human beings, every product has a lifespan at the expiration of which it is dead; it is dead in terms of its capacity to generate sales and profits on account of its perishable distinctiveness. As a corollary, therefore, products too have their childhood, adolescence, youth and old age. This has been described as life-cycle in human beings. When applied to products, it is termed as Product Life Cycle.

Product life cycle has been defined as "an attempt to recognise distinct stages in the sales history of the product" and a "generalised model of sales and profit trends for a product class or category over a period of time". But essentially the PLC concept is a simple one. It has three key elements;

(i) Products move through the cycle of introduction, growth, maturity, saturation and decline or obsolescence at different speeds.

(ii) Both sales volumes and unit profits rise correspondingly till the growth stage and fall correspondingly after maturity stage. However, during the maturity stage sales volume rises but unit profits fall.

(iii) The functional emphasis required for successful product management changes from stage to stage on account of changes in the economics of profitability.

Illustrate the five distinct stages through which a product normally passes through in its life cycle. But before we could elaborate on these stages it may be pertinent to know the following:

(i) Not all products introduced in market essentially pass through all the stages of PLC. It is just possible that the product may travel to the first and second stage and then dies out.

(ii) There is no definite line of demarcation between one and the subsequent stage. The succession is a merging one.

(iii) A product may not be in an identical stage in all the market segments; it may be in the second stage in one segment whereas in the third stage in another segment at a point of time.

(iv) The time-span of each stage in PLC in respect of each product may vary. Thus, a product may stay for longer or shorter duration in a particular stage

This is the first stage in the life of a product. In this stage the product is new and distinctive. Her, new product means "a product that opens up an entirely new market replaces an existing product, or significantly broadens the market for an existing product". This stage is characterised by slow rise in sales and profit margins, few direct competitors, high income group buyers, frequent product modifications, high production and marketing costs, narrow product-line high prices, limited distribution, and primary demand cultivation.

In growth stage, the product achieves considerable and widespread approval in market. Sales increase sharply and at an increasing rate. The number of competitors increase considerably and there are first major product improvements. Although the contribution to saie is maximum from the high income group buyers, now middle income group buyers also contribute to the sales. There is a scramble for distribution outlets and dealers also adopt multiple product-line policy. Although price soften in this stage, the profit margin continues to rise. Now there is a selective demand cultivation.

In maturity stage, the maturity of product is reflected in terms of its capacity to face competition. In this stage sales do rise but at a decreasing rate: profit margins, however, decline. The product covers mass markets. New product models oriented towards style becomes an annual phenomenon. There is further softening of product price and shrinkage in dealers simplify their product line. Market segmentation, trade discounts, and institutional brand loyalty become important tenets of company's marketing strategy. One of the most "important features of this stage is that there is a great shake-out of marginal firms form. the market as competition becomes desperate.

In this saturation the market is saturated with the product and is dominated by the replacement sale. It is fully matured as measured by the ratio of replacement sale to the first time purchases of product by buyers. During this stage, the rise and fall of sale is dependent on the basic economic factors- demand and supply. Markets are highly segmented and the number of competitors also stabiliSes. Annual product models and competitive cost structure are conditions of survival in this stage. Profit margins also continue to decline in this stage of PLC.

In the obosoelescence stage the product loses its distinctiveness and dies out in terms of both sale and profit margins. The decline in sale is permanent and product travels back to the core markets. product line gets narrow and primary demand cultivation again becomes important. To begin with prices soften but subsequently stablise and the increase. As a result, profit opportunities increase in the latter phase of this stage. Those who survive this stage become product specialists. In India, the glaring examples of products in the obsolescence stage include gramophone, lantern, ultramarine and, in a way, electric radio.

The concept of product life cycle has lived through controversy about its usefulness as a marketing tool. While exclaiming its theoretical proposition and the analogy with human organism, it is often alleged that the concept does not have a practical relevance. Even it is said to have 'little validity'. Some of the doubts raided about its relevance and problems encountered in using it include the following:

1. Many products fluctuate with the economy rather than conform to the traditional product life cycle pattern. Or example, steel, coal and cement.

2. Broad range of consumer and speciality products are not affected by normal life cycle pressures. For example, drugs patent medicines, bicycles, etc.
3. A substantial number of products, not subject to typical life cycle pattern, are protected by the economies of their production-distribution process. For example patenting helps a company to neutralise the facts of life cycle.
4. Real product histories do not subscribe to the position that products pass from to the successive stage as a matter of course.
5. It is difficult to identify the stage of PLC in which the products is currently placed.

Notwithstanding the doubts raised about its relevance and practical problems encountered in using it, it may be said with some degree of reasonableness that product does die out over a period of time and the intervening period between its introduction and decline is beset with events which are manageable. The concept is an important forecasting, planning, and control tool in the hands of markets.

Predictive Tool. Since a products has a predictive life pattern and the problems likely to be encountered in different stages of PLC are known, the management is pre-warned of the likely changes in the product position. For example, behaviour patterns of sales, profits, dealers, competitors, in different stages re known. Although it is rather difficult to forecast these changes with any degree of exactness, it undoubtedly provides a preview of the broad spectrum of product events likely to occur.

Planning Tool. Once product life pattern and the behaviour of forces impinging on it are known, management is better placed to plan its strategy in advances so as to fully exploit the product potential. Product modifications, promotion and pricing strategies and dealer motivation programme may be planned much earlier than the market conditions warrant. This becomes possible owing to the predictive signals provided by PLC.

Control Tool. In case of a multi-product company when a number of products are simultaneously offered in the market, not all of them fare identically. Some fare better, some not, when their position in the PLC is monitored, it may indicate the types of changes required in the marketing strategy so as to fully exploit its/their potential and attain maximum market share. Thus, it serves as an important control tool.

In recent years, manufacturing firms worldwide have been directing increasing attention to the need for improving productivity in order to strengthen their competitive position. To monitor and evaluate productivity changes, and to communicate and reinforce this new emphasis on productivity improvements, appropriate measures of productivity are required.

Productivity measurement can generate information that may be useful for management control purposes in two ways. First, such measurement may identify dimensions on which productivity improvements are possible, in which case targets may be generated to guide future operations.

The productivity measures may be employed to identify products or processes for which the firm has a competitive edge in productivity or similarly evaluate new technologies or investment projects that are likely to increase the firm's profitability. The second role for productivity measures in management control systems arises from their use in evaluating the performance of managers. In conjunction with the usual profit or cost accounting system, a productivity measurement system can be designed by the corporate managements so that it motivates the divisional managers to select actions that are consistent with the overall corporate plans and priorities.

Recent surveys, however, have documented that most large corporations do not use direct measures of productivity. Instead, they continue to use surrogates for productivity, such as labour variance, capacity utilization, or production cost standards. Sumanth's survey of 61 manufacturing companies indicated that partial productivity measures were used in 19.3% of the cases, aggregate productivity measures were used in only 0.3% of the cases, and simple surrogate measures were used in 80.4% of the cases. Furthermore, considerable confusion prevails about the definition and implementation of productivity measures. This is likely due to the fact that the direct productivity measures that have traditionally been used are simplistic, and they generally do not reflect the complex nature of most production processes encountered in practice.

In particular, the traditional approaches assume linearity, separability, and other restrictive features for the production technology to simplify the calculations. As a result, improvements in productivity as measured by the traditional approaches are frequently found, in practice to be inconsistent with improvements in the firm's competitive position and its short-term or long term profitability. This arithmetic simplicity may have been necessitated in the past by computational concerns.

However, with the increasing availability of inexpensive computing facilities, it is imperative that new productivity measure be developed that are appropriate for todays technologies.

A management control system is sometimes described as consisting of a device for measuring what is actually happening, a device for assessing the significance of the measured quantity relative to a standard, and a device for influencing the behaviour of managers, with evaluation of performance based on this measure and standard.

Similarly, a productivity measurement system requires first a proper definition and development of a productivity index that reflects the actual productivity considerations in complex technologies. Second, it requires benchmarks for comparison purposes. These benchmarks, or standards, may be based on the information about the organization's performance in the past. Such information need not be restricted to just the performance in the preceding period. The standards could also be based on the performance of other similar organizations. This is particularly appropriate for corporations with a number of similar plants or branches or divisions which are evaluated relative to each other. Such benchmarks could also be developed from extensive engineering simulation models. This approach is appropriate for evaluating the productivity impact of new or potential technologies.

Finally, a productivity measurement system must be integrated with other systems for evaluating managerial performance. Productivity measurement is not very meaningful without an appropriate accounting and reporting system to support it.

However, currently in most corporations, much of productivity oriented information remains at the shop floor level and is rarely reported to higher levels of management. If productivity accounting is to be employed for management control purposes it must be defined and developed carefully, and integrated with existing accounting and reporting systems, and further, it must maintain consistency with other corporate objectives such as profit maximization.

Productivity, as defined in this framework, measures the extent to which the actual input consumption exceeds the minimum inputs necessary to produce the actual input levels. The minimum input consumption is determined in a manner consistent with out current knowledge of the available production technology. Thus, a distinction is made between resources controllable by the responsible manager, and resources that are fixed, or beyond his discretionary control.

In a manner analogous to responsibility accounting, the productivity variations are analyzed to emphasize which manager controls what parameters of the firm's operations, and to what extent each manager is responsible for the observed productivity variations. For the price of the output relative to the labour usage rate depicted by the relative price line, it is also apparent that profits will be maximized if, in fact, the activity level is increased. But this implies a reduction in the traditional productivity measure. In this situation, therefore, the criterion of increasing "productivity" leads to a decision that is contradictory to the objective of increasing profits. This remains the fundamental problem with the traditional methods, where productivity improvement does not always imply profitability improvement.

❐

8

Productivity and Work Study

Policy formulation in modern times has become a very complicated and time consuming phenomenon. Business enterprises now-a-days wants to plan their future strategies from its past performance. There are number of measures *viz.* Productivity, Profitability, Rate of return etc. to illustrate the past performance. All these indicators are some sort of direct or indirect relationships between input and output factors. But none of the measures is able to determine or evaluate the overall performance of an enterprise.

The only way of raising the living standards of the society is to increase productivity. Productivity can be increased by increasing output from each unit of input.

THE CONCEPT OF PRODUCTIVITY

Productivity refers to the physical relationship between the quantity produced (output) and the quantity of resources used in the course of production (input). It is the ratio between the output of goods and services and the input of resources consumed in the process of production.

$$\text{Productivity (P)} = \frac{\text{Output (O)}}{\text{Input (I)}}$$

Output implies total production while input means land, labour, capital, management, etc.

Productivity measures the efficiency of the production system. The efficiency with which resources are utilised is called productive efficiency. Higher productivity means producing more from a given amount of inputs or producing a given amount with lesser inputs. At the level of a plant or an industry productivity is an output-input ratio. But at the macro level, productivity is a measure of performance of an economy or country. It denotes the ratio of available goods and services to the available resources of the society.

IMPORTANCE OF PRODUCTIVITY

The concept of productivity is of great significance for undeveloped and developing countries. In both the cases there are limited resources which should be used to get the maximum output *i.e.*, there should be tendency to perform a job by cheaper, safer and quicker ways. The aim should be optimum use of resources so as to provide maximum satisfaction with minimum efforts and expenditure. Productivity analysis and measures indicate the stages and situations where improvement in the working of inputs is possible to increase the output.

The productivity indicators can be used for different purposes *viz.* comparison of performances for various organisations, contribution of different input factors, bargaining with trade unions etc.

Definitions of Productivity

(i) Productivity is a measure of how much input is required to produce a given output *i.e.* it is ratio of output to input.

(ii) Productivity is the ratio between the amount produced and the amount of resources used in the course of production. The resources may be any combination of materials, machines, men and space.

(iii) European Produdivity Council defines "Productivity is an attitude of mind. It is a mentality of progress, of the constant improvement of that which exists. It is the certainly of being able to do better than yesterday and continuously. It is constant adaptation of economic and social life to changing conditions. It is the continual effort to apply new techniques and methods. It is the faith in human progress."

(iv) According to Peter Drucker, "Productivity means a balance between all factors of production that will give the maximum output with the smallest effort."

(v) I.L.O. generally takes productivity to mean, "The ratio between the volume of output as measured by production indices and the corresponding volume of labour input as measure by production indices and the corresponding volume of labour input as measured by employment indices."

(vi) Organisation of European Economic Community (OEEC) defines productivity as the ratio between the production of given commodity measured by volume and one or more of the corresponding input factors also measured by volume.

Thus there can be a number of measures indicating the level of performance corresponding to each input.

FACTORS INFLUENCING PRODUCTIVITY

Productivity is the outcome of several factors. These factors are so interrelated that it is difficult to identify the effect of anyone factor on productivity. These factors may broadly be divided into two categories—human factors and technological factors.

1. Human Factors

Human nature and human behaviour are the most significant determinants of productivity. Human factors may further be classified into two categories as given below:

(i) **Ability to Work.** Productivity of an organisation depends upon the competence and calibre of its people—both workers and managers. Ability to work is governed by education; training, experience, aptitude, etc., of the employees.

(ii) **Willingness to Work.** Motivation and morale of people is the second important group of human factors that determine productivity. Wage incentive schemes, labour participation in management, communication system, informed group relations, promotion policy, union management relations, quality of leadership, etc., are the main factors governing employees' willingness to work. Working conditions like working hours, sanitation, ventilation, lighting, temperature, safety measures and welfare amenities like housing, schools, clubs, libraries, subsides canteen, company transport, etc., also influence the motivation and morale of employees.

2. Technological Factors

Technological factors exercise significant influence on the level of productivity. The main technological factors are as follows:

(a) Size and capacity of plant.

(b) Product design and standardisation.

(c) Timely supply of materials and fuel.

(d) Rationalisation and automation measures.

(e) Repairs and maintenance.

(f) Production planning and control.

(g) Plant layout and location.

(h) Materials handling system.

(i) Inspection and quality control.

(j) Machinery and equipment used.

(k) Research and development.

(l) Inventory control.

(m) Reduction and utilisation of waste and scrap, etc.

MEASUREMENT OF PRODUCTIVITY

Measurement of Productivity has been defined as the ratio of output and input. An increase in productivity means an increase in output that is proportionately greater than an increase in inputs. But measurement of outputs and inputs is not a simple matter. When a single product is being manufactured output can be measured in physical terms, *e.g.*, number of units produced, weight, volume, etc. But in most of the industries more than one product is being manufactured. When an industry produces some by-products the problem becomes all the more complicated.

Measurement of output posses similar problems. Input factors are many and varied. Some of them may not be measurable at all *e.g.*, managerial skills. When it is difficult to compare the output and inputs in physical terms, they have to be converted into money terms for the purpose of comparison. Then productivity is defined as the ratio of net value of output to the net value of input, all expressed at constant prices. But price fluctuations create errors in measurement. Monetary measurements do not measure correctly the changes in quantity. Measurement of productivity is even more difficult in service enterprises.

Productivity may be measured either on aggregated basis or on individual basis. In the first case output is compared with all the input factors taken together: This is known as total productivity. In the second case output is compared with anyone of the input factors and this is called partial productivity or factor productivity.

$$\text{Total Productivity Index} = \frac{\text{Total Output}}{\text{Total Input}}$$

$$= \frac{\text{Total production of goods and service}}{\text{Labour} + \text{Materials} + \text{Capital} + \text{Energy}}$$

This index measures the efficiency of the entire organisation in the use of all the resources. It is a strategic yardstick for evaluating the operating efficiency of the entire plant or firm.

FACTOR PRODUCTIVITY INDICES

In order to means the efficiency of individual operations or specific factors of production, productivity indices for individual inputs are computed.

Labour Productivity Index

Labour productivity index is the most common measure of productivity. The labour input is measured in terms of man-hours. One man working for one hour is called man-hour.

$$\text{Labour Productivity Index} = \frac{\text{Output in units}}{\text{Man - hours works}}$$

This index does not indicate the idleness of labour due to machine breakdown, power failure, etc. The factory attendance may be used as gross man-hours and actual working time as net man-hours. Comparison between the two would indicate the extent of the idle time.

$$\text{Land Productivity Index} = \frac{\text{Total output}}{\text{Machine hours worked}}$$

$$\text{Material Productivity Index} = \frac{\text{Total output}}{\text{Quantity of materials used}}$$

$$\text{Land Productivity Index} = \frac{\text{Total output}}{\text{Area of land used}}$$

TECHNIQUES TO IMPROVE PRODUCTIVITY

Productivity can be considerably improved by improving the performance of various factors affecting productivity. The measures to improve productivity can be:

(i) Better planning and training of employees, improved jobs and communication and effective management through CPM/PERT methods.

(ii) Use of time and motion studies to study and improve work performance. It enables to assess the quantum of work which can be used for planning and control.

(iii) Better transportation and material handling system.

(iv) By providing work incentives and other benefits to workers.

(v) Workers involvement in decision making and working of organisations.

(vi) Improvement in technology of production process and nature of raw material and its quality.

(vii) Simplification, standardisation and specialisation techniques.

(viii) Better and efficient utilisation of resources at the disposal of the enterprise.

(ix) Use of linear programming and other quantitative techniques for better decision making.

(x) ABC analysis to identify more important items and then apply inventory control to reduce capital investment.

(xi) Value engineering to reduce material content by good design.

MEANING OF PRODUCTION ORDER

It is necessary that detailed information about the nature of items to be produced, the manufacturing system, etc. should be provided for effective and proper implementation of production planning activities. The sequence of operations involving men, machine and material of the system should be properly analysed and described in a systematic manner. In short, the systematic arrangement of the information to carry out the production planning activities of an organisation is known as Production Order.

Through Production Order, the production control measures can be applied effectively. It also provides guidelines for economic and efficient location and layout of plant and equipment.

It can also be termed as the graphical representation of the activities performed by men, machine and materials of a manufacturing system. It is an asset for formulating detailed and efficient production strategy.

MAIN OBJECTIVES OF A PRODUCTION ORDER

The following may be the objects of a production order:

(i) Providing valuable information about the nature of the production, their specifications, volume of production, time to be taken in production process, and time schedule of various activities involved in the production process.

(ii) Enabling various production departments to take appropriate action at specified time.

(iii) To start the control system working.

(iv) Supplying basic information for evaluating the performance of the production process in terms of cost, time and quality.

(v) Maintaining a balance between work systems and techniques.

(vi) Standardisation of plant layout, systems and procedures.

(vii) Elimination of unnecessary, useless and ineffective motions and activities.

(viii) To make possible the maximum utilisation of men, materials and machines and to increase overall productivity.

(ix) To make efforts to reduce the cost production

MEANING OF WORK STUDY

Work study is 'a management service based on those techniques, particularly method study and work measurement, which are used in the examination of human work in all its contexts, and which lead to the systematic investigation of all the resources and factors which affect the efficiency and economy of the situation being reviewed, in order to effect improvement.'

This definition indicates clearly where present-day work study differs from earlier job improvement schemes: a systematic discipline has been set up, providing a framework in which to work. Regrettably, work study has been endowed with a glamour which leads new comers to believe that it is a panacea for all the ills which arise in production/operations. This, of course, is not so: it is one of a number of equally important management tools and cannot replace good management, although it may indicate areas requiring investigation.

Traditionally, work study is associated with 'shop-floor' or direct labour. When applied to indirect work, the term 'organisation and methods' (normally abbreviated to O & M) is used. The techniques of the O & M man are exactly those of the work study practitioner, but applied to clerical and administrative procedures, and in non-manufacturing environments.

In a Joint Industrial Training Board report on Training for Work Study Practice, the following excellent statement occur:

Work study attains its benefits through, firstly, investigation of the current situation, examining especially any apparent weaknesses (for example, poor performance by an operating team or machine or the high cost of a job): this diagnosis is followed by the determination and introduction of appropriate improvements in operating methods. The investigation and review will cover operating methods, selection to type of equipment, usage of equipment, layout, supply and usage of materials, availability of ancillary services, *e.g.* materials handling, organisarion of work, effectiveness of planning procedures and progress control, and the potential effect of the investigation on overall cost and profitability.

By virtue of its far-reach in nature, the inception of work study must be undertaken most carefully. For example, in examining the procedures for handling and processing documents, investigations may show that a significant cause of inefficiency is the time the computer takes to process the information. This might appear to be a criticism of the software developed by the data-processing department, which in turn may be revealed to be conditioned by the general financial policy of the company, limiting the size and power of computer purchased. Thus, what may start as a simple improvement of method programme may call into question the action of a number of senior executives. Such a situation could well cause considerable resentment and in some cases active opposition. An equally difficult situation is the employment of a work study practitioner in a department without adequate managerial support, so that any suggestions or improvements are not implemented. This results in bitterness on the part of the work study practitioner and work study itself being brought into derepute.

At the outset of any work study programme, therefore, it is vital that all concerned should understand the principles, techniques and limitations of work study. As with any face of management, success depends upon the cooperation of the people concerned. and positive steps must be taken to obtain the goodwill of those whose work is to be studied. Secrecy, or the appearance of secrecy, must be avoided at all costs. The ideal situation is one where work study is not considered as a separate entity but as an integral part of all activities. It is highly desirable that all levels of management down to shop-floor/office supervisor level appreciate the scope and limitations of work study. Indeed some of the techniques can be used effectively by management without the need for excessively long training periods to become proficient.

Work study has two closely related facets: method study, an examination of the ways of doing work, and work measurement, which is the assessment of the time which a job should take. Both are carried out systematically and follow very similar patterns.

Work Study

Method Study	*Work Measurement*
1. Select task to be studied.	1. Select tasks to be studied.
2. Record the facts.	2. Record the facts.
3. Examining the facts.	3. Analyse the facts.

Contd.

Method Study	*Work Measurement*
4. Develop and define the new method.	4. Measure the task.
5. Install the hew method.	5. Compile the standard time.
6. Maintain.	6. Define method and its related time.

GENERAL RELATIONSHIP BETWEEN METHOD STUDY AND TIME STUDY

Work Study concerns itself with better ways of doing things and control over the output of those things by setting standards with respect to time. Productivity which is, generally speaking, a ratio of output to input, is of great importance for the healthy running of any organisation; it assume particular importance for developing countries like India who have to compete favourably with other countries in the international market and make optimal use of scarce resources. Although usually the concepts of Work Study relate to a manufacturing organisation, they are equally valid for other than manufacturing situations where services—if not goods—are generated.

The means of improving ways and means of doing things in called Method Study. The primary purpose of improving 'methods' is to save time, and therefore, effort of labour and machinery. Hence a measurement of the work involved in any job and the setting of the standards (for control purposes) of the time normally expected and the effort involved will be necessary. This aspect of setting work standards for comparison, control and other managerial action purposes is termed as Work Measurement. Since the standards are mentioned in time units required to perform a job, given a particular work setting and method, Work Measurement is also alternatively called Time Study. Method Study and Time Study together comprise Work Study.

The study of 'methods' of accomplishing a job by the movement of human limbs and eyes, etc. is termed as Motion Study. This is a part of Method Study.

COMPONENTS OF WORK STUDY

There are two main branches of Work Study namely *(i)* Method Study and *(ii)* Work Measurement.

Work Study

Method study	*Work measurement*
1. Select the task to be studied.	1. Select task to be studied.
2. Collection, recording and presentation of facts.	2. Record the facts.
3. Analyse the facts.	3. Analyse the facts.
4. Develop new methods.	4. Measures the tasks.
5. Install the new methods.	5. Define the method and related time.
6. Maintain the methods.	7. Maintain the work.

BASIC PROCEDURE OF WORK STUDY

The basic procedure of work study consists of the following steps:

(i) Define the problem.

(ii) Obtain all relevant facts.

(iii) Examine the facts critically and objectively.

(iv) Consider the alternatives and decide which one to follow.

(v) Act on the decision.

(vi) Follow up the development.

OBJECTIVES OF WORK STUDY

Work study deals with the techniques of method study and work measurement, which are employed to ensure the best possible use of human, machine and material resources in carrying out a specified activity.

Objective. Work study is concerned with finding better ways of doing work and avoiding waste in all its forms. As such the objective of work study is to assist management to obtain the optimum use of the human, machine and material resources available to the organization for the accomplishment of the work upon which it is engaged.

The objective has three aspects:

* The most effective use of plant and equipment

* The most effective use of human effort

* The evaluation of human work.

Work study has two broad areas, *viz.*, method study and time study.

Method study is concerned with finding the facts about a situation, and after a critical examination of these facts, developing a new and better method of doing that work. It is defined as the existing and proposed ways of doing work and the development and application of easier and more productive methods.

Time study is concerned with the establishment of time standards for a qualified worker to perform a specified job at a defined level of performance.

Method study must precede time study before any attempt is made to measure and set standards for the various jobs concerned.

Method Study

It is the systematic recording, analysis and critical examination of existing and proposed ways of doing work and the development and application of easier and new production methods.

Areas of Application of Method Study. It can be applied to any field of work, but the most important areas where it plays a major role in improving productivity are as follows:

* Improved layout of office, working areas of factories
* Improved design of plant and equipment
* Improved use of materials, plant, equipment and manpower
* Most effective handling of material
* Improved flow of work
* Standardization of methods and procedures
* Improved safety standards
* Better working conditions

Steps in Method Study

Methods improvement involves systematic, orderly and scientific approach to problems. One should have an open mind, maintain a questioning attitude, collect all relevant facts, consult others including workers, list reasons/causes for various effects.

Decision must be taken after listing out all alternatives and evaluating them critically. Based on these guidelines, the steps in method study are explained below.

1. **Select.** Select the work to be studied.
2. **Record.** Record all the relevant facts of the present (or proposed) method by direct observation.
3. **Examine.** Examine the facts critically in sequence, using special critical examination sheet.
4. **Develop.** Develop the best method, *i.e.* the most practical, economic and effective method, under prevailing circumstances.
5. **Install.** Install that method as standard practice.
6. **Maintain.** Maintain that standard practice by regular routine check.

Among all the Steps, Step 2 and Step 3 need detailed discussion, which are discussed in the following sections.

Recording

In order to carry out any investigation, data or relevant facts pertaining to the existing method must be collected and recorded. There are a number of recording techniques developed to simplify and standardize the work.

The recording may trace the movements of men, material or details of various processes. The principle is to use the simplest technique which will contain all relevant information needed for investigation.

The different recording techniques are charts, diagrams and models. The most commonly used recording techniques to cover most of the activities are shown in Table 1. The different symbols which are used in process charts are explained in Table 2.

Examine Step

This is the most important step in method study. This step aims: to eliminate the activity altogether if it is unnecessary, to combine it with other activities, and to change the sequence of activities so that work delay is reduced and simplify the activity to reduce the work content or time consumed.

In this step, we will have to ask a series of questions. The questions may be classified into primary questions and secondary questions.

Table 1 : Recording Techniques

	Information Recorded
(1)	*(2)*
Charts	
1. Outline process chart	Principle operations and inspection of the processes.

Contd.

(1)	*(2)*
2. Flow process chart	Activities of men, material or equjpment are analysed into five events. Operation, inspection, transport, storage and delay.
3. Two-handed process chart	Movement of two hands or limbs of the operator.
4. Multiple activity chart	Simultaneous/interrelated activities of operators and/or machines on a common time scale.
5. Simultaneous motion cycle (SIMO)	Movement of body members of the operator, expressed in terms of therbligs on a common time scale.
Diagrams and Models	
1. Flow diagram	Path of men, materials and equipments on a scale model.
2. String diagram	Same as above except for the variation that it uses string to trace the path.
Photographic Aids	
1. Cyclegraph	Movement of hand obtained by exposing a photographic plate to the light emitted from small bulbs attached to the operator's fingers.
2. Chrono-cyclegraphs	Modification of cyclegraph in which record is made using flash lights.

Table 2: Symbols Used in Process Chart

Symbol	*Activity*	*Purpose for which Used*
○ (Circle)	Operation	Indicates main steps in a process, method of procedure usually, the part, material or product concerned is modified or changed during the operation.
□ (Square)	Inspection	Indicates any type of inspection, check, measurement, visual scrutiny for quality and/or quantity.
⇨	Transport	Indicates movement of workers, material or equipment from place to place.
D	Temporary storage or delay	Indicates a delay in the sequence of events.
▽ (Inverted tringle)	Storage	Indicates controlled storage in which material is received into or issued from stores under some form of authorization, or an item is retained for reference purposes.

Primary Questions

Purpose	What is the purpose of the event? Why is it necessary?
Place	Where does the event take place? Why there?
Sequence	When does it occur? Why then?
Person	Who carries out the work? Why that person?
Means	How is the purpose achieved? Why that particular way?

Secondary Suestions

Purpose	What else could be done?
Place	Where else could it be done?

Sequence	When else could it be done?
Person	Who else could do it?
Means	How else could it be done?

Alternatives. When each of the above questions is applied to any event, number of alternatives would emerge. When these have been established, ask the following questions.

Purpose	What should be done?
Place	Where should it be done?
Sequence	When should it be done?
Person	Who should do it?
Means	How should it be done?

Principles of Motion Economy (Ergonomic Considerations at Work)

The improvement of any method is generally accomplished using the ideas chosen from the alternatives thrown up during the critical examination phase of the method study. To aid critical examination, certain rules or principles may be used. These are called principles of motion economy. These can be classified into the following three categories.

1. Related to the use of the human body.
2. Related to the arrangement of the work place.
3. Related to the design of tools and equipment.

Principles Related to the Use of the Human Body

(a) The two hands should begin as well as complete their motion at the same time.

(b) The two hands should not be idle at the same time except during rest periods.

(c) Motions of the arms should be made in opposite and symmetrical directions and should be made simultaneously.

(d) Momentum should be employed to assist the worker wherever possible, and it should be reduced to a minimum if it must be overcome by muscular effort.

(e) Ballistic movements are faster, easier and more accurate then restricted or controlled movements.

(f) Rhythm is essential to the smooth and automatic performance of an operation and the work should be arranged to permit any easy and natural rhythm wherever possible.

Principles Related to the Arrangement of the Work Place

(a) There should be a definite and fixed place for all tools and materials.

(b) Tools, materials and controls should be located close to the operator and directly in front of the operator.

(c) Gravity feed bins and containers should be used to deliver materials close to the point of use.

(d) Drop deliveries should be used whenever possible.

(e) Materials and tools should be located to permit the best sequence of motions.

(f) The height of the work place and the chair should preferably be arranged so that alternate sitting and standing at work are easily possible.

Principles Related to the Design of Tools and Equipment

(a) The hands should be relieved of all work that can be done more advantageously to a jig, a fixture or a foot operated device.

(b) Two or more tools should be combined wherever possible.

(c) Tools and materials should be pre-positioned wherever possible.

(d) Where each finger performs some specific movements such as in typewriting, the load should be distributed in accordance with the inherent capacity of the finger.

(e) Handles such as those used on cranks and large screw drivers should be designed to permit as much of the surface of the hand to come in contact with the handle as possible.

Time Study

This was originally proposed by Frederick Taylor and was later modified to include a performance rating (PR) adjustment. The time study is considered to be one of the most widely used means of work measurement. Basically, by using time study, an analyst will be taking a small sample of a single worker's activity, and using it to derive a standard for tasks of that nature.

The steps of time study are as follows:

Step 1. First select the job to be studied. Breakdown the work content of the job into smallest possible elements. Then inform the worker and define the best method.

Step 2. Observe the time for appropriate number of cycles (such as 25 to 50).

Step 3. Determine the average cycle time (CT)

$$CT = \frac{\Sigma \text{ times}}{\text{No. of cycles}}$$

Step 4. Determine the normal time (NT)

$$NT = CT\ (PR)$$

where, PR is the performance rating.

Step 5. Determine the standard time using the following formula.

$$ST = NT\ (AF)$$

where

$$ADF = \frac{1}{1 - \%\ \text{Allowance}}$$

AF being the allowance factor.

In Step 2, n can be calculated using the following formula.

$$n = \frac{z^2[n_1 \Sigma x^2 - (\Sigma x)^2]}{h^2 (\Sigma x)^2}$$

where

n_1 = Preliminary sample size

x = recorded stopwatch times

h = half the precision interval in % (for example, if the precision interval is ± 5%, then h = 0.05)

z = the standard normal deviate for the desired confidence level.

Example 1. In a welding shop, a direct time study was done on a welding operation. One inexperienced industrial engineer and one experienced industrial engineer conducted the study simultaneously. They agreed precisely on cycle time (shown below) but their opinion on rating the worker differed. The experienced engineer rated the worker 100 percent and the other engineer rated the worker 120 percent. They used a 0.10 percent allowance fraction.

Cycle Time (in minutes)	*Number of Times Observed*
20	2
24	1
29	1
32	1

From the above statement,

(a) Determine the standard time using the experienced industrial engineer's worker rating.

(b) Find the standard time using the worker rating of inexperienced industrial engineer.

(c) Comment on the reliability of time study engineers.

Solution.

(a) Rating the worker at 100% by the experienced Industrial Engineer

$$\text{Cycle time (CT)} = \frac{20 \times 2 + 24 \times 1 + 29 \times 1 + 32 \times 1}{5}$$

$$= 25 \text{ minutes.}$$

$$\text{Normal Time (NT)} = \text{CT} \times \text{PR}$$

$$= 25 \times 100\% = 25 \text{ minutes}$$

$$\text{Standard Time (ST)} = (\text{NT})/(1 - \%\text{A})$$

$$= 25/(1 - 0.10) = 27.78 \text{ minutes}$$

(b) Rating the worker at 120% by the inexperienced Industrial Engineer

$$\text{Cycle time (CT)} = 25 \text{ minutes}$$

$$\text{Normal time (NT)} = \text{CT} \times \text{PR}$$

$$= 25 \times 120\% = 30.00 \text{ minutes}$$

$$\text{Standard time (ST)} = \text{NT}/(1 - \%\text{A}) = 30/(1 - 0.10)$$

$$= 33.33 \text{ min.}$$

(c) Comment. The results in part (a) and part (b) show differences in normal time and standard time. The task of estimating performance rating of a worker requires certain experience. So, we can rely on the results obtained by the experienced industrial engineer. The consistency in rating skill can be improved by repeatedly seeing rating films and/or by attending short courses on performance rating.

Work Sampling

Work sampling is also a technique for establishing standard times of activities. This method was introduced by L.H.C. Tippett in 1934. This method is more suitable for analyzing group activities and repetitive activities which take longer duration.

If a given individual performs more than one activity, then the time standard for each activity may be computed using this method.

For example, on a printing press, a single worker will be doing composing, proof reading, printing, cutting etc. The time standards for these activities may be determined using the work sampling method.

In this method, the standard time of a specified activity is determined by computing the proportion of time the worker spends on that activity.

The percentage of the total observation a person is engaged in a given activity approximates the percentage of the total work time spent in that activity. Assume, for example, that during a 8-hour study period an analyst made a total of 100 observations and 10 of those observations showed the worker was inspecting the size of components produced on his machine. It would be assumed that 10/100 or 10 percent of the time was spent on inspection. Ten percent of 8 hours is 48 minutes. The proportion of time is computed by observing the operator at random intervals. Let us assume that the operator has produced 40 components during the 8-hour duration. Then the average time spent for inspection on component is 1.2 minute (48/40 min.). This time is taken as the observed time. Later, the analyst must adjust this time for performance rating of the operator and allowances.

The steps for the work-sampling method are listed below:

1. (a) Select the job which is to be studied

   (b) Inform the workers about the method study

   (c) Prepare a detailed list of activities of the job.

2. Decide the total duration of observation.

   Total duration of observation = No. of hour/shift × No. of shifts/per day × No. of days

3. Determine the number of observations to be made.

$$n^* = \frac{Zpq}{h^2}$$

where

Z = Standard normal statistic at a given confidence level

p = Value of sample proportion

q = 1 − p

h = Half the precision interval (Half of the width of the confidence level)

This is only a rough estimate. As the study progresses, if the value of p is more than p ± h, then again the value of n should be revised.

4. Prepare a tour schedule to take the specified number of observations over the specified time duration.

5. Record performance rating of the workers and their activities as per the schedule.

6. Determine the acceptable number of units produced during the period.

7. Compute the percentage of working on a given task using the following formula

$$\text{Percentage of working} = \frac{\text{Frequency of performance of a task}}{\text{Total number of observations}} \times 100$$

8. Determine the normal time

$$NT = \frac{(\text{Total time})\ (\%\ \text{of working})\ PR}{\text{No. of acceptable units produced}}$$

9. Determine the standard time (ST)

$$ST = NT \times AF$$

$$= NT \frac{1}{1 - \text{allowance percentage}}$$

Example 2. A job consists of three work elements and all are performed by the same operator. An analyst conducted work sampling to determine the standard time for the job. The duration of the study is two shifts each with 400 minutes of effective time. The details of observations are summarized in the following table. The total number of acceptable units produced during the study period is 150 units. Determine the standard time by assuming allowance of 10%.

Work Number	*Frequency of Performance*	*Performance Rating*
1	70	80%
2	80	120%
3	50	110%

Solution.

Total duration = 2 x 400 = 800 minutes

Total number of observations = 200

The calculations for determining normal time and standard time of each of the work elements are summarized in the following table. From the table, it is clear that the standard time of the job is equal to 3.06 minutes.

Work Element Number	*Percentage Working*	*Observed Time (minutes)*	*Standard Time (minutes)*
1	(70/200) × 100 = 35%	(400 × 0.35 × .80)/150 = 0.75	0.75/0.9 = 0.83
2	(80/200) × 100 = 40%	(400 × 0.40 × 1.2)/150 = 1.28	1.28/.9 = 1.42
3	(50/200) × 100 = 25%	(400 × 0.25 × 1.1)/150 = 0.73	0.73/.9 = 0.81
			Total = 3.06

PROCESS CHARTS

These are 'charts in which a sequence of events is portrayed diagrammatically by means of a set of process chart symbols...' Their purpose is to provide an unambiguous, succinct record of a process so that it may be examined, analysed and—desirably—improved, usually away from the workplace.

Five symbols have been generally agreed and are in current use. These are illustrated in Fig. 1.

It is useful to differentiate between two types of operation:

(a) 'do' operations where work is actually performed on the material or equipment resulting in an increase in added value;

(b) 'ancillary' operations where material or equipment is prepared, cleaned down, or put away.

○ Operations: '... usually the part, material, product or document... is modified or changed.'

⇨ Transport: '.... movement of workers, materials or equipment from place to place' without otherwise furthering the process.

▽	Permanent Storage:	'... a controlled storage...'
D	Delay or Temporary Storage:	'... a delay... for example, work waiting between consecutive operations or... temporarily laid aside.'
□	Inspection:	Inspection... for quality and/or... quantity.'

Fig.1 Charting Symbols

Cross-hatching may be used to emphasise the 'do' operation, as in following Fig.2.

Distances are recorded to the left of the transport symbol, and brief descriptions are written on the right of the symbol.

These symbols, combined in a process chart, give a rapid picture of a process showing clearly where it is worked on, where it is transported and so on. The care with which this recording is done will largely determine the final success of the study.

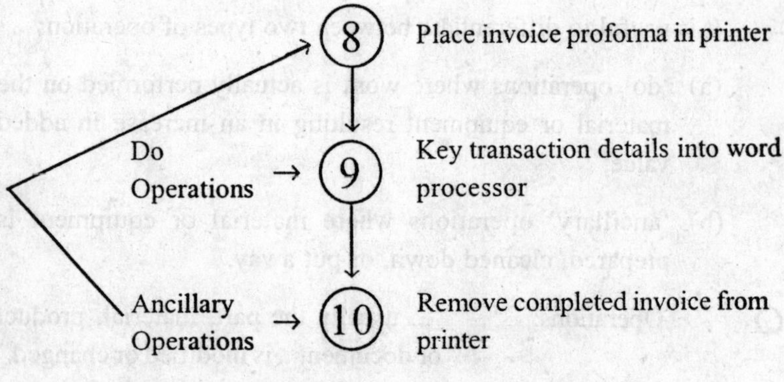

Fig. 2. Emphasizing 'do' operations by hatching

There are basically two types of process chart, differing in the level of detail recorded:

(a) Outline Process Chart. In this, the overall picture of the sequence of events and of the introduction of materials in a process is given by recording operations and inspections, using only two symbols (the cirde and the square) of the five available.

(b) Flow Process Chart. This provides considerably more detail than the outline process chart, and all five symbols are used. Row process charts refer either to the man (or machine/equipment), *i.e.*, to the activities performed by the man, or to the material (the activities carried out upon the material) and not normally to both simultaneously. Pre-printed forms are often prepared within larger organisation.

TIME-SCALED CHARTS

These are charts where two or more activities which are proceeding concurrently or simultaneously are shown on a common time scale. Again, there are broadly two set of time-scaled charts, differing in the level of detail:

(c) Multiple Activity Chart. This chart, which may be considered to be a vertical Gantt chart, is used to show the time relationships between two or more workers, machines or materials. Essentially, a vertical column is elected for each, and the work performed is recorded as shading within the column. Time is recorded on the left and a brief description of the activities on the right. From the chart, the ratio of working to non-working time can be determined, and an attempt at balancing can be made.

(d) Simultaneous Movement Chart (SIMO Chart). In this the movements of two or more parts of a worker's body are recorded. The movements are generally of very short duration—of the order of milliseconds—and the preparation of a SIMO chart usually requires a frame-by-frame analysis of a cine firm of video tape of the work being studied. The elements of work may be recorded by therblig symbol, which are first used by Gilbreth, hence the name—therblig is Gilbreth spelt backwards (almost!). There are now 17 therbligs covering such elements as grasp, hold, unavoidable delay. There are a number of varieties of SIMO charts which do not use therblig symbols, but employ one or other of the predetermined motion time systems (PMTS) codes. These codes usually carry with them time values for the performance of the individual elements being recorded, and the PMTS charts are most frequently prepared as a means of work measurement. Whilst SIMO charts can enable imbalances to be detected, they are difficult to prepare, and likely to be expensive both in time and equipment. They are used only if very great justification can be demonstrated.

MOVEMENT CHARTS

When movement is to be recorded, one or other of the movement charts is employed:

(e) Travel Chart. In complex situations it is sometimes confusing to try to use a flow diagram, and a travel chart (see following Fig.) can be used. In this, the number of movements made over a period of time can be recorded. Movement is always assumed to start with the lefthand row title and move to the column headings, so that movements from department 7 to department 4 and from department 2 to department 16 are as shown by the two crosses. By adding up the crosses in the rows, the 'movement out' can be found, while summing the columns gives 'movements in'.

(f) Flow Diagram. This displays the workplace and the locations of the various activities, drawn to scale. The five standard symbols are used, and the diagrams again refer to worker, material or machines equipment. Effectively, it can be considered to be a flow process chart drawn upon a scale drawing of the workplace.

(g) String Diagram. Here again a scale drawing is used which is mounted upon a wooden panel. A preliminary survey identifies the locations of terminal points, and a fine string is would between these pins to represent movement, supplementary pins being inserted where direction of movement change. The advantage of string over pencil marks on a piece of paper is that repeated journeys over common paths can be shown without risk of obliteration or confusion.

Unwinding and measuring the strings will enables the distances moved to be discovered. The string diagram will display vividly faults in a layout which cause bottlenecks, back or cross-tracking or other movement difficulties.

TO
DEPARTMENT

	1	2	3	4	5	6	7	8	9	10	11	12	13	14	15	16	17	18	19	20
1																				
2																				
3																				
4																				
5																				
6																				
7																				
8																				
9																				
10																				
11																				
12																				
13																				
14																				
15																				
16																				
17																				
18																				
19																				
20																				

Fig. 3. Travel Chart

□

9

Materials Management

Materials are any commodities used directly or indirectly in producing a product or service, such as raw materials, component parts, assemblies, and supplies. Managing materials in most companies is crucial to their success because the cost of buying, storing, moving, and shipping materials accounts for over half of a product cost. Productivity basically means driving down the cost of doing business, and doing the job of materials management better is increasingly seen as the key to higher productivity in many U.S. firms today. Operations managers are working hard to develop better ways of managing materials so that on-time deliveries quality, and costs can be improved so that their companies can survive in an increasingly competitive world.

A materials system is the network of material flows within a production system, including materials at suppliers, in transit from suppliers, in receiving, in raw-materials warehouses, in in-process inventories, being processed in production departments, being moved between the production operations, being inspected in quality control, in finishedgoods warehouses, and in transit to customers. In short, a materials system includes all the materials present in a production system between the suppliers and the customers. A materials system of manufacturing plant. Studying material flows the acquisition, storage, movement, and processing of raw materials, components, assemblies, and supplies is a good way to understand manufacturing. Also, services such as retailing, warehousing, and transportation companies can be viewed as systems of material flows. In these systems, all organisational functions are critically affected by the planning and control of the materials system.

Materials management is all the management functions related to the complete cycle of materials flows, from the purchase and internal control of materials to the planning and control of work in process to the warehousing, shipping, and distribution of the finished products. Some organisations have centralised their diverse materials management functions under one department headed by a materials manager or vice-president of materials. This executive position coordinates all the activities of the materials system and bears total responsibility for the continuous supply of materials of low cost and specified quality when and where operating departments and customer require them. The responsibility of the materials manager is immense, a reality underscored by their typically high salaries, which rank with those of the highest industry positions.

Material management can be defined as "that aspect of management function which is primarily concerned with the acquisition, control and use of materials needed and flow of goods and services connected with production process having some predetermined objectives in view".

Most manufacturing concerns spend more than 60% of the money they take in, for materials, *i.e.,* materials soak up a substantial portion of the capital invested in an industrial concern. This emphasise the need for adequate materials management and control because even a small saving in materials can reduce the production cost to a fair extent and thus add to the profits.

Materials management may be thought of an integrated functioning of the different sections of a company dealing with the supply of materials and other related activities so as to obtain maximum coordination and optimum minimum expenditure on materials.

Materials management involves controlling the type, amount, location, movement, timings of purchase of various materials etc. used in an industrial concern.

Objectives of Materials Management

(i) To minimize material cost.

(ii) To procure and purchase materials of desired quality when required at the lowest possible the cost of the concern.

(iii) To reduce investment tied inventories for use in other productive purposes and to develop high inventory turn over ratios.

(iv) To purchase, receive, transport (*i.e.,* handle) and store materials efficiently and to reduce the related costs.

(v) To trace new sources of supply and to develop cordial relations with them in order to ensure continuous material supply at reasonable rates.

(vi) To cut down costs through simplification, standardization, value analysis, import substitution etc.

(vii) To report changes in market conditions and other factor affecting the concern, to the concern.

(viii) To conduct studies in areas such as quality consumption and cost of materials so as to minimize cost of production.

(ix) To modify paper work procedure in order to minimize delays in procuring materials.

Functions of Materials Management

(i) Materials planning

(ii) Procurement or purchasing of materials

(iii) Receiving and warehousing

(iv) Storage and store administration

(v) Inventory control

(vi) Standardisation, simplification and value analysis.

Principles of Materials Management

The following principles should be followed in the development and operation of an effective materials handing system:

(i) The number and frequency of movements should be minimised. The best handling is 'no handling'. As this is not possible the objective should be 'minimum handling'. All types of handling and rehandling should be minimised.

(ii) The time and distance involved in handling should be minimised wherever possible.

(iii) Whenever possible flow line and gravity should be used to move materials.

(iv) The handling should as far as possible be combined with the production equipment.

(v) Materials should be deposited as near to the point of use as possible.

(vi) Continuous and straight line movement is more efficient than irregular movement.

(vii) Materials handling equipment should be simple and consistent with the nature of materials and speed of movement. For example, for moving materials over inclined planes, gravity rollers are more appropriate than powered conveyers.

(viii) Fixed routes should be established for all handling devices.

(ix) Utilisation of handling equipment should be kept as high as possible.

(x) Materials handling system should be flexible so as to accommodate changes in products, plant layout, volume of output, etc.

Importance of Materials Management

Materials management department plays a vital role in the success of an enterprise. A significant portion of capital is invested in materials and well planned and well designed and well designed materials management operations can lead to considerable saving in the capital expenditure. It is of great importance to production, marketing, engineering and finance departments of an enterprise. The advantages or benefits from effective materials management operations can be outlined as:

(i) Regular supply of the material is ensured, reducing the chances of any interruption in production process.

(ii) Procurement costs and transportation costs associated with are materials are checked.

(iii) Efficient store and stock control minimises waste of material.

(iv) Inspection of material at the time of procurement minimises the possibility of finished product being rejected by the consumer.

(v) Timely supply of raw material and other inputs can be assured.

(vi) Better utilisation of labour, capital and equipment.

(vii) Congestion stores and at different stages of production can be avoided by an effective materials management system.

(viii) Length of manufacturing cycle is reduced to minimum.

(ix) Slight changes in material costs will exert a great impact on a firm's profit picture.

(x) Shortages can be eliminated.

Classification of Materials Handling Equipment

(i) Industrial Trucks. For moving mixed or uniform loads intermittently over various paths with suitable surfaces:

(a) Forklift trucks;

(b) Highway trucks;

(c) Crawlers;

(d) Electric haulage trucks.

(ii) Cranes and Hoists. For moving materials in varying loads intermittently to any point within a fixed area.

(a) Bridge crane;

(b) Jib crane;

(c) Electric overhead crane;

(d) Hoist-electric and pneumatic;

(e) Lifts;

(f) Jacks and Winches.

(iii) Conveyors. For moving uniform loads continuously from point to point over fixed paths.

(a) Roller conveyor;

(b) Belt conveyor;

(c) Mobile conveyor;

(d) Chutes;

(e) Trolley;

(f) Monorails.

Materials Handling Devices

A large number of tools and techniques are used for handling materials. The device and method of handling depend upon the type of materials, quantity and frequency of handling and the distance involved. Some of the major materials handling devices are given below.

(i) Cranes. A crane is used for intermittent movement of materials of different size and weight within a fixed area. It is more flexible than a conveyor but not as flexible as industrial trucks. Cranes are usually of three types: jib crane, bridge crane and gantry crane. Jib crane is used for loading and unloading of work pieces on machines.

(ii) Hoists. A hoist is able to move materials vertically and horizontally in a limited area. It is used primarily when materials must be lifted prior to being moved from one point to another. For example, if a part is large or heavy, the operator may find it necessary to use a hoist for loading and unloading the machine. Then, a crane may be employed to move the part to another work station. Cranes and hoists are able to carry objects through the overhead space in the plant. As a result they utilize less floor space. They are good means of positioning materials in a particular location. But a hoist is capable of serving only a limited area. Air hoist, electric hoist and chain hoist are important types of hoists.

(iii) Conveyors. A conveyor moves materials between two fixed points. It creates a relatively fixed route. Conveyors are employed primarily in continuous manufacturing where the loads are uniform and materials move from one work station to another specific work station. The rate of movement and location are fixed and materials can move continuously. Conveyors can bypass cross traffic. Conveyors can be of several kinds, *e.g.*, belt, roller, wheel, chute, apron, slot, trolley, screw, bracket, pneumatic. Belt conveyor is used to feed materials continuously to inaccessible points, *e.g.*, feeding coal and iron in a steel plant. Once put on the belt, materials are taken to the machine automatically as the belt is continuously moving.

(iv) Industrial Trucks. These are used to pick up and move materials intermittently through different routes. In such cases unit loads are used and distances are moderate. Industrial trucks are also useful for handling materials of mixed size and weight. These trucks are powered by hand, electricity or gasoline. An industrial truck does not occupy space permanently. Industrial trucks can be of different types, *e.g.*, forklift trucks, platform trucks, straddle carriers, etc. a forklift truck is often used to pick up materials and arrange them vertically in storage.

Choices of Materials Handling Equipment

The choice of materials handling equipment involves proper balancing of production problems, the capabilities of equipment available and the human factor involved. Production problems consist of the desired volume of production the type of material to be handled and the nature of plant layout. The skill, safety and attitudes of employees are important human factors which should be considered in selected materials handling equipment.

Within these considerations, the following factors should be kept in view while selecting materials handling equipment.

(i) **Supervision Required.** Automatic equipment requires less supervision than non-automatic equipment.

(ii) **Space Requirements.** The space required to install and operate the equipment is an important factor in selection.

(iii) **Cost.** The purchase price, installation costs, labour costs, salvage value and depreciation charges affect the cost of equipment. Operating costs should not be high.

(iv) **Load Capacity.** Equipment selected should have the adequate capacity to carry the required load of materials.

(v) **Power Requirements.** The equipment should be such that it can be operated with the available power.

(vi) **Flexibility.** As far as possible, the equipment should have the flexibility to handle more than one class of material. It should be adaptable enough to meet the material handling requirements in terms of load, movement, etc.

(vii) **Ease of Maintenance.** Equipment should be such that maintenance is easy and can be done at reasonable cost.

(viii) **Speed.** Rapidity of materials movement should be considered subject to limits of the production process or plant safety.

Duties of Materials Manager

Material management embraces all functions concerning with ordering, storage and movement of materials *i.e.*, purchasing, production control, stores, traffic and physical distribution.

The responsibilities of materials manager can also be described under following heads:

(i) **Purchasing.** Purchasing department buys materials in amounts authorised by requisitions received from the production control and stores department. Its main operations in this context are:

(a) Selection of suppliers and issue of purchase order.

(b) To expedite delivery of material from the suppliers.

(c) Acting as a liaison between suppliers and other departments of the enterprise.

(d) To look for new products, materials and suppliers that can contribute to company's profits. Material manager acts as company's eyes and ears' to the outside world and report on changes in market conditions and ether facters that can influence operations and activities of the enterprise.

(ii) **Production control.** This is dene by:

(a) Determining requirements of materials and parts to be purchased and manufactured.

(b) Schedules production and purchasing precesses of parts and material.

(c) Issues work order to manufacturing departments and purchase order to suppliers.

(iii) Inventory and Stores Control. It keeps detailed and upto date record of inventory, on order status and potential demand for each production part and material. It is also responsible for non-productive stores like office supplies, perishable goods etc.

(iv) Traffic. It controls in bound shipments of purchased materials and outbound shipment of carriers.

(a) Selection of carriers.

(b) Auditing invoices from carriers and filing claims for refund in case of excess charges of damaged shipments.

(c) Develeping techniques to reduce transportation costs.

(v) Physical distribution: finished goods are meved from the production line to the warehouse and finally to the customer.

Factors Responsible for Providing Economy in Materials Management

There are a number of ways to achieve economy in material management operations but some of them given below need careful attention and concentration:

(i) Volume of Purchases. With large size orders the organisation can have more bargaining power and less expenditure on procurement process *i.e.* material purchases can be done in economic quantities.

(ii) Plant Near to the Source of Materials. in this situation transportation, inspection and same other costs are automatically reduced. This leads to economy in cast of production.

(iii) Fluctuations in Prices of the Materials. The department of materials management should be in continuous touch with the market of the material. The purchase policy should be formulated with a view to safeguard the losses due to unforseen and unwarranted price fluctuations.

(iv) **Design and Engineering of the Product.** The design of the product should not involve complicate operations in its production process. The complex operations system generally leads to waste of material at different stages of the production process. This leads to increase in per unit cost of production.

(v) **Design of Equipments.** Simple design of tools and other equipment required to perform the operations involved in production process reduces the chances of waste and thus provides economy in production.

(vi) **Inspection of the Material** before placing the order and many other measures prior to actual procurement of the material leads to sufficient economy.

(vii) **Some Sub-parts which are Uneconomical to Manufacture** can be purchased from expert and specialised agencies. This can provide economy in production.

SIGNIFICANCE OF STORS

It is servicing facility, inside an organisation, responsible for proper storage of the material and then issuing it to respective departments on proper requisition. The custodian of stores is generally known as Storekeeper or Store-controller. Those items which are not in use for some specific duration *e.g.* spare parts and the raw-materials are called as Stores and the building or space where these are kept is known as Store room. Alfordand Beatty say that store-keeping is that aspect of material control which is concerned with the physical storage of goods. In the words of maynard, the duties of store-keeping are "to receive materials, to protect them while in storage from damage and unauthorised removal, to issue the materials in the right quantities, at the right time, to the right place and to product these services promptly and at least cost."

The significance of store-keeping has not been properly recognised by various enterprises. In most organisations store-keeping is not given its due position in the organisational setup. Stores are generally located in ill-equipped and badly and poorly ventilated buildings. The executives of stores management are generally paid less in comparison to executives of other departments. These factors are responsible for mis-management of stores resulting in discrepancies in issue of materials, loss of items in stock, mistakes in vouchers etc. All these results in undue delay in production.

It is an established fact that more than 70% of the capital of an enterprise is invested in stores. Thus for efficient and economic utilisation of capital the importance of stores cannot be ignored. The management of stores should be entrusted to experienced, sincere and efficient personnel and the location of stores should be at some proper and safe place.

OBJECTIVES OF STORE-KEEPING

(i) Easy location of the items in store.

(ii) Proper identification of items.

(iii) Speedy issue of material.

(iv) Efficient utilisation of space.

(v) Reduction in need of material handling equipment.

FUNCTIONS OF STORES

Stores play a vital role in the operation of a company. It is in direct touch with the user departments in its day to day activities. The most important purposes served by the stores is to provide uninterrupted service to the manufacturing divisions. Further, stores is often equated directly with money, as money is locked up in the stores the functions of stores can be classified as follows:

(i) To receive raw materials, components, tools, equipments and other items and accounts for them.

(ii) To provide adequate and proper storage and presentation to the various items.

(iii) To meet the demands of the consuming departments by proper issues and accounts for the consumption.

(iv) To minimise obsolescence, surplus and scrap through proper codification, presentation and handling.

(v) To highlight stock accumulation, discrepancies and abnormal consumption and effect control measures.

(vi) To ensure good house keeping so that material handling, material presentation stocking, receipts and issue can be done accurately.

(vii) To assist in verification and provide supporting information for effective purchase action.

STORES SYSTEM

Well designed Stores System and procedure ensure timely information for decision making. "Function of Stores starts even before material moves in the inventory." Stores System can be broadly classified in two categories (i) Closed and (ii) Open.

Closed	*Open*
1. All materials are stores in a closed/controlled area.	There is no specific storage area Stores are maintained in the form of suitable/conventional locations.
2. No other person than the stores personnel is permitted in the area.	Every individual has access to any storage facility.
3. Materials can leave or enter the storage area only be authorised documents.	After the receipt of the material it is delivered to respective department to expendite the production activity.
4. Maximum Physical Security.	Chances of Pilferage high.
5. Tight accounting control of inventory material.	Less emphasis on the accounting control of the material.

VARIOUS TYPES OF STORE HOUSES

In stores depots according to their functions and utility may be divided into the following broad categories:

(i) Main or central stores,

(ii) Sectional or Branch Stores Depot,

(iii) Tool stores Depot,

(iv) Ware Houses.

(a) Main or Central Stores

The functions of the main or central stores depot are:

(i) To receive all the materials, tools equipments etc.;

(ii) To issue the material to sectional or branch stores depots, tools to the tool stores depots and equipments to the various departments and when required by them and

(iii) To take steps for the replenishment of stock. The main stores depot should be under the charge of stores officer. Of course, the actual handling of stores would be done by the store keeper and his assistants. Thus, the central store is a whole sale supplier to the other units, departments, and sub store depots (sectional or branch stores depots) which operate on a retail basis and are engaged in issuing goods directly to the users of the materials.

ADVANTAGES OF CENTRALISED STORAGE SYSTEM

(i) Minimum possible stocks of spares, equipment, tools and fixtures are to be kept, thus avoiding unnecessary blockade of money.

(ii) The range of goods becomes wider and benefit the users more than is possible under small restores depots.

(iii) Scientific and better methods of stock control becomes possible.

(iv) Storage cost can be reduced, since bulk stores always take less space.

(v) Economy through bulk purchases is possible since these purchases are cheaper.

(vi) Efficient and successful organisation of inspection and verification becomes possible.

(vii) Standardisation becomes easier.

(viii) Determination in stores, can be minimised through a more regular turn over of stocks.

(ix) Co-ordination between the central store and the different departments can be improved.

DISADVANTAGE OF CENTRALISED STORAGE SYSTEM

(i) Because of duplication of work, handling and transport costs are increased.

(ii) More staff may be required to handle huge stocks.

(iii) Recurrent storages at the point of usage may occur, if the organisation is not efficient.

(iv) If the sub stores are not rigidly controlled, the stock investment tends to rise.

(v) Increased documentation work may involved extra cost.

(vi) Risk of determination, fire, pilferage and theft is increased manifold.

(b) Sectional or Branch Stores Depot

The sectional or branch stores depot is located in each section, unit, department or branch from where the materials are drawn by the later group. This depot, in turn, draws its requirements from the main or central stores depot to which it places its requirements from time to time. The main stores depot issues the materials to the sectional stores depot for a certain period say a fortnight or a month. These sub stores are especially recommended for big business and industrial houses, in order to facilitate the prompt issue of materials of varied specifications and quality to different production centres. The following are the main advantages of a sectional stores depot:

(i) The requirements of each department can be promptly and efficiently supplied.

(ii) If regular supplied are received, unnecessary hold ups and delays in work are avoided.

(iii) The disadvantages faced by the central stores depot are eliminated. That in fact, is the major advantage of a sectional store.

(c) Tool Stores Depot

Tool stores depot even if there is a centralisation of storage facility is generally maintained as a separate depot in large industrial enterprises. This store is responsible for issuing tools, spare parts and other accessories to different sections in general, and production department in particular. The tools are drawn from the main store once and then they are issued by the stores depot as and when they are required by the departments. The main advantage of such a store is to relieve the main stores depot from the burden of executing the retail requisition of the departments. In this way it helps in smooth and efficient running of all the departments without any stoppage of, or daily in work. Another advantage is that proper and up to date records of tools, which are temporarily issued on loan basis, can be more easily maintained than would be done in the case of central stores.

(d) Ware Houses

Ware Houses are the godowns which take the responsibility of keeping and storing goods and providing ancillary services in order to help the small and medium sized traders and manufacturers who, because of technical and economic reason may not like to have their own store house.

These ware houses undertake to preserve the goods in a scientific and systematic manner so as to maintain their original value, quality and usefulnees, for which they charge a certain prescribed rent, at fixed rate in advance. Thus, we say that a ware house is a stores depot not in the strict sense of the term but in a broader sense. It functions are:

(i) To keep the goods in safe custody till these are claimed back by their owner.

(ii) To preserve the goods so that they do not lose their value, quality and usefulness.

(iii) To undertake these duties against prescribed charges, known as rent, paid by the owner of the goods.

(iv) To work as an agent of the owner (trader or manufacturer) by

(a) undertaking the job of loading and unloading the merchandise on and from ships, railways etc.,

(b) getting clearance from customs authorities on behalf of the owner,

(c) keeping the sale proceeds (if authorised) till they are claimed by the owner, and

(d) honouring hundies, bills etc., on the security of goods ware housed.

MATERIALS PLANNING AND INVENTORY CONTROL

Methods for Pricing the Materials Issued

Each item inside the inventory has come value associated with it. This value depends on the price, duration of the item inside the inventory, procurement cost, storage costs etc. Generally the time of purchase and time of issue of any item are different and the market price of the items also vary with time. Thus for costing purposes the problem of pricing at the time of issue is of great significance. The fundamental consideration in this problem is whether the price of the item at the time of purchase or price of the item in market at the time of actual issue or a compromise between the two should be adopted or not.

Before entries are made to the stores ledger for the materials issued, it is necessary to determine the price to be charged and the concerned departments are debited with it. When materials are made into products, their money value is taken out of the materials account and added into the account showing the value of the work in process. There are many methods of pricing. Some of them are given below:

(i) First In First Out Method (FIFO)

In first in first out method the materials received first are issued first. The materials are issued in chronological order. The recently received materials remain in stock. Whenever a requisition for materials issue is presented to the store-keeper he will use the price of the first lot and then of the second and third lot etc., when the quantity of the first, second lot is exhausted. When prices are fluctuating then the cost of different batches of production will be different. This method is suitable when prices are falling because material issues will be priced at earlier (bigger) figures while costs of replacements will be low, on the other hand, when prices are rising then materials will be issued at lower prices and replacement costs will be higher. This method is useful for materials which are subjected to obsolescence or deterioration.

Advantages of FIFO Method

(a) Actual cost of the item is used in pricing.

(b) Method is appropriate for those items which are likely to deteriorate or become obsolete with time.

(c) In case of falling price it inflates the issue price.

Disadvantages of FIFO Method

(a) Issue price of the same item may be different if used by different departments and issued from different lots.

(b) The price charged is not related to the current market price of the item.

(c) Frequent price fluctuations may lead to increase in the work of stores department.

(ii) Last In First Out Methods (LIFO)

In last in first out methods the last received materials are issued first and ending inventory consists of earlier acquired materials. This methods is also known as replacement cost method because the latest purchased goods will correspond to the current market prices except that goods were not purchased much earlier. The inventories will be valued at oldest lots on hand and these values will be quite different from current invoice prices.

Last in first out method is suitable during rising prices because goods will be issued from the latest received lots at prices which are closely related to current market prices. The current costs will also be matched to current income. This method is able to show lower profits because of increased charge to production and closing stock figures will also be low as they will be valued at earlier prices. The taxable liability will also be low thus enabling the concern to retain more money in the business.

A comparison between two jobs will not be possible if these jobs were started at the same time but materials to the second job were issued from a different lot, the earlier lot having been exhausted. The materials may be priced at two or more prices even in the same voice.

(iii) Average Cost Method

Here the average cost of the material in stock is calculated by dividing the total value of items available in stock by the number of items in stock. Here average cost is used for the valuation of issued material. The main disadvantage of this method is that whenever fresh lot of items arrive in the stock the average cost has to be revised again.

(a) Simple Average Cost

In this method the prices of all lots in stocks are averaged and the materials are issued on that average price, for example three lots of materials are in stock and the prices per unit of these lots are Rs. 2, Rs. 3, and Rs. 4 of first, second and third lots respectively. Then the average price will be

$$\frac{(2+3+4)}{3} = \text{Rs. } 3$$

Though this is a simple method of pricing materials but particularly this method does not give good results. The total cost of materials is not observed in this method. The following example will explain this point.

10,000 units were purchased @ Rs. 2 per unit.

15,000 units were purchased @ Rs. 3 per unit.

20,000 units were purchased @ Rs. 4 per unit.

The total cost of material will be:

$$10{,}000 \times 2 = 20{,}000$$

$$15{,}000 \times 3 = 45{,}000$$

$$20{,}000 \times 4 = 80{,}000$$

$$\underline{\text{Rs. } 1{,}45{,}000}$$

The simple average price issue in this case is Rs. 3 per unit and total amount, will come to Rs. 1,35,000. The under absorbed amount in this case will be Rs. 10,000. Because of this defect weighted average method is preferred.

(b) Weighted Average Method

In this method the total cost of all the materials is divided by the total number of items in stock. The price calculated in this way will be used for issue of materials upto the time a fresh purchase has not been made. After a fresh purchase, has not been made the quantity will be added to the earlier cost. A fresh price is calculated by dividing the changed total cost by the number of units in stock after the purchase is made. A new price is calculated where even a fresh purchase is made. Taking the earlier example, the weighted average price will be:

$$\frac{10,000 \times 2 + 15,000 \times 3 + 20,000 \times 4}{10,000 + 15,000 + 20,000}$$

$$\frac{1,45,000}{45,000} = \text{Rs. } 3.22$$

The weighted average price method recovers the whole cost of materials. This method is suitable when price fluctuations are frequent because it smoothes our fluctuations by taking into account total cost and total quantity of materials.

(iv) Base Stock Method

In this method same quantity of materials is assumed to be necessary for keeping the concern going. The quantity is not issued unless otherwise there is an emergency. This material which is not issued as is kept in stock known as a base stock. The earlier material received are kept as a base and are valued at the price on which they are acquired.

This method is not an independent method. It is used alongwith some other methods such as FIFO, LIFO, Average price method etc. After maintaining the base quantity in stock the issues are priced at one of the methods mentioned above. The purpose of this method is to issue materials at current prices. This aim will be achieved only when LIFO method of pricing the material is used.

(v) Other Methods

(a) Standard Price Method

Some standard price is fixed for each item without any consideration of its actual price. The standard price is then charged for the issued material. The fixation of standard price is based on the fluctuations in price of the item in past and exception in future.

The procedure enables the organisation to have a costing of finished products such that possibility of losses due to price increase is minimised to a great extent.

The standard price is fixed after careful examination of the current market price, price trends and market conditions. It is fixed for some specific period which can be a month, quarter or year. After the expiry of the period stipulated, standard price is again reviewed.

(b) Inflated Price Method

Here the cost incurred by the stores department in receiving, encoding, storing, handling, inspection and expenses due to some normal wastages are added to the price of the material to get the inflated price.

(c) Replacement Price Method

It is price at which the items issued can be replaced in stock at the time of issue *i.e.*, the material issued is charged at the prevailing market price. The difference between charged price and the actual purchase price is adjusted to the "price fluctuations reserve account". This difference reflects the performance of the purchase department.

ACCOUNTING SECTION

The stores department has to maintain upto date account of the value of items in stock, so that correct price is charged at the time of issuing the materials. Besides this the account of expenditure made on various stores operations and services is also to be properly maintained. The accounts section exercises financial control over stores. The goods receipt book is maintained for all arrivals, making the receipt in triplicate, a copy of which is sent to accounts section and the other to the store section. The stores section enters the details given in the receipt in stores ledger indicating date and amount of receipts as well as the price of the items. Similarly at the time of issue the details of the items are subtracted from the receipts entries in stores ledger and balance is recorded. Requisition slips are issued for each item issued from store.

Stock Taking or Checking

This implies physical checking of items in store to see that these are in accordance with the entries of stores ledger. In the maintenance of store records mistakes are bound to occur due to human involvement in the process. The checking should be done by an individual not belonging to the stores department.

The checking provides a control on the activities of stores department. The different methods of stock-checking are:

(a) Fixed Annual Inventory System. A special team is deputed to check and count the material inside the stores at the end of each financial year. The method is appropriate for organisations which have some vacations or which operate in some particular periods only *e.g.*, sugar industry etc. In other cases this system is not desirable as there will be unwanted loss to the organisation in closing the activities for stock verification.

(b) Perpetual Inventory System. In this system the stock control department maintains upto date and systematic records of each and every transaction made inside the stores department. There is system of continuous verification of stock. The entries on bin cards and stores ledger should tally with each other. In case of discrepancies thorough investigation is made. A credit note in the case of shortage and a debit note in the case of surplus stocks is prepared and the records are adjusted accordingly.

The following are the advantages of this method:

(i) There is no need to stop the production for checking.

(ii) No dislocation in stores operations.

(iii) Checking is done in a systematic way, thus reducing the chances of errors.

(iv) Mistakes, discrepancies are spotted more quickly. Important and expensive items can be checked more frequently.

(v) Facilitates the preparation of interim profit and loss accounts.

(vi) avoids excessive inventory maintenance.

(c) Low Point Inventory Method. In this system the verification of stocks is done during a period when the level of the inventory is at low level. The main merit of this method is that lesser number of items are to be counted which results in less effort and time is required for the checking operation. The disadvantage is that there is an unbalanced burden on the stores personnel.

(vi) Market Price Method

In this method, the price charged to production are not costs incurred on the materials but latest market prices. The market prices may either be replacement prices or realisable prices. The replacement prices are used for the materials which are kept in stock for use in production and realisable price are used for the goods kept for resale. The prices of issue for materials are always the replacement prices. The actual prices paid for acquiring the materials are not considered at the time of issue of materials. Ever issue is paid at the replacement price of that day. It reflects the latest priced charged to production. This method is a check on the efficiency of the purchasing department. If prices paid are more than the market prices, it shows efficiency and if actual prices paid are lower than the market prices, it will show efficiency.

Market price method is not generally used because of a number of difficulties. It becomes difficult to select the market price because different prices prevail in different markets. This method brings in human bias in the selection of market price. The charging of more or less prices than the price actual paid will bring in the elements of profit or loss which is unnecessary.

WORKING OF STORES DEPARTMENT

The stores department performs the functions of receiving, storage, store accounting and issuing. The following are the details of the activities of stores department:

(i) Receiving

The items ordered by purchase department are received by this section. The supplier delivers the items along with other documents to receiving section of stores department. The consignment is properly checked and entered in goods inward note. The discrepancy if any is also recorded in this note.

(ii) Receipt System

When a purchase order is placed, a copy of it is sent to the stores department indicating quantity and delivery date. The purchase orders should be arranged chronologically so that total volume of receipts at any time may be estimable.

Outside suppliers: On despatching items, normally send an advice note to the stores showing date of despatch, carrier details, description of the consignment and the value of items. The ensures quick and easy clearance of bills etc.

The purchase copy, suppliers note and transporter information/ consignment note enables the stores manager to organise and plan for expeditious clearance of materials and minimise costly demurrage.

Internal Suppliers. Whenever materials are received from internal divisions or returned from user departments transfer notes and returns to stores documents are usually used for this purpose. The format of the goods inward note is shown below:

Goods inward note		**No..........**
Date of receipt	Consignor	Consignor Advice
....	....	Note No.........
Types of Packages	No. of Packages	Order No.
....	....	....

Description of item	Quantity Recog. undamaged	Standard price	Value

Details of damage/
Shortages

The stock entry Signature ....
Has been made Date ....

Signature of Inspector
....
Date..........................

Receiving section in stores department can be centralised, semicentralised or decentralised. In a centralised receiving department all categories of items are received, checked and inspected at one common place. In semi-centralised light weight items are received, checked and inspected at one common place whereas heavy weight or items of unmanageable size are received, checked and inspected at the place of storage. In both cases the records are maintained in the same stock book. In a decentralised system all items are received, checked and inspected by their respective departments.

The building where receiving section is located should have sufficient space for loading, unloading and inspection of the consignments. Receiving and despatching sections should be at a distance from each other to avoid confusion among incoming and outgoing items.

In case of stores keeping of finished goods, the upto date position of stocks inside the stores should be regularly communicated to marketing department of the organisation.

(iii) Stores Section

This is a place where all materials received by the stores department are kept with protection against deterioration and pilferage. They are stored in such a way that their location is easily identified at the time of issue. According to Kimball and Kimball, "A well developed stores system necessitated a system of identifying nomenclature so that location of all materials is easily found ".

Now the various store operation *viz.* location, procedure layout, equipment and identification of stores section are described in detail :

(a) Location in Stores Section. Stores are to provide space to the materials till these are issued to the respective departments of the enterprise. Stores are in the form of covered sheds, buildings and open space. Generally the storing place should be situated near the operating departments but there are many other considerations which influence their location *e.g.* certain categories of items like explosives or other sensitive items should not be stored with general class of items. Gaseous items like oxygen cylinders etc. should be stored in more protective sheds. Some items may require air-conditioned space or space at some desired level of temperature.

(b) Working Procedure. The stores incharge receives the materials from receiving sections alongwith goods inward note. The material is classified and coded according to their nature and use. The coded sign is inscribed on the items for identification. Items may also be identified by different colours. The items are then stored at assigned shelves or places inside the store. For quick and easy identification of the item's category, a bincard is tagged with each shelf.

Card No.	Stores Bin Card		Part No.
Description		Location	
Date	IN	OUT	STOCK

The bin card contains upto date information about the receipt, issued and balance of the respective item in the stock. The materials from store section are issued to respective departments on the instructions from despatch section.

(c) Layout to Stores Section. The layout of the stores section should be conductive to the materials to be stored and equipment *viz.*, shelves, racks, almirah, handling equipment etc. There should be enough space for materials handling and labour movement. A good stores layout is characterised by:

(i) Flexibility in management.

(ii) Convenience in physical counting of materials.

(iii) Items used sparingly should be easy to locate.

(iv) Efficient protection against deterioration and pilferage of materials.

(v) Better stock control but minimum routine work like record maintenance etc.

(vi) Efficient use of floor space and height.

(vii) Safely from hazards, insurance etc.

(viii) Proper illumination and ventilation.

(ix) Proper security arrangements, so that no person other than stores staff can enter the store.

(x) Heavy and bulky items should be stored as low as possible.

(xiii) Shelves and bins should not be very deep.

(xii) Minimum handling and transportation of materials.

(d) Stores Equipments. A good store is equipped with various types of tools/equipments for handling, measuring and weighing the materials. The equipment should be such that stores investment and operating expenses are reduced.

The various modes of storing are open and closed shelves, cabinets, stacking, pallets and skids, bins, stacking boxes, gravity feed racks, outdoor platforms etc. The facilities can be of wood or steel. Wooden equipment is safe for delicate items and can be installed quickly. It is inexpensive but is rather inflexible. Steel equipment is more flexible with advantages of more strength, fire resistance and easy maintenance?

(e) **Material Handling Facilities.** These basically depend upon the nature of items as well as the size and shape of the storage space. It also depends on how much frequently an item is used in production operations. The material handling equipments in stores can be rolleys, mobile jigs, cranes, conveyer belts etc.

There should also be proper weighing and measuring instruments at the time of receiving and issuing the materials.

(f) **Identification of Materials in Stores.** "There shouid be a place for everything and everything should be in its place". Provision of a good identification system in stores assists those who try to keep everything in place. Depending on the size and nature of the organisation, the store can have a variety of items in stock. It may not be possible to remember and locate these items inside the store simply by their names. The task can be simplified by proper coding of the items as well as their location. Identification can be done by:

(i) Tagging some piece of paper or cloth with the items.

(ii) Labels may be fixed on the items.

(iii) The coded number or any other identification mark may be embossed on the items.

(iv) Painting or colour coding of items.

Advantages of coding items:

(i) An asset in keeping records.

(ii) Facilitates quick identification.

(iii) Mechanised accounting is possible.

(iv) Eliminates the chances of duplication of items.

METHODS OF CODING

Generally alphabets, numerals or a combination of the two is used for codification of items. The following methods can be used for code construction:

(a) **Mnemonic Method.** Here alphabets closely associated with the name of the item are used *e.g.* MT can be used for some metallic item. This method is useful when few type of items are to be stored.

(b) **Random Method.** Here both alphabets or numerals can be used randomly. But the method is rather arbitrary.

(c) **Scientific Method.** The items are divided into a number of groups and each group is given some code. The further sub-grouping is done on the basis of classification of item in any group, its shape, function etc.

Then complete code of the item is written by combining the sub-codes of groups and sub-groups for that item.

LOCATION CODING

Storeroom is divided in blocks of storage units and each block is identified by lateral block letter and a longitudinal block letter. Within each block every row of shelves is given a number. Each row is divided vertically into columns and horizontally into shelves. Blocks and Rows are identified by painted signs.

Sometimes items requiring special protection for storages *viz.*, rust/corrosion proof space of metal parts are stored in dry areas. It is an asset for easy and quick location of items when the size of the store is very big. Each place is coded by alphabets or numerals. The location can be identified in terms of the number of the warehouse, row number, column number, rack number, shelf or bin number etc. Location of any item inside the store can also be decided in three ways:

(i) Fixed Location.

Here some fixed place is designated to each class of items. The basis can be *(a)* Supplierwise *(b)* itemwise *(c)* utility of the item etc.

(ii) Random Location.

Items are placed according to the availability of space in store at the time of receiving the items. This method can be applied when the number of items to be stored is few and store-keeper is efficient in remembering the location of each item.

(iii) Zonal Location.

Generally the whole inventory is divided into three Zones namely *(a)* Bulk Zone, *(b)* Reserve stock and *(c)* Indirect material like spares and consumable items. This approach tries to avail full benefit of the space and other storage facilities.

ISSUE SECTION

This section handles the issue of materials when required by some department of the enterprise. A storeroom does not always issue a material in the same units in which it is purchased as the materials are purchased in gross and issued in dozen. The standard unit of issue for a material is usually defined as the smallest quantity likely to be issued inventory is always recorded in standard units. Some items like powdered material, nails, screw etc. can be dispensed more efficiently of weight then by actual count. Materials carry some money value and in order to avoid malpractices and to curb the tendency of waste, the items should be issued against proper requisition. The material requisition is a request to the stockroom to issue materials. It gives details of the type and quantity of the material, the use to be made of them and is duly signed by some authorised person.

JUST-IN-TIME MANUFACTURING

The goal of Just-in-Time (JIT) manufacturing is not new. The basic desire for continued reductions in material resource requirements is quite common in the minds of many business managers. The means by which the goal of JIT is now being accomplished is considered to be new.

The JIT may sometimes be a by-product of a Companywide Quality Improvement (CQI) programme or it may be one of a number of specific goals in such a programme. Either way, CQI is fundamental to the achievement of JIT. Companywide quality improvement is a type of management approach used in Japanese companies. Later, this is being rapidly adopted by many world's leading companies.

Overview of JIT

The primary goal of JIT is to achieve zero inventory within an organization as well as throughout the entire supply chain. This is achieved by questioning each and every aspect of stock at raw materials stores, in-process buffers, etc. This is primarily to find out important causes for unnecessary stock at various points. A detailed analysis of these causes would further breakdown the major causes ilito a wide range of reasons for holding excessive stock.

By way of illustrations, let us consider the problem of raw material stock. These may be held because the suppliers' quality is unpredictable. Further analysis may show that if many suppliers are used, each of them will have his own unique shortcomings. In one case, material specifications may be of dubious quality. In others, difficulties may be evident in the ability to hold tolerances, and so on. These deficiencies in themselves will also lead to further unique undesirable aspects. In addition, deliveries may be erratic or quantities supplied may vary from contract requirements.

Raw materials may also be held for internal reasons such as inaccurate forecasting, machine breakdown, quality related losses on current products and a host of other causes. All these are outside the scope of the materials control department and would require considerable collaboration across several functions before improvements can be made.

"Just-in-time" is not a jargon term for a new concept. It represents a goal. That goal is the ultimate total elimination of inventory, minimal work-in-progress and is monitored by a constant reduction in so-called working capital. It can be achieved only as a result of a fundainental change in management thinking and industrial cultural values.

Basic Principles

In JIT, the key theme is to work without buffer stock/with minimal buffer stock. To achieve this objective, identify every point in the organization where buffer stocks normally occur. Then critically examine the reasons for such stock, if any.

A set of possible reasons for maintaining high stock is listed below.

* Unreliable or unpredictable deliveries
* Poor quality from suppliers
* Increased variety of materials
* Machine breakdown
* Labour absenteeism
* Frequent machine setting
* Variation in operators' capabilities
* Schedule changes
* Changing product priorities
* Product modifications

Universal Problem Solving Sequence

Dr. Juran states that every problem solving, every breakthrough, follows a universal sequence of events. Avoiding this sequence is likely to lead to erroneous premises and non-solutions. All successful projects follow the sequence mentioned below.

Symptom → Cause → Remedy

The diagnostic steps are as follows:

Symptom

↓ Theories of causes

Test theories to find true cause

Cause

↓ Identify possible remedies

Select remedy

Test remedy and implement

Remedy

Overcome resistance to change.

Hold the gains.

Push/Pull Production

Basically, production can be classified into two categories.

1. Produce on demand (pull system)
2. Produce to forecasts of demand or make to stock (push system).

Some companies have a policy of not producing anything until a customer is found. At the other extreme, in other companies products may be made in large quantities in the hope that supply and demand can be matched by advertising and by giving high visibility to the product, as in the case of domestic products sold in supermarkets.

Kanban Systems—Pull System

Kanban system is a kind of production system which operates based on the information contained in cards, called "Kanbans". There are two types of Kanbans namely, Withdrawal Kanban (WK) and

Production Order Kanban (POK). For the purpose of working of the Kanban System, production line is divided into Preceding Process (PP) and Succeeding Process (SP). Withdrawal Kanban contains information on how much materials (raw material/semi-finished material) the Succeeding Process should withdraw. Production Order Kanban contains information on how much quantity the Preceding Process should produce. Kanban system brings immediately any problem in the system to the notice of the concern person for corrective action. If a company aims to implement the Kanban system, it should have a well designed maintenance system and motivated workforce.

The steps followed in the Kanban system are summarized below.

1. Carrier of the succeeding process is sent to the stores of the preceding process with a necessary number of Work Order (WKs).

2. The carrier of the succeeding process withdraws items from the stores against each work order. While doing this, it detaches the POK associated with the corresponding physical units and places it in the Kanban Receiving Post.

3. At the same time, it attaches a WK to physical units. If the carrier has more than one WK, it should be done properly based on one-to-one correspondence.

4. When the physical units are taken for processing which are associated with a WK, the WK must be placed in the WK post.

5. In the previous process, the POK which was placed in the Kanban Receiving Post is shifted to the POK post. The sequence by which the POKs are placed in the POK post is as per First Come First Served (FCFS) principle.

   The items are produced against POKs as per FCFS basis among various POKs. The physical units (semi-finished) and POK must be moved as an integral pair.

6. When the physical units are completed, then the units and the respective POK are shifted to the store-X which receives the output from the previous process. The carrier of the succeeding process will withdraw these units when necessary.

COMPUTER INTEGRATED MANUFACTURING AND FLEXIBLE MANUFACTURING SYSTEM

Manufacturing industry has progressed through the phases of Industrialization, Mechanization, Automation (Computerization) and Integration (Linking). Productivity improvement is the main thrust in all these phases.

Integration of automated industry is now recognized by the widely accepted label of 'Computer Integrated Manufacturing' (CIM). Factory integration enables better organization of material and information flows. Part of CIM concept is the application of Flexible Manufacturing System (FMS) technology.

An FMS is a system in which all the aspects of CIM automation and integration are found in one system. A machine tool is a part of an FMS just as an FMS is a part of the total CIM environment.

Computer Integrated Manufacturing

Until recently, integration of information and data transfer was always manual, usually using paper as the transfer medium. With the advent of computers and electronic data communications it has been possible to integrate manufacturing activities without the need to push paper.

In addition, each functional area of management is considered as an island performing its normal role. Within a functional area, like production management, the various sub-areas are working in isolation. If the functional areas and the various sub-systems in each functional area are interconnected by powerful computers for the purpose of data transfer and information flow, the productivity of the organization would be increased to a larger extent. The integration of these areas by proper computer hardware and software for effective functioning of the organization is the goal of CIM.

There are two aspects of CIM. They are organizational part and operational part. The various elements in each of these are listed below.

1. Organizational part includes the following:
   * Corporate services
   * Finance
   * Business planning
   * Marketing
2. Operational part (Advanced Manufacturing Technology-AMT) consists of the following:
   (i) Computer Aided Engineering (CAE)
      * Computer Aided Process Planning (CAPP)
      * Computer Aided Planning (CAP)
      * Computer Aided Quality Control (CAQC)
      * Computer Aided Design (CAD)
      * Computer Aided Design and Drafting (CADD)
      * Materials Resource Planning (MRP)

   (ii) Computer Aided Manufacturing (CAM)
      * Flexible Manufacturing System (FMS)
      * Flexible Manufacturing Cell (FMC)
      * Flexible Manufacturing Assembly (FMA)
      * Direct Numerical Control (DNC)
      * Data Acquisition System (DAS)

— Production Data Acquisition

— Machine Data Acquisition

* Area Controller (AC)

* Cell Controller (CC)

* Flexible Assembly System (FAS)

The different types of computer which are used in CIM are as follows:

(a) Mainframes

(b) Mini Computers

(c) Micro Computers

(d) Personal Computers (PCs)

(e) Programmable Logic Controllers (PLCs)

(f) Robotic Controllers (RCs)

(g) Work Stations

Flexible Manufacturing Systems (FMS)

FMS is the latest level of automation to achieve ever more productivity and flexibility from manufacturing facilities. An FMS is a collection of production equipment logically organized under a host computer and physically connected by a central transport system. The objective of the FMS is to simultaneously manufacture a mix of piecepart types. Also, the system should be flexible enough to sequentially manufacture different piecepart type mixes without costly, time consuming and changeover requirements between mixes.

FMS consists of two types of equipment namely, primary and secondary. The primary equipment adds value to the components being manufactured. Secondary equipment supports the primary equipment in achieving this goal.

The equipments in an FMS are as follows:

1. Primary Equipment:

   (i) Work Centres:

   * Universal machining centres (Prismatic FMS)
   * Turning centres (Rotational FMS)
   * Grinding machines
   * Nibbling machines

   (ii) Process Centres:

   * Wash machines
   * Coordinate measuring machines
   * Robotic workstation
   * Manual workstation

2. Secondary Equipment:

   (i) Support Stations:

   * Pallet/Fixture load/Unload stations
   * Tool commissioning/setting area etc.

   (ii) Support Equipment:

   * Robots
   * Pallet/Fixture/Stillage stores
   * Tool stores
   * Raw materials stores
   * Transport units (pallets/stillages) etc.

Types of FMS. There are different types of FMS. Important five types of FMS are given below.

* Sequential FMS
* Random FMS
* Dedicated FMS
* Engineered FMS
* Modular FMS

In a sequential FMS, the planning and preparation for each piecepart are done one after another. A random FMS manufactures any random mix of piecepart types at any given time. Dedicated FMS manufactures continuously the same, but a limited mix of piecepart type for extended periods. Engineered FMS will manufacture the same mix of part types throughout its lifetime. Modular FMS is a sophisticated FMS which enables the users to expand the capabilities of any of the four earlier FMS types in stepwise fashion.

Applications of FMS. The FMS philosophy is applied to Metal-cutting, Metal forming, Assembly, Metal joining (welding etc.), Surface treatment, and Testing and Inspection.

TOTAL QUALITY MANAGEMENT

Nowadays, customers demand products/services with greater durability and reliability at the most economic price. This forces producers to strictly follow quality procedures right from design till shipment and installation of the products. So the goal of any competitive industry is to provide a product or service at the most economical costs, ensunng full customer satisfaction. This can be achieved through Total Quality Management (TQM); because, quality is not a technical function, but a systemic process extending throughout all phases of the business, *e.g.* marketing, design, development, engineering, purchasing, production/operations.

As per Feigenbaum, it is' an effective system for integrating the quality development, quality maintenance and quality improvement efforts of various groups in an organization so as to enable marketing, engineering, production and service at the most economical levels which allow for full customer satisfaction.

Scope of Total Quality Management

Total quality management guides the coordinated actions of people, machines and information to identify and fulfil customer quality requirements.

The total quality management is applied to many stages of Industrial Cycle which are listed below:

* Marketing
* Engineering
* Purchasing
* Manufacturing
* Mechanical
* Shipping
* Installation and Product Service.

Benefits of TQM

The benefits of TQM can be classified into the following two categories:

* Customer satisfaction oriented benefits
* Economic improvements oriented benefits.

Customer Satisfaction Oriented Benefits. The benefits under this category are listed below:

* Improvement in product quality
* Improvement in product design
* Improvement in production flow
* Improvement in employee morale and quality consciousness

* Improvement in product service

* Improvement in market place acceptance.

Economic Improvements Oriented Benefits. The benefits under this category are as follows:

* Reductions in operating costs

* Reductions in operating losses

* Reductions in field service costs

* Reductions in liability exposure.

Fundamental Factors Affecting Quality

The nine fundamental factors (9 M's) which are affecting the quality of products and services are: markets, money, management, men, motivation, materials, machines and mechanization, modern information methods and mounting product requirements.

1. Market. Because of technology advancement, we could see many new products to satisfy customer wants. At the same time, the customer wants are also changing dynamically. So, it is the role of companies to identify needs and then meet it with existing technologies or by developing new technologies.

2. Money. The increased global competition necessitates huge outlays for new equipments and process. This should be rewarded by improved productivity. This is possible by minimizing quality costs associated with the maintenance and improvement of quality level.

3. Management. Because of the increased complex structure of business organization, the quality related responsibilities lie with persons at different levels in the organization.

4. Men. The rapid growth in technical knowledge leads to development of human resource with different specialization. This necessitates some groups like, System Engineering group to integrate the idea of all specialization.

5. Motivation. If we fix the responsibility of achieving quality with each individual in the organization with proper motivation techniques, there will not be any problem in producing the designed quality products.

6. Materials. Selection of proper materials to meet the desired tolerance limit is also an important consideration. Quality attributes like, surface finish, strength, diameter etc. can be obtained by proper selection of material.

7. Machines and Mechanization. In order to have quality products which will lead to higher productivity of any organization, we need to use advanced machines and mechanize various operations.

8. Modern Information Methods. The modern information methods help in storing and retrieving needed data for manufacturing, marketing and servicing.

9. Mounting Product Requirements. Product diversification to meet customers' taste leads to intricacy in design, manufacturing and quality standards. Hence, companies should plan adequate system to tackle all these requirements.

Quality Control Activities During Product Cycle

The quality control activities during production cycle can be classified into the following three categories.

* New design control
* Incoming materials control
* Product control.

New Design Control. This has the following tasks:

* Selling quality products
* Engineering quality products
* Planning quality products.

Incoming Materials Control. This accounts for the following three tasks:

* Buying quality materials

* Receiving and inspecting quality materials

* Manufacturing quality parts and products.

Product Control. This involves the three important activities:

* Inspecting and testing quality products

* Shipping quality products

* Installing and servicing quality products.

Operating Quality Costs

Quality cost in companies can be classified into the following two categories:

* Costs of control

* Costs of failure to control.

Costs of Control. The costs of control can be divided into cost of prevention and cost of appraisal.

Costs of Prevention. The costs incurred to avoid defects and non-conformities from occurring are accounted under cost of prevention. The following activities involve the costs of prevention.

* Quality planning

* Process control

* Design and development of quality information equipment

* Quality training and work force development

* Product-design verification

* Systems development and management.

Costs of Appraisal. Costs of maintaining quality level by means of evaluation procedures like, inspection, test, quality audits, etc. are accounted under cost of appraisal. These are mentioned below:

* Test and inspection of purchased materials
* Laboratory acceptance testing
* Laboratory or other measurement services
* Inspection
* Testing
* Checking labour
* Setup for test or inspection
* Test and inspection equipment and material and minor quality equipments
* Quality audits
* Maintenance and calibration of quality information test and inspection equipment
* Product engineering review and shipping release
* Field testing.

Costs of Failure to Control. These are nothing but the costs due to defects and non-conformities of products. This can be further classified into internal failure costs and external failure costs.

Cost of Internal Failure. Internal failure costs include costs which are incurred within the company such as scrap cost, spoilage cost, rework cost, material-procurement cost and factory contact engineering.

Cost of External Failure. External failure costs are the costs due to unsatisfactory quality outside the company such as:

* Complaints in warranty
* Complaints out of warranty
* Product service
* Product liability
* Product recall.

ISO 9000 SERIES

ISO stands for International Organization for Standardization. It is an international body which consists of representatives from more than 90 countries. The national standards bodies of these countries are the members of this organization. BIS (Bureau of Indian Standards) is the Indian representative to ISO. ISO and IEC (International Electro Technical Commission) operate Jointly as a single system. These are non-governmental organizations which exist to provide common standards on international trade of goods and services.

ISO 9000 standards expect firms to have a quality manual that meets ISO guidelines, document quality Procedures and job instructions, and verification of compliance by third-party auditors.

ISO 9000 series has five international standards on quality management which are listed below:

1. ISO 9000
2. ISO 9001
3. ISO 9002
4. ISO 9003
5. ISO 9004

The tasks of each of these standards is listed in the following Table 1. The systems requirements of ISO 9001, ISO 9002 and ISO 9003 are presented in Table 2.

Table 1 : ISO 9000 Series

Standard	*Objectives/Tasks*
ISO 9000	This provides guidelines on selection and use of quality management and quality assurance standards.
ISO 9001	It has 20 elements covering design, development, production, installation and servicing. This is applicable for the industries which are doing their own design and development, production; installation and servicing.
ISO 9002	It has 18 elements covering production and installation. It is the same as ISO 9001 without the first two tasks, *viz.*, design and development. This is applicable for the units excluding R&D functions.
ISO 9003	It has 12 elements covering final inspection and testing for laboratories and warehouses.
ISO 9004	This provides guidelines to interpret the quality management and quality assurance. This also has suggestions which are not mandatory.

Benefits of ISO 9000 Series

ISO 9000 series provides several tangible and intangible benefits which are listed below:

(a) This gives competitive advantage in the global market.

(a) Consistency in quality, since ISO helps in detecting non-conformity early which makes it possible to take corrective action.

(c) Documentation of quality procedures adds clarity to quality system.

(d) ISO 9000 ensures adequate and regular quality training for all members of the organization.

(e) ISO helps the customers to have cost effective purchase procedure.

(f) The customers while making purchases from companies with ISO certificate, need not spend much on inspection and testing. This will reduce the quality cost and lead time.

(g) This will help in increasing productivity.

(h) This will aid to improved morale and involvement of workers.

(i) The level of job satisfaction would be more.

Table 2 : Systems Requirements

S. No.	*Systems Requirements*	*ISO 9001*	*ISO 9002*	*ISO 9003*
1.	Management Responsibilities	Present	Present	Present
2.	Quality System	Present	Present	Present
3.	Product Identification and Traceability	Present	Present	Present
4.	Inspection Status	Present	Present	Present
5.	Inspection and Testing	Present	Present	Present
6.	Inspection Measuring and Test Equipments	Present	Present	Present
7.	Control of Non-conforming Products	Present	Present	Present
8.	Handling, Storage, Packaging and Delivery	Present	Present	Present
9.	Document Control	Present	Present	Present
10.	Quality Recrds	Present	Present	Present
11.	Training	Present	Present	Present

Contd.

S. No.	Systems Requirements	ISO 9001	ISO 9002	ISO 9003
12.	Statistical Techniques	Present	Present	Present
13.	Internal Auditing	Present	Present	Not Present
14.	Contract Review	Present	Present	Not Present
15.	Purchasing	Present	Present	Not Present
16.	Process Control	Present	Present	Not Present
17.	Purchaser Supplied Product	Pcesent	Present	Not Present
18.	Corrective Action	Present	Present	Not Present
19.	Design Control	Present	Not Present	Not Present
20.	Servicing	Present	Not Present	Not Present

Steps in ISO 9000 Registration

The following are the steps in ISO 9000 registration:

1. Selection of appropriate standard from ISO 9001, ISO 9002 and ISO 9003 using the guidelines given in ISO 9000.
2. Preparation of quality manual to cover all the elements in the selected model.
3. Preparation of procedures and shop floor instructions which are used at the time of implementing the system. Also document these items.
4. Self-auditing to check compliance of the selected model.
5. Selection of a registrar and making application to obtain certificate for the selected model.

A registrar is an independent body with knowledge and experience to evaluate any one of the three models of the company's quality system (ISO 9001, ISO 9002 and ISO 9003). Registrars are approved and certified by accreditors. As an example. RAB (Registrar Accreditation Board) of USA is an accreditor of registrars. National

Accreditation Council for Certification Bodies (NACCB) is an accreditor of registrar in U.K.

The registrar, on successful verification and assessment will register the company.

Before selecting a registrar one should know the following:

* Accreditors of the registrar.
* Background and credibility of the registrar.
* Cost of registration through the proposed registrar.
* Expected harmony between the company and the potential registrar while working towards implementing ISO model in the company.

❐

10

Quality Control

When a customer considers the purchase of a product or service, he weighs the value he will receive against the asking price before making his decision. There is no exact method or formula for this because the process usually differs for each customer, according to his individual needs or desires. However, a general classification of those factors that contribute to the value of a product or service would inciude:

1. The price of the product or service
2. The operational capabilities of the product
3. The designed appearance
4. Any associated services rendered
5. The general quality of the product or service.

The price of the product (factor 1) would be weighed against the sum of factors 2-5 to determine the level of value. Factors 2 and 3 are dependent on product design, which attracts and sells the customer. Factor 4 covers any services that might be included, such as the warranty or installation of a product, as well as services purchased, such as those of a barber, a plumber, or an auto mechanic. Factor 5, general quality, is concerned not only with the quality of the workmanship but with the quality of factors 2-4, which are also weighed against the price. The quality of design and the quality of service are evaluated by the customer, and since quality, like value, cannot be determined objectively, it must be judged according to the standards of the customer.

Another aspect of quality that the customer considers is the quality of the product when used over a long period of time. The word "lemon" best describes the product which fails to satisfy the customer over a long period. A business must consider quality over time (reliability) if it does not want to lose future customers. The tendency of the buying public to stick to brand names is a good example of the customer's willingness to pay a slightly higher price to minimize the risk of receiving an unknown product of poor quality.

A business must consider many factors in determining the level of quality its products. Competitive price standards will influence the choice of quality level. A lower quality than that offered by a competitor at the same price will mean that fewer customers will buy the product, and some of these will be disappointed. Conversely, a quality too high above competitors levels may mean that too much emphasis is placed on quality with the result that profit margins are not as large as they could be. As with any other product parameter, money is required to improve quality or to maintain a high standard. This is not to imply that a business should not strive for the best quality in its competitive field, but only that it should not strive to be so far ahead of competition that economic returns are adversely affected.

Since quality is such a nebulous and often variable term, how does one go about defining it so that design and production can be oriented and controlled to assure meeting quality standards? First, it should be emphasized that a company is in business to serve a customer, and thus all its standards must be customer-oriented. This is accomplished in various ways, depending on the product. Market surveys, customer specifications, industry and company standards and practices, and customer drawings are all used by industries to determine quality standards. These quality standards are often expressed in terms of standards developed by the industries themselves, by technical organizations, or by government agencies. Standards are actually the backbone of mass production methods because they provide interchangeability between manufacturers. A house-wife can go into any supermarket and buy a 60-watt light bulb and know that

the bulb will fit her lighting fixture and give light comparable to every other manufacturer's 60-watt light bulb.

Thus two critical characteristies for a light bulb manufacturer are that each bulb must be mechanically interchangeable in a standard fixture and that the average wattage of the bulbs must be 60 watts, plus or minus some nominal tolerance. All other quality characteristics are relatively insignificant, because the sales appeal to the customer is limited if these two characteristics are not met. Most products contain many such standards as well as quality characteristics more difficult to define whose determination constitutes the first phase of setting quality levels.

The value in quality of our factors 2 and 3 (comparative operational features and design) is something that a customer weighs when he purchases a product. He not only weighs his choice against similar products (such as another Ford, Chevrolet, or Plymouth automobile) but also compares his choice to both a Volkswagen and a Cadillac to determine the relative value of the product level. Another example would be that of a man who decides that the value received from buying several \$10 watches and scrapping them as they fail outweighs the purchase of \$100 watch which will have a longer life and a higher prestige value. This, then, is comparative value measured by the customer's terms. Thus the quality of design and manufacture of the \$100 watch is not the only factor in determining value, because there may be one or more alternative choices for the customer to make, and he is the one that decides what his measure of value and quality will be.

These examples are used to emphasize that the customer usually has alternative choices in purchasing, that value and quality must be customer-oriented, and that quality standards must reflect the customer's wishes. Even though value cannot be expressed as a mathematical equation, it may be defined as quality for the price, or

$$\text{Value} = \frac{\text{quality}}{\text{price}},$$

with quality reflecting quality of design or service as well as manufacturing quality.

Not only is quality a variable term as far as characteristics are concerned, but the emphasis customers place on characteristics will vary. The couple who are searching for a new car is typical. The wife compares cars for appearance, color, shape and other visual characteristics, while the husband compares the maintenance aspects, operational characteristics, and economy. There will usually be some compromise, because anyone car or model will not embody all the desired features. A company, in planning the design of a car, must consider the desires of all types of customers. This is the main reason for the variety of models and the "extras" available within each automobile product line. In addition, the large companies cater to several different groups of customers by having several product lines with overlapping price ranges to satisfy the greatest number of potential customers. The automobile industry thus provides a good example of variations in quality due to different customers considering different products to be of the greatest value.

When there are various uses for a product, the quality of each use should be considered. A building contractor, in deciding on the type of home to be built in a new development for a predetermined price, must consider the customers he plans to attract in determining the quality of materials and the type of layout. A family with five young children will choose a different style home than a family with one teen-age child and a family head who does a lot of entertaining of business associates. The first family will look for the most rooms and space for the money 'while the second may desire extensive landscaping, built-in appliances, and more expensive fixtures. The two homes would be quite different, but their value in terms of sales price and tax assessment would be the same. Many other products have more than one use. The same model automobile with identical accessories might be used by a farmer, a salesman, an elderly school teacher, or a city dweller, but the use and what would be expected of the car would vary greatly from user to user. Again, each of the potential customers and his needs would have to be considered.

Not only must quality of product be considered, but the quality of services rendered must be evaluated and determined. In a service-industry company, the quality of service is the product, and less than competitive quality would soon mean that the company would be out of business. Quality of service also applies to service features of products. Installation, warranties, periodic checkups, and money-back guarantees are all additional features that add value to a product. The change from a one year to a two-year warranty on an automobile does add value to the product, and so does an increase in time between periodic grease jobs, brake adjustments, and coolant changes.

Quality of service is also associated with the product in service industries such as hotels, restaurants, and department stores, in which the level of service is associated with the quality of the product. The quality of the services offered in a self-service department store are quite different from those in a women's dress shop, and part of this difference in value is reflected in the prices. Again, it is the customer who decides what he considers the value to be, and each business must cater to the customer's desires within its competitive field.

Quality of product is not limited to elimination of defects but is part of the design and service planning. since quality control personnel are charged with coordinating the quality of a company's outputs, they must consider customer requirements, including design and associated services. Too often, however, quality control programmes are limited to the elimination of customer rejects or returns for defective workmanship. To achieve quality, the programme should be allied more closely to marketing inputs and less closely to manufacturing requirements.

What is Quality Control?

In any large modern business, a systems approach to any business function is required to assure maximum operational effectiveness. This is as true for quality as it is for accounting, drafting, or production control. The quality programme should extend into every contributing function of the business and should integrate the quality efforts of each function into measurable administrative entities. Thus a quality system may be defined as a network of administrative procedures designed to deliver a quality product to the customer.

Within this framework, the role of the quality control organization is to provide and coordinate a system which ensures that the operation will produce an optimum quality product at minimum product cost. The actual responsibilities of the quality control organization are to define, plan, coordinate, and measure the quality efforts of the business as well as to perform those activities normally associated with the quality control function. Because of the support nature of a quality control organization and the lack of adequate means of rating its performance, the direction and goals of the quality programme must be based on a quality philosophy rather than on the performance of tasks subject to direct measurement.

Organization and Management

The organizational level and the structure of the organization for quality control depend on so many relevant factors, such as type of product, size of operation, type of business, and management philosophy, that no single organization can be denoted as typical. However, all quality control organizations should have well-defined responsibilities and authority and should have the organizational freedom to identify and evaluate quality problems and to initiate, recommend, and provide solutions. Such an organization would generally report to the plant manager or the manufacturing manager, depending on the type of business.

Whatever the level at which the quality control function reports, and whatever form it takes, one of the crucial criteria for a successful quality programme is management endorsement. Such endorsement by top management does not authorize the quality control organization to run the business, but it does imply that the quality philosophy and goals should be an integral part of overall operational planning. Quality personnel should make it clear to management that the quality programmes and plans that must be emphasized are those that lead to quality improvement at the planning stages of the product.

When top management succumbs to the pressures of monthly shipping schedules, it is quite understandable that the quality effort may be misdirected. If a mutual quality philosophy is not established by both quality personnel and top management, the quality programme can degenerate into periodic end-of-the-month programmes involving drastic sorting and reworking or continual changing of tolerances and lowering of standards.

Two quality control axioms reflect the direction that the quality programme should take: *(1)* Quality must be designed and built into the product, and *(2)* quality cannot be inspected into the product. These help to explain why bigger and better inspection programmes are not the answer to improvement of quality. A popular concept of quality control by the uninitiated is that the quality organization is a super inspection force that uses statistics to justify its rejections. In practice, this concept unfortunately sometimes proves to be true, but in actuality it is in direct contrast to the quality philosophy expressed by the two axioms.

The quality control function should consist of two elements: quality engineering (or planning) and inspection (or appraisal). According to the most modern concepts, emphasis should be placed on the planning function, since good planning will lead to a more effective appraisal function. Although organizational structure, number of personnel, and type of personnel will depend on the individual operation, adequate support should be given at the planning phase if the appraisal phase is to be carried out successfully and programme goals are to be met.

In addition to quality goals, the quality manager should be responsible for cost goals and related measures. In any competitive business, it is the duty of each functional manager to reduce unit cost through effective use of the facilities and personnel assigned to him. Although many quality costs cannot be segregated in the quantitative sense, one of the areas that quality control management must develop is measurement in terms of costs. This includes both quality control costs for the overall operation and specific costs for the elements of the quality function.

Again, the role of the quality organization is to ensure optimum quality product at minimum product cost.

History of Quality Control

The alert customer of any era has always demanded value in any product that he purchased. To ensure at least a minimum standard of quality, each succeeding era has required change and progress in the methods of measurement and in the standards used to determine the goals.

Before the era of measurement, all aspects of quality were of a general nature and all were bargaining points in a transaction. The feel, look, size, appearance, or any other characteristic of a product were determined by the craftsman as he manufactured his product. They were generally designed around some physical attribute. A tailor, for instance, made a suit using the customer as model.

The first attempt to standardize measurements was made about 5,000 years ago by the Egyptians, when the "royal cubit," credited with being a prime factor in the erection of the pyramids, became the master standard for linear dimensions. During this same era the Egyptians developed inspection standards for squareness, horizontal level, and vertical plumb. Over the next 2,000 years, the Egyptians, Greeks, and Romans developed many of other basic measures as standards for their trade and commerce. Thus it might be said that the first attempt at quality control occurred in this era, when many characteristics were subject to quantitative measurement and craftsmen were beginning to base their work on numerical requirements.

The method of production was through the use of individual skills and basic tools until the early 1600's, at which time, the use of machines to supplement human skills began in earnest. Nevertheless, until about 1800 the quality of the product continued to depend on the skill of the workman in fitting, filing, or adjusting as the product was being built or assembled. Many new measuring devices assisted in improving the accuracy of individual parts and the ability to make more precise measurements. This era also introduced the assembly line technique, in which more than one person contributes to the overall product and the owner or manager of the operation is the judge of quality.

The first needs for interchangeable parts occurred during the American Revolutionary War, when mass production of many military items was attempted. The use of jigs, fixtures, and gauges during the production cycle by the operators was the first step in the mass production techniques of today. Gauging, particularly the "go-no go" type, was initiated and developed during the following era, but the owner or supervisor of the shop was still responsible for quality.

As large corporations and businesses took shape during the late 1800's, the use of inspectors became more prevalent. This lessened the operating burden of the foremen and provided a standard for the quality within an area. Inspectors had been used in other than industrial operations before this time, particularly by the federal government in connection with subcontractors, but the use of inspectors for in-process type operation was initiated during this period. The responsibilities and scope of the inspector's job were enlarged, during the First World War, and government inspectors increased in stature.

In most changes or advances in quality control the leaders have been the military and the greatest changes have been made during a war or as a result of one. World War II brought statistical quality control into the picture with its standard deviations X and R charts, and other statistical tools. The main difference between the present quality thinking and that of the statistical era is that statistics in now a tool of the system and not the system itself.

Again, under the impetus of war, a new phase was born about 1954. This was the quality system, complete with written descriptive procedures conforming to specification MIL-Q-5923 and its several sister documents. Generally, in an informal way, this new requirement forced a formal quality system on industry and introduced the need for full-time engineering activities for quality. Thus emerged the quality control engineer, whose initial duties were to assure customer representatives that quality procedures were adequate, that they were being followed and that corrective action was being taken when necessary.

After a few years the primary requirements of MIL-Q-5923 has been mastered by quality personnel and quality engineers began to look for new fields to conquer. In 1961 the concept of total quality control was first introduced by A. V. Feigenbaum in a book by that title and served to describe those areas where quality programmes should be applied. This concept utilized a quality systems approach and emphasized planning and measuring methods to ensure product quality rather than increased inspection programmes. The following outline represents a typical quality system.

Quality engineering (new design, reliability, purchased materials, processes, instrumentation)

Quality measuring programmes

Product and process control (process control engineering appraisal programmes, audit programmes)

Statistical techniques

Special studies

Advanced quality planning

Customer quality relations and complaint analysis

Quality training

Administration of the quality system.

To summarize the present concept of quality control might be described as a systems approach with the emphasis on planning.

The Challenge of Quality Control

Despite the fine philosophy incorporated into the quality system and the outstanding results achieved in specific areas by some companies, many opportunities remain to advance the state-of-the-art. These advances will probably occur in techniques, methods, and programmes rather than in the quality control philosophy.

To make the planning phase effective, new techniques and programmes must be developed and the overall programme must be sold to those responsible for designing its functions. In addition, new methods must be developed for appraisal and instrumentation so that quality appraisal advances can keep pace with mechanization and automation as they are introduced into production.

Quality costs and effectiveness ratios must be developed for the Quality functions so that effort will be expanded in the right areas and the effects of new methods and programms can be measured in quantitative terms. The lack of good measuring tools has continually hampered quality management in demonstrating the effectiveness and value of quality programmes.

The introduction of new materials, tighter tolerances, and new sciences have provided a real challenge to quality personnel. The best example is the impact of the space sciences and their by-products (including reliability) on quality efforts. Continuing advances and changes will be the rule for years to come, so there appear to be no limits to the development of quality control in the foreseeable future.

The subject of quality cost was mentioned earlier. Quality control, since it is primarily and generally a staff function above and beyond that of normal productive workers, must pay for itself. Another way of looking at quality cost is not as a cost burden as such but as a benefit to be gained. Top management always understands and appreciates the dollar sign. It must do so to survive. One way of indicating the benefit of quality control is to relate the resulting reduction in defects, scrap work, and what have you, to the dollar sign. For example, it can be said that in a particular company each I percent reduction in the scrap and reject rate represents a savings and is therefore "money in the bank." If the scrap and reject rate prior to the establishment of a quality control programme is running at 10 percent, and a 5 percent reduction in quality cost can be derived by the establishment of such a quality control program, the benefit is obvious to all concerned. The challenge, therefore, concerns the ability of the quality control engineer to relate the quality cost to be the overall productivity of the organization. Quality control is necessarily both a long and a short-term asset, rather than a long-term liability.

Quality Control Functions

There can be no uniform list of functions performed by every quality control organization, because most quality organizations vary according to personalities, level within the company, technical capabilities, nature of the industry, size, and utilization of company manpower. From the outline prescribed in the preceding sections a general outline of the functions typically performed by many quality organizations can be made. While it is not necessary that all these functions report within a single quality organization, it is necessary that management (including quality management) recognize that tasks performed by other organizational elements must be oriented toward the same quality cost and quality goals.

Engineering, Appraisal, and Administration

The functions can be divided into three general categories: engineering, appraisal, and administration. The following outline is by no means comprehensive, but it will provide reasonably concise guidelines to the functions listed under the various categories.

Engineering

Customer Quality Analysis. Analysis of customer quality requirements for the marketing function for purposes of quality planning. It is incumbent upon the quality control engineering organization in concert with the marketing and sales organizations to see that the customer gets exactly what he is looking for, not what the sales department or the marketing department thinks the customer is looking for. This may be accomplished by customer surveys that are free from biases exerted by the sales and marketing departments.

Design Phase Functions. Functions performed during the design phase of a product, such as reliability studies, design reviews, quality planning, manufacturing process capability, and pilot run evaluations.

Vendor and Sub-contractor Surveys: Preaward. Surveys performed prior to the award issuance of a purchase order, which will determine the supplier's capability to supply the components, parts, or materials specification on a continuing basis and with the minimum amount of rejection. Postaward-Surveys necessary to ensure continued compliance with specifications and requirements on the part of a supplier.

Inspection Planning. Planning and preparation of inspection and test instructions for all phases of the manufacturing quality control appraisal function.

Quality Information Equipment Design and Procurement. Design and purchase of all inspection and test equipment needed to perform the appraisal functions.

Vendor Coordination. Coordination with suppliers and sub-contractors to rectify quality control problems, should they occur.

Equipment Calibration Planning. Planning of methods and cycles for the calibration of all quality information equipment.

Material Dispositions and Corrective Actions. Disposition of all rejected material and corrective action where applicable.

Cost Analysis. Analysis of quality costs on responsible projects.

Failure Analysis. Analysis of rejects to determine causes and to take corrective actions.

Systems Audits. Periodic audits of the instructions, procedures, and products to ensure compliance, to evaluate quality, and to uncover trouble areas.

Customer Complaints and Coordination. Review of customer complaints, coordination with customers, and modification of the quality programme.

Special Studies. Such as evaluation tests and process capability studies.

Statistical Planning and Analysis. Mathematical or statistical support required for the quality programme.

Appraisal

Receiving Inspection. Inspection of parts, components, and materials from outside sources.

Vendor Inspection. Inspection of vendor's material or witnessing of tests at the vendor's facilities.

In Process Inspection. Mechanical visual electrical, chemical, or other inspections for the purpose of determining product quality during the steps of the production cycle.

Final Inspection. Final product inspection plus any preservation, packing, or shipping inspections.

Calibration and Maintenance. Of quality information equipment.

Process Controls. All process controls used in conjunction with inspection efforts.

Record Systems. Tabulation of data for reject summaries, rating systems, failure analyses, and other statistical reports.

Drawing Controls. Control of instructions, procedures, and drawings to be used for inspection purposes.

Administrative

Programme Planning. Planning for allocation of resources such as facilities, personnel, and equipment.

Measurement Analysis. Analysis of general trends such as reject rates and quality costs on a nonproduct basis.

Quality Training. Training to improve the effectiveness of quality personnel.

Long-Range Planning. For new methods, techniques, and skills, including changes in the industry state-of-the-art.

The Quality Control Engineer

What should the quality engineer be doing in his position and what type of responsibilities should he have? There is no simple answer to these questions because they involve philosophies, principles, and work elements that vary with the size of the business and the type of industry. However, the objective of any quality control organization is to ensure an optimum quality product at a minimum product cost. To attain this objective, the quality engineer utilizes engineering techniques to:

1. Ensure a product design that will have a minimum of quality defects;
2. Plan and coordinate a quality appraisal programme that will result in satisfied customers;
3. Take effective corrective action on defects found in the manufacturing process and make sure they do not recur;
4. Reduce the quality costs within his sphere of control.

In describing the work elements of a quality engineer, general terms will have to be used because of the wide differences in industries. However, to do an effective job it is necessary that the quality engineer possess both the technical knowledge of the industry and the engineering concepts inherent in quality engineering. The size of the organization and the nature of the product will determine the extent to which the quality engineer can specialize in technical knowledge and associated quality concepts such as reliability engineering, test and inspection design, and statistical specialties. In many companies, engineers engaged in reliability engineering and test equipment design do not report to the quality control organization, but they should be consulted when the overall quality programme is developed.

Since the early 1940's when the concept of quality control engineering was conceived, many attempts have been made to categorize the various work elements of the quality control engineer.

Today the American Society for Quality Control has a standing committee at the national level, which continually reviews work elements in the light of current trends, innovations, and changes in the industrial climate. The General Professional Council of the Society defines these elements as follows.

A Broad Definition of Quality Control Engineering Activities

The ultimate objective of all Quality Control (QC) endeavor is to provide quality assurance for the finished product and to assure optimum quality costs for that product. To accomplish this objective, every producer needs an integrated programme for the control of product quality including its reliability elements comprising the basic work elements described herein. The totality of the work elements is not, of course, intended to describe the work of any single QC Engineer, nor the work of any particular QC Organization. A QC Engineer may specialize in only one or a few of these elements and still be performing legitimately professional work. QC Engineering encompasses the planning, the control, the evaluation, and the reporting of all quality aspects of the product from its conception through manufacture, processing, storage, delivery, installation, maintenance, and repair to the end of its service life.

All the functions of an organization have specific responsibilities for product quality. QC Engineering does not seek to usurp any of these functions. However, it does afford an effective means of providing each supervisor and engineer with specific and overall quality and cost views to enable him to make decisions leading to optimum product cost and quality.

In like manner, of course, all functions of an organization contribute to the reliability elements of product quality. Ultimate reliability cannot exceed that which is designed into the product. Continued achievement of the design reliability is dependent upon strict control of all material and process characteristics which maintain the integrity of the design. Logically, therefore, those activities related to product reliability are appropriately reflected in all the principal work areas of the Basic Work Elements.

In the new design area, QC Engineering aids in the development and analysis of new products and processes, and work to eliminate future quality problems. Economical incoming material control procedures, which include supplier process controls, are the responsibility of QC Engineering. Inplant process and product control and evaluation and assurance of the quality and reliability of finished goods are also prime QC Engineering responsibilities. Finally, QC Engineering includes evaluation of in-process, finished, field inventories. All of these elements make up the hard core of QC Engineering.

The activity which ties together and directs the planning, control, evaluation, and reporting of all the quality aspects of the production task is truly engineering. It is characterized by creative work. Statistics, technical process and product knowledge, and practical shop experience are combined in attaining the goal of optimum quality product at lowest possible cost.

General QC Engineering

Certain work elements of QC Engineering are general in nature and have application in all phases of the QC job. Regardless of the area of his specialization, several or all of the following elements comprise and important part of the QC Engineer's job.

Training. Prepare current educational material for conducting training programmes in all aspects of quality control, including Statistical Quality Control (SQC). Train at all levels of the organization. Keep abreast of new developments in the field for purposes of training and application.

Quality Standards. Develop and implement quality standards where needed in the organization. Train members of the organization in their use.

Measurement and Analytical Facilities. Determine, recommend, and/or design measurement and analytical facilities required to make evaluations of product quality and reliability. Develop and maintain an economic programme for periodic precision and accuracy checks, for calibration and for maintenance of all jigs, fixtures, physical testing, measurement, and analytical facilities.

Methods and Procedures. Develop forms and instructions to be used for collecting, analyzing and reporting quality and reliability data. Institute procedures for identifying responsibility and for implementing corrective action.

Discrepant Material. Establish and implement clear concise procedures for the disposition of discrepant material. Determine responsibility and the proper allocation of extra costs involved.

Audit of the QC Programme. Provide methods and arrange for auditing and reporting the implementation, effectiveness, cost, and savings of the QC Programme.

New Design QC Engineering

Quality Control Engineering activities in the new design field thread through all the preproduction activities from conception of the product to trial runs. Application of QC Engineering effort in this phase of the job means an improved, less costly product, incorporating all the knowledge obtained from previous designs or research. Quality Control Engineering will minimize process control problems from the day production begins. Several or all of the following specific activities are involved in this area.

Product and Process Research. Conceive and analyze designed experiments and tests to gain further knowledge of the variables affecting component, product, and process quality and reliability. Devise means of evaluating other manufacture's designs. Analyze and report results.

Specifications. Prepare and present data summarizing field, manufacturing, and vendor complaints on previous designs. Recommend to design engineering specifications which will eliminate these problems from the new design.

Tolerances. Use statical methods to predict overall tolerances of proposed designs based on previous process capability studies.

Submit to design engineering tolerance recommendations which enable desired overall tolerances to be met and at the same time allow individual dimension tolerances to be within process capabilities.

Initial Samples. Plan tests, inspections, and statistical studies on initial product samples. Analyze results to verify realization of design quality and reliability objectives.

Methods of Achieve Quality Production. Recommend to production engineering process improvements including fixtures, tools, jigs, inspection, and testing devices required to achieve process control and maintain desired quality and reliability.

Final Design Analysis. Analyze tolerances, specifications, and dimensions of final design to assure that the product can be manufactured as planned. Make recommendations to design engineering on tolerance problems for possible modification.

Trial Runs. Determine parameters of trial lots to be measured and controlled. Analyze results. Predict the performance of future production lots. Prepare a report of trial data for design engineering and for a permanent record.

Controls of Production Lots. Summarize all the information learned in Steps 1 to 7 and make recommendations for use in establishing economical methods of measuring and controlling production.

Incoming Material QC Engineering

The control of overall product quality is inseparably linked with the quality of purchased material. QC Engineering, therefore, has a contributing responsibility in the selection of suppliers and a direct responsibility for economic control of the quality of incoming materials and for providing evaluation and feedback to other functions to assure the procurement of quality materials at the most favourable cost. The following QC Engineering functions provide for the accomplishment of this objective.

Supplier Capability. Evaluate supplier quality performance capability and develop quality performance ratings for use by Purchasing in their selection and development of material suppliers.

Quality Requirements. Provide suppliers, through Purchasing, with clear, concise quality and reliability requirements. Follow up to assure adequate understanding and supplier action to meet these requirements.

Certification. Work with suppliers to establish quality certification plans based on adequate procedures and controls at suppliers' plants to minimize the cost of assuring the quality of incoming materials.

Inspection Methods. Develop, install, and maintain inspection and analytical procedures including economical sampling plans to determine the quality level of incoming material. Insure compatibility of these procedures between supplier and incoming inspection.

Documentation and Feedback. Establish and monitor systems for recording and reporting supplier conformance to quality and reliability requirements.

Process QC Engineering

Utilizing statistical, engineering, and administrative QC methods, develop, install and maintain economic process controls to achieve and retain process capabilities. The objective of these controls is to maintain operating costs while product quality is retained or improved to acceptable standards. The following are several specific techniques QC Engineers may use to accomplish process control.

Capability Studies. Make capability studies of production equipment and processes. Determine the measurements to be taken, the analysis of data, and the action to correct undesirable conditions.

Process Controls. Establish measurements and process controls to maintain economic control and to detect entry of any factors that might adversely affect product quality or reliability.

Provide adequate written and verbal instructions to personnel performing process control activities.

Periodic Review. Review process controls periodically to adjust for changing conditions and to minimize process control costs.

Trouble Shooting. When out-of-control conditions develop, assist operating and engineering personnel to identify and eliminate causes, using statistical techniques where applicable.

Designed Experiments. When either quality or cost of a controlled process is unsatisfactory, design and conduct experiments to point-out imprcvements and desirable changes of product specifications. Recommend or authorize changes necessary to effect improvement.

Product Evaluation QC Engineering

Develop, install, and maintain inspection practices and product evaluation procedures to ensure that only acceptable quality product is shipped. To accomplish this objective, QC Engineering activity should encompass the following functions.

Inspection Methods. Develop, install, and maintain inspection and analytical procedures to determine the quality level and permit the acceptance of satisfactory product. Ensure compatibility of these procedures between process and product acceptance.

Sampling Plans. Develop and implement economic sampling plans and procedures.

Feedback. Provide for both routine and special feedback and analysis of inspection results so that corrective action can be taken when necessary.

Quality Levels and Defect Classifications. Develop and implement quality levels and appropriate defect classifications for quality rating of completed product and associated packaging compatible with consumer requirements and capabilities of the production processes.

Auditing. Develop and install methods and procedures for auditing, evaluating, certifying and reporting the quality and reliability of product shipped.

Complaints. Analyze customer complaints and field reports. Identify causes and responsibility, and initiate corrective action.

Inventory Evaluation QC Engineering

The deterioration of materials and finished products in use or in storage is an important problem to both producers and users. Economical, reliable evaluation, factual analysis, and engineering judgment applied to inventory quality problems provide management with deterioration curves, maintenance requirements, and feedback information to maximize life. These functions of QC Engineering minimize costs and maximize product service ability.

Sampling. Apply economical statistical sampling procedures to appraise inventory, quality.

Quality Projection. Using the results of periodic samples, establish and interpret deterioration curves to enable management to maintain desired levels of acceptable quality stocks.

Feedback. Based on sampling results, provide feedback to design, purchasing, and production which will aid in maximizing inventory serviceable life.

Process Controls. Provide and implement process controls for repair, maintenance, reprocessing, and disposition of materials and products in inventory or service.

Management Inventory Policies. Recommend, on the basis of inventory quality and reliability history, those inventory policies which will result in optimum quality and cost of maintaining serviceable materials or products.

Special Studies and Activities of QC Engineering

Under this heading fall those work elements which will result in wider and more complete use of SQC techniques. General in nature and not directly connected with day-to-day quality problems, they should nevertheless be part of every QC Engineer's responsibilities.

New Techniques. Develop new techniques and approaches for the analysis of quality problems.

Special Studies. Assist in applying SQC methods and principles to other management functions such as Operation Research, Safety, Finance, and other administrative applications.

Advancement of QC Engineering. Promote the objectives and applications of SQC through activity in professional organizations. Contribute to the advancement of QC Engineering through the preparation of technical papers for presentation at meetings, seminars, and conventions, and for publication in company and national magazines and in books.

Job Descriptions and Requirements

Due to a lack of standards for quality control engineering both industrywide and at the academic level, it has (more or less) been left to various authors to develop clear job descriptions. Feigenbaum does this in *Total Quality Control* and Juran in his *Quality Control Handbook.*

Like the quality control work elements, the job requirements for quality control engineer are constantly changing, but again we will exercise our prerogative and "freeze" the definitions and job descriptions into a categorical listing. Following the list of job descriptions is a list of quality control and reliability topics and related subtopics referred to throughout the engineering job descriptions. Obviously the more complex the job level, the more familiar an individual must be with the various topics. In industry many cases exist where an individual, for whatever reason, may progress from the non-professional or technician level to the ranks of the professional quality control engineer. The total range of quality control and reliability job descriptions within the scope of this text is therefore cited.

The technician programme provides for a balanced combination of experience, on-the-job training, and formal study. The professional programme is organized about the accumulation of both experience and credits for a combination of required and optional study topics. These study topics are built around course outlines, defined in terms of formal study equivalents (2-3 hours of instruction for a period of from 10-12 weeks).

Within the technician category, ratings are, in ascending order, Apprentice, Technician, and Senior Technician. Specialties within this category may include Inspection and Test, Process Control, and Test Equipment Calibration and Repair. Within the engineer category ratings shall be, in ascending order, Engineer, Senior Engineer, and Master, with provision for specialization as appropriate for individual career development plans.

Technical Ratings

Specific requirements for the technical ratings in Inspection and Test and Process Control are as follows:

Apprentice. Successful completion of a basic course in General Quality Assurance at least 24 class hours in length, or successful completion of 6 months in a formal on-the-job training programme supervised by a Technician or higher rating.

Technician. Successful completion of a basic course in General Quality Assurance and at least 6 months of formal on-the-job training supervised by a Senior Technician or higher, or successful completion of at least 12 months formal on-the-job training supervised by a Senior Technician or higher rating.

Senior Technician. Successful completion of an advanced course in General Quality Assurance of at least 24 class hours in length and a minimum of 12 months satisfactory performance in a Technician rating, or successful completion of a basic course in General Quality Assurance, at least 6 months formal on-the-job training supervised by a Senior Technician or higher rating, plus 12 months satisfactory service in a Technician rating. In addition, a candidate for Senior Technician must have demonstrated ability to supervise and direct work of others and to supervise on-the-job training programmes.

Specific requirements for Technical Ratings in Test Equipment Calibration and Repair are as follows:

Apprentice. Successful completion of a basic course of at least 6 months duration in electrical and mechanical measuring equipment, electronics, or radio and TV repair, and at least 6 months formal on-the job training under a Technician or higher rating, or at least 12 months formal on-the-job training conducted and supervised by a Senior Technician or higher rating, or successful completion of an applicable technical course at least 12 months in duration.

Technician. At least 12 months satisfactory performance as an Apprentice under supervision of a Technician or higher rating, or successful completion of an advanced course in electronics plus 6 months satisfactory performance as an Apprentice, or successful completion of a 2-year course in electronics or measurements technology.

Senior Technician. Successful completion of an advanced course in electronics or measurements equivalent to the second 6 months of a 12-month electronics or measurements course plus at least 1 year satisfactory service as a Technician under the supervision of a Senior Technician or higher rating, or successful completion of a 2-year course in electronics or measurements technology with at least 6 months of satisfactory performance under supervision of a Senior Technician or higher rating.

Engineering Ratings

The ratings within the Engineering category will be based upon successful completion of a specified number of studies (see Classification of Topics, page 43), and in addition will include provisions for satisfactory performance and allowance for professional education in engineering and allied sciences.

Quality Assurance Engineer. A degree of Bachelor of Science or Arts in engineering, science, or mathematics, at least 1 year of satisfactory performance in the profession of Quality Assurance and successful completion of basic and advanced topical studies in Quality Assurance Engineering, or at least 2 years satisfactory performance as a Senior Quality Assurance Technician with successful completion of at least two topical studies [in each of Categories I and 2 in addition to Topics 2a and 2b].

Reliability Engineer. A degree of Bachelor of Science or Bachelor of Arts in engineering, science, or mathematics, at least 1 year of satisfactory performance in the profession of Reliability and successful completion of topical studies in Basic and Advanced Reliability or Basic Reliability and Frequency Distribution, or 2 years satisfactory performance as a Senior Quality Assurance Technician with successful completion of at least two topical studies [in each of Categories 1 and 2 in addition to Topics 1j and 1k or Topics 1i and 1j which are required].

Senior Quality Assurance Engineer. At least 2 years satisfactory performance as a Quality Assurance Engineer plus successful completion of at least 10 topical studies [selected five each from Categories 1 and 2, except that, as an option, a substitution for not more than one in each of Categories 1 and 2 may be selected from Categories 5 and 6, but not more than one selection from each optional category].

Senior Reliability Engineer. At least 2 years satisfactory service as a Reliability Engineer plus successful completion of at least 10 topical studies [selected five each from Categories 1 and 2, except that, as an option, a substitution for not more than one in each of Categories 1 and 2 may be selected from Categories 5 and 6, but not more than one selection from each optional category].

Test and Calibration Engineer (Specially). A Bachelor of Science or Arts degree as appropriated the applicable measurements speciality plus at least 1 year successful perform in Test, Measurements, or Calibration and successful completion of Topic 1h and an appropriate subtopic [selected from topic 2c], or two years satisfactory performance as a Senior Test Equipment Calibration and Repair Technician plus successful completion of six study topics [including at least Topic 1 hand one option from Category 1, subtopic selected from Topics 2d and 2e].

Test and Calibration Engineer (General). A Bachelor of Science or Arts degree in engineering or science plus at least 1 year completion of [Topic 1h and subtopic 2c (1) and one topic selected from Topics 2d and 2e].

Senior Test and Calibration Engineer. At least 2 years satisfactory performance as a Test and Calibration Engineer (Special or General plus successful completion of at least 10 topical studies [including Topic 1h and at least two options from Category 1, Topics 2d and 2e, subtopics 2c(1) and at least two additional subtopics in Topic 2c from Category 2, but not more than one topic each from Categories 3,4,5, or 6].

Classification of Topics For Quality Assurance Engineering Ratings

1. Technical, theory

(a) Statistics, variables

(b) Statistics, attributes

(c) Analysis of Variance, basic

(d) Analysis of Variance, advanced

(e) Design of Experiments

(f) Process Control, basic

(g) Process Control, advanced

(h) Measurements

(i) Frequency Distributions

(j) Reliability, basic

(k) Reliability, advanced

(l) Stochastics

(m) Operations Analysis

(n) Operations Research.

2. Technical, applied

(a) Quality Control Engineering, basic

(b) Quality Control Engineering, advanced

(c) Inspection and Test

(1) General	(5) Visual
(2) Electrical	(6) Physical
(3) Mechanical	(7) Chemical
(4) Dimensional	(8) Other (as approved)

(d) Measurement Systems

(e) Metrology

(f) Test Equipment Design (Value Analysis)

(g) Electronics Data Processing

(h) Reliability Measurement and Prediction

3. Management

(a) Organization

(b) Quality Cost Control Systems

(c) Motivation and Recognition (Zero Defect)

(d) Communications

(e) Accounting Systems

(f) Programme Planning

(g) Reliability Programme Management

(h) Specification Management

4. Personnel and Career Development

(a) Training

(b) Personnel Counseling

(c) Career Programming and Development

5. Research (quality assurance and reliability)

(a) Theoretical

(b) Applied

(c) Methods and Techniques

6. Associate

(a) Industrial Engineering, basic

(b) Industrial Engineering, advanced

(c) Electronics Engineering, basic

(d) Electronics Engineering, advanced

(e) Physics

(f) Chemistry

(g) Fluid Mechanics

(h) Optics and Optical Measurement

(i) Mechanical Engineering

(j) Other (as approved)

❑

11

Material Planning Budgeting

Following the development of spreadsheets, word processing, and database software for personal computers, there has been an explosion in the development of project scheduling software. At one time, there were around 150 packages known to exist; as of this writing the number available is not known, but probably six packages account for 95% of all sales. Still, there are a lot of packages available, and trying to select one that will meet your needs is like trying to navigate through a strange country with no road map. The proper approach is to set up a comparison matrix and enter data for the packages being considered and make a selection based on the unit that has the biggest "bang for the buck."

Some years ago, Applied Business Technology Corporation, the producers of Project Workbench, developed a methodology for evaluating software, which was intended to be used by their clients to compare Workbench to other programmes. Their methodology is reduced to a comparison matrix, into which you can place checkmarks or "yes-no" responses. However, the matrix is based on philosophy which seems sound, and with their permission, the following guidelines are extracted from their methodology. The evaluation of any management productivity tool should be closely related to the management process that it impacts. For project management software, tbe software should be closely related to the role of the project manager that is, to what the project manager actually does. The methodology is therefore driven by the "business of project management," rather than disconnected "features" that are unrelated and perhaps irrelevant to the day-to-day activities of a project manager.

This approach is different from that taken by many trade publications in which evaluations are totally feature-driven (*e.g.*, "Does it have a relational database? "Does it print the Gantt chart sideways?" and so on). The features approach is misleading, since it does not ensure that the feature is properly designed or even useful to a project manager for getting the job done.

The evaluation methodology should relate the functionality of the software to the following activities that are normally performed by a project manager:

— Creating an initial project plan

— Refining that plan

— Tracking status versus plan

— Replanning the remainder of the project

— Reporting status

— Supporting departmental management

— Using other tools/methodologies of the organization

The methodology developed by ABT is based on these seven functions. Each function is stated in the form of a question, and each of these is supported by a set of detailed sub-questions. "How easy is it to create the initial plan?" would be an example of a detailed question directly related to the role of the project manager. "Can a project manager enter incomplete data about an activity?" is an example of a detailed question supporting the basic question shown above. A detailed question may support more than one basic question.

The complete methodology examines the following areas:

Summary. Summarizes the major findings about the product, its primary marketplace, what it does, how it does it, and its strengths and weaknesses.

Systems Architecture and User Interface. Aescribes the architecture of the system (*i.e.*, its command structure and data-entry modes) and considers how easy it is to learn and use the system. Also included is an assessment of the user manual, tutorial, and help function.

Functionality. Considers the capabilities of the software, structured in the basic/detailed question format discussed above. The basic questions are as follows:

— How easily can the initial plan be created?

— How easily can the plan be refined?

— How easily can the remainder of the project be replanned?

— How well is information reported, to the project team and to management?

— How well is department management supported?

— How well are I other tools/methodologies interfaced to or made use of?

Capacity Limitations. Considers the limits in terms of the number of tasks, resources, etc., which can be handled by the system.

Marketing Information. Covers the pricing structure, support, training, user base, and general corporate information.

Control and Evaluation

Proper project control and evaluation are necessary if project objectives are to be met. Therefore, the design of a project control system is very important, as is the practice of proper evaluation methods. Before such systems can be designed, it is essential to understand the basic concepts and principles of control and evaluation. As the dictionary definition says, to evaluate a project is an attempt to determine if the overall status of the work is acceptable, in terms of intended value to the client once the job is finished. Project evaluation appraises the progress and performance of a job compared to what was originally planned. That evaluation provides the basis for management decisions as to how to proceed with the project. The evaluation must be credible in the eyes of everyone affected, or decisions based on that evaluation will not be considered valid. The primary tool for project evaluation is the project audit, which is usually conducted at major milestones throughout the life of the project.

We saw that the last phase of a project involves a post-mortem analysis, which is conducted so that the management of projects can be improved. However, such an audit should not be conducted only at the end of the project. Rather, audits should be conducted at major milestones in the project, so that learning can take place as the job progresses. Further, if a project is getting into serious trouble, the audit should reveal such difficulty so that a decision can be made to continue or terminate the work.

One project that was terminated when it was learned that the new product being developed was going to reach the market too late, and because of its late entry the company would never recover its investment. The cost to terminate the job was in excess of $100 million! Naturally, no organization accepts such a loss without serious soul-searching, but it was better in this case to cancel the job rather than to continue "throwing good money after bad."

Following are some of the general reasons for conducting periodic project audits:

— Improve project performance together with the management of the project.

— Ensure that quality of project work does not take a back seat to schedule and cost concerns.

— Reveal developing problems early, so that action can be taken to deal with them.

— Identify areas where other projects (current or future) should be managed differently.

— Keep client(s) informed, of project status. This can also help ensure that the completed project will meet the needs of the client.

— Reaffirm the organization's commitment to the project for the benefit of project team members.

Project Control

Control is an attempt on a day-to-day basis to keep project work on track. It consists of measuring the status of work performed, comparing that status with what was planned to be accomplished to date, then taking corrective action to get back on target if a deviation is discovered. The need for a good plan, against which progress can be compared. In this chapter, the focus will be on attempting to assess or measure actual progress, which is not always such an easy task, as we shall see.

One important distinction about control should be made. The word control often refers to power, authority, command, or domination. Another meaning, however, is that of guiding a course of action to meet a predefined objective. This is the meaning of control that should be applied to project control systems. Based on these ideas, here are some premises of management control systems.

Work is controlled—not workers. The objective is to get the work done, not make workers "toe the line." Authoritarian management generally leads to resentment and an atmosphere that stifles creativity, which is just the opposite of what is needed. Control should be viewed as a tool that the worker can use to work more effectively and efficiently.Control is based on completed work. To determine if the work process is achieving objectives, the product produced is examined. In the case of a complex task, the work is subdivided (to the work-package level, for example) and the smaller units are monitored. Each task must have a well-defined output (or deliverable), and there must be standards for evaluating the completed work.

Control of complex work is based on motivation and self-control. Control must be exercised by the person, doing the work or by someone else. Control by someone other than the worker has a number of problems. Control is likely to degenerate into control of the worker, rather than the work. There is the need for communication between the worker and controller, which may not, take place properly. Finally, the controller probably does not know the work as well as the worker, and cannot establish reasonable checkpoints as required. The worker is in the best position to establish a course of action and monitor his or her own progress.

Self-control is part of the job of every knowledgeable worker. This should be clearly spelled out to those individuals. The best set of control procedures will not work unless the people involved are motivated to make it work. Methods of obtaining control data must be built into the work process. That is, the person doing the work must be able to tell where he or she is at any given time. When driving, we use road signs to tell us where we are, and we compare those to our map to see if we are on course. If a brick wall is being constructed, it is easy enough to count the bricks actually laid (or measure the height of the wall) so that figure can be compared to the plan. As has been pointed out previously, however, knowledge work is harder to measure and usually will be an estimate of progress.

As a further consideration, only data that is actually required for control should be collected. The control process should not be a burden. Control data must go to the person who does the work. Consider a Pilot. Do you give information about the plane's position to the pilot's boss? Of course not. Yet this is often done in organizations, and results in a manager, receiving more control data than he can possibly use. A control system is designed for the routine. A thermostat, turns a furnace on or off to control temperature. If cannot compensate for an empty fuel tank. A control system is designed to cope with the routine: exceptions must be given special handling. It must, then, be decided what is routine and what is not. Control of a complex process is achieved through, levels of control. That which is exceptional at one level may be routine at the next higher level. Only the most pressing problems should find their way to the top level of control.

CHARACTERISTICS OF A PROJECT CONTROL SYSTEM

There are four basic activities that must be performed to have a satisfactory control system. These are as follows:

1. Planning performance
2. Observing actual performance
3. Comparing actual and planned performance
4. Adjusting as required

Comparing performance against plan can be difficult when the work cannot be quantified. When work can be quantified, deviation from plan is called variance. For non-quantifiable work, performance must be judged subjectively.

Objectives

The control system must focus on objectives. The designer of the control system should answer these questions:

— What is important to the organization?

— What are we attempting to do?

— Which aspects of the work are most important to track and control?

— What are the critical points in the process at which controls should be Placed?

The important should be controlled. However, what is controlled tends to become important. Thus, if budgets and schedules are emphasized to the exclusion of quality, only those will be controlled.

Response

A control system should focus on response-if control data does not result in action, then the system is ineffective. That is, a control, system must use deviation data to, initiate corrective action or it is not really a control system but simply a monitoring system.

Timeliness

The response, to control data must be timely. If action occurs too late, if will be ineffective.

Human Factors

The system should be easy to use. In particular, the control system should be designed for the convenience of people and net machines.

Flexibility

One system is not likely to be correct for all projects. It may need to be scaled down for small projects and beefed-up for large ones.

Simplicity

The smallest control effort that achieves the desired result should be used. Any control data that is not essential should be eliminated. However, one common mistake is to try to control complex projects with systems which are too simple.

COMPONENTS OF A PROJECT CONTROL SYSTEM

In its simplest form, a project control system can be represented by a first-order feedback system. The system has inputs, outputs, and a process for transforming those inputs to outputs, together with a feedback loop to ensure that the system, continues processing inputs according to its design. The outputs are monitored, compared to some pre-set standard, and if the outputs are not correct, that information is fed back as an input to the system to correct for the deviation.

This feedback system is a very simple one. It is not very elegant and has some serious limitations as a model of how to achieve control in project management. For those readers unfamiliar with feedback systems, a good analogy for the first-order system is the thermostat in one's home. In the winter, the system provides heat and the desired room temperature is preset by adjusting the thermostat to the proper level.

It should be clear that every system is designed to work properly only under certain conditions. For example, the home heating system might be designed to maintain the room at 70 degrees Fahrenheit so long as the outside temperature does not go below minus 30 degrees. When the outside temperature drops below that level, the heater will run continuously, but the room temperature will begin to drop below the preset level of 70 degrees. To maintain the desired room temperature, the system would have to increase its heating capacity, but it cannot do this. Thus, it keeps running, without being able to adequately heat the house.

In a similar manner, a project may run into unexpected obstacles, which fall outside the boundaries for which the project control system was designed. Everyone is following the plan to the letter, but they are not getting the desired result. What is needed is to change the approach. However, a first-order control system does not have that capability. Something more flexible is needed.

There are inputs, processes, outputs, and feedback. However, the third-order system feeds information about the system outputs to a comparator, which weighs them against the original plan. If there is a discrepancy, that information is passed to an adjust element, which must decide if the discrepancy is caused by something being wrong with the process, the inputs, or the plan itself.

Once that determination is made, the adjust element calls for a change in the plan, inputs, or the process itself. Note also that the adjust element has an arrow going back to the monitor. If a deviation is detected, the monitoring rate is increased until the deviation is corrected, then monitoring is decreased to its original level.

The real-world analogy is that if you were monitoring progress on a project weekly and a problem occurred, you might begin to monitor daily. If the problem becomes, serious enough, your monitoring rate might increase to several times each day. Once the problem has been solved, you would revert to your weekly monitoring. Comparing performance against plan can, be difficult when the work cannot be quantified.

This often leads to strange results. Suppose a member of the project team has agreed to design a new golf club, and has promised to finish it in ten weeks. At the end of week one, she reports that the design work is 10 percent complete. At the end of week two, the work is 25 percent complete.

In week three she hits a small snag and gets a little behind, but by week five she has gotten ahead again. Everything goes pretty well until week eight, when she hits another snag. At the end of that week she has made almost no progress at all. The same is true the following week, and the following, and the following .What happened? For one thing, the 80/20 rule got her. In the case of knowledge work, it says that 80 percent of the work will be consumed by 20 percent of the problems encountered, and they will always happen near the end of the job.

The real issue, though, is how she measured progress in the first place. Chances are at the end of the first week, she reasoned some what like Cathy, of comic strip fame who said to herself, "Im at the end of the first week on a ten-week job. I must be 10 percent complete." And she would be in good company, because that is exactly what a lot of people do when estimating progress on knowledge work.

It is for this reason that two practices are advisable. First, work should be broken into small "chunks" that permit progress to be monitored fairly frequently, perhaps at intervals no greater than two weeks. Second, tangible deliveribles should be used as signposts to show progress. In design, a drawing is tangible evidence of progress. The same is true with software development. Printed code or written functional specs are evidence that work is complete. Having it "in one's head" is impossible to verify.

Project Audit. Ideally, a project audit should be conducted by an independent examiner, who can remain objective in the assessment of information. However, the audit must be conducted in a spirit of learning, rather than in a climate of blame and punishment. If people are afraid that they will be "strung up" for problems, then they will hide those problems if at all possible.

Even so, this is hard to achieve. In many organizations the climate has been punitive for so long that people are reluctant to reveal any less-than-perfect aspects of project performance. Chris, Argyris has described the processes by which organizations continue ineffective practices. All of them are intended to help individuals "save face" or avoid embarrassment. In the end, they also prevent organizational learning.

To say it simply, there is no such thing as constructive criticism when you are the target of it. Criticism—even in the form of "we could have done this, better"—hurts, and we generally avoid being hurt if possible. For that reason, it takes organizations time and considerable effort to develop a climate in which project auditing, can be done in a true spirit of cooperation and a desire to learn and improve.

Audit Report. There may be varying degrees of audits conducted, from totally comprehensive, to partial, to less formal, cursory examinations. A formal, comprehensive audit should be followed by a report, which should contain as a minimum the following:

(1) ***Current Project Status.*** This is best shown using earned value analysis. However, when earned value analysis is not used, status should still be reported with as much accuracy as possible.

(2) ***Future Status.*** This is a forecast of what is expected to happen in the project. Are significant deviations expected in schedule, cost, performance, or scope? If so, the nature of such changes should be specified.

(3) ***Status of Critical Tasks.*** The status of critical tasks, particularly those on the critical path, should be reported. Tasks that have high levels of technical risk should be given special attention, as should those being performed by outside vendors or subcontractors, over which the project manager may have limited control.

(4) ***Risk Assessment.*** Have any risks been identified that highlight potential for monetary loss, project failure, or other liabilities?

(5) ***Information Relevant to Other Projects.*** What has been learned from this audit that can and should be applied to other projects, whether presently in progress or about to start?

(6) ***Limitations of the Audit.*** What factors might limit the validity of the audit? Are any assumptions suspect? Is any data missing or suspect of contamination? Was anyone uncooperative in providing information for the audit?

The simpler and more straightforward a project audit report, the better. The information should be organized so that planned versus actual results can easily be compared.

Project Budget. The project manager actively participates in the three elements of cost management. These are cost forecasting, cost reporting, and cost containment, frequently referred to as cost control. Initial decisions are important. On a process facility, once the type of facility, the process, the capacity, the location, the general arrangement of the equipment, and the specification philosophy have been selected, the theoretical minimum cost of the proposed facility is set. This cost probably will remain unknown as it is only rarely calculated. The goal of all of those involved with the project should be to complete the work at a figure close to the minimum cost. For non-process facility projects, a similar analogy may be used. After only a very few basic parameters are established, the theoretical minimum cost of the project is fixed.

Cost Forecasting. At any stage during the project, the total predicted cost consists of four components: *(1)* the defined elements, *(2)* the contingency, *(3)* the escalation, and *(4)* the job growth. If the forecast is made early in the project, the defined elements will be less precise, the contingency on that number must be higher as must the escalation. Job growth is very difficult to fix. Probably, past corporate experience is the best basis for setting this number. As the project develops, all of these number become progressively more precise until they merge as defined elements to form the total job cost at completion.

Cost Reporting. Cost reports are statements of funds that have been expended as of a designated date. They may cover funds committed and funds billed. Two important requirements of the reporting function are: *(1)* the need for timeliness, and *(2)* the importance of accuracy. Cost management and accounting accuracy are different. For the former only that accuracy essential for subsequent analytical use is needed. The project manager cannot wait for accounting accuracy in order to produce meaningful forecasts or to order corrective action.

Cost Containment. Cost containment is, by far, the most important component of cost management. Cost Containment, works hand in hand with constructability throughout the project. The true minimum cost of a facility is established early with acceptance of a few basic definitions. It follows that there are the areas where the results of cost containment can be most fruitful. A project should be programmed to conduct cost containment reviews on each of the documents that set the true minimum cost. Each should be examined to ascertain that all on the stipulated provisions and conditions are really needed. Those that are superfluous should be discarded before production engineering is started.

Throughout the project, CCRs should be held to review the work that is underway to make sure that the minimum cost definitions are being followed. As the project develops, the detailed project execution plans should be reviewed from the cost containment standpoint. If substantial amounts of money can be save by making modifications to the plan, the project manager should order the changes made.

Estimating and Estimates. An estimate, very simply, is a prediction of the final cost. Very early in the project, the scope definition, component pricing and quantity takeoffs will be very approximate and other cost information will be sparse. It follows that an early estimate will be much less accurate because of these limitations. We try to compensate for this by adding a contingency to account for costs that are a part of the intended work scope, but which have not yet been completely defined. We also try to adjust for anticipated changes in present day costs by adding escalation.

The project manager should not spend money to develop estimates that are any more accurate than are required for the intended purpose. Initial estimates, espacially, are made with very little firm data. These estimates are used for early project screening to determine the viability of the project. Although estimates may be classified in many ways, classifications generally follow those listed below. Each estimate type lists the estimating methods, the type of backup information required and the expected accuracy. Accuracies are given by percentage limits that the final costs will not underrun or exceed. The four usual estimate types are listed in chronological order.

Common Types of Estimates

Viability Estimate. This type of estimate is made from a preliminary scope definition from historical cost curves for the type of facility, or by scaling up or down from the return costs for another similar plant. Accuracy is from –25 to +40 percent.

Appropriation Estimate. An appropriation estimate is prepared from a more developed scope definition using a multiplier on estimated major equipment costs and is sometimes referred to as a factored estimate. It has an accuracy of from –15 to +25 percent.

Approximate Estimate. Approximate estimates also make use of the factoring method. The difference is that the final scope definition is available and the equipment costs will normally have been quoted by suppliers and are fairly firm. The range of accuracy goes from – 10 to + 15 percent.

Definitive Estimate. This estimate is prepared using material takeoffs, quoted equipment and material prices. About forty percent of the engineering for the project will have been completed to do a definitive estimate. The accuracy is considered to be from –5 to +5 percent. This type of estimate is required for a lump sum bid.

Computerised Estimates. Computer programmes for developing cost estimates are being used for making appropriation and approximate estimates. Some of these programmes generate some of the costs from an historical data base. Computer software programmes are also being introduced that will progressively refine estimates up to the final cost report.

Relationship with Work Breakdown. In order to provide an orderly progression through each of these types, the early estimate should be prepared based on the appropriate level of the work breakdown structure. The earlier estimate will be tied only to the upper levels of the WBS, while the definitive estimate will be tied into work packages and activities. The latest and most accurate estimate is used as a source for the project budget development or as a basis for variance analysis.

Job Growth

Job growth is an insidious adversary for the project manager. It frequently comes in the guise of a 'better' way to do something, often late in the job-something not required by the objectives, but something which cannot be objected to except for the attendant costs, schedule delays, and general disruption to the work. The project manager must hold firm with a policy of "no changes" for all work outside the approved scope unless the proper evaluations have been made, additional funds provided, and the work approved by the owner/client prior to starting work on the change.

Of course, some companies want be able to make late changes on project work. Any project closely associated with current research and development, new technology, or state-of-the-art equipment design must expect late breaking changes even as the project reaches its final stages. These companies should understand when they approve such projects that there will be changes and these will cost money over and above the estimated costs of the defined scope of work. They must also realize that this never represents a proper use of the contingency money approved for the project.

There are compelling arguments for providing, or at least realizing that additional funds will be needed for the project to cover job growth.

— Historical records will indicate the extent of the company's record of overruning projects due to job growth. This is largely a result of the particular environment: set by the management of the company.

— Many projects initially are marginally viable. Common sense dictates that you don't add extra money onto a project in this situation.

— Senior management is not accustomed to allocating and approving money that does not cover a specific benefit. Job growth, by its very definition, cannot be pinpointed in advance.

There are also persuasive arguments for not being concerned with this funding until it is actually required. There is no universal solution to the dilema of providing funds for job growth. It is very much a matter for The management of each company to set guidelines as to how they want job growth handled. The project manager must be aware of these guidelines; or he should discuss how he should handle job growth on his project with his own manager.

Even though the terms project estimate and project budget are sometimes used interchangeably, they are different. An estimate is made as a prediction of what each activity, work package or total project will cost. The budget is a tool used to control expenditures. The estimate and the budget may be the same for many activities or work packages, and differ from others. The total budget shown for the overall project may be different from the estimate for the total project. Estimates are used to obtain the corporate appropriation of money for the project. The estimate may be adjusted upward or downward to set the approved level of funding for a project.

The practice of "padding" the estimate deserves mention. The project manager should insist on complete honesty in the preparation of the estimate. Individual activities and work package contingencies should be calculated based upon the risk analysis for each item. Then all of the contingencies should be lumped together as a separate line item at the end of the estimate. If everyone involved is honest, the result will be a proper basis for fixing the project budget. If senior management has a discernable pattern of arbitrarily cutting the appropriation requests, the project manager will have to protect himself accordingly.

The estimate thus serves as a basis, for both the appropriation and the budget. The budget is a control tool. If the amount of money approved for the project is lower than the estimate, then the project budget will also have to be lower than the estimate. The approved budget should never exceed the approved appropriation, and it normally is lower.

The estimate should be broken down according to the work break down structure. The budget, however, must be expressed in these same WBS terms. Each ac~ivity and work package must have an .identifiable budget. It will also have a definite schedule. Both cost and schedule parameters are needed in order to exercise proper project control. The criteria for broader controls at higher levels of the WBS are achieved through a rollup of the data for the activities and work packages. Once the final project control budget has been approved, it cannot change unless the scope of work is changed by means of an approved change order. The budget can not be changed to exceed the funds approved for the project.

There are various other reasons for having a project budget that differs from the project estimate. One of the principal reasons is the desire to set more challenging performance goals for the project team. It might be imprudent to change the estimate. itself because this act would represent a variance from the historical performance records. Keeping the costs of each activity within its budge is the responsibility of a designated individual as indicated by the work breakdown structure assignments.

Budgeting the Work

The initial control budget maybe derived from the viability or the appropriation estimates. As the subsequent estimates are developed, the margin for error is reduced by better definition, quantities, and prices. The control budget is then adjusted as may be necessary to reflect the new information. This does not mean that the project manager has carte blanche to increase the budget, but he should be sure that the interim control budgets track the input from the latest estimate. When the final control budget is prepared, it is submitted for approval. After the final control budget has been adopted, it is never changed without an approved scope change. It can never exceed the appropriated funds.

If the system is working right, the estimate for the original scope win decrease slightly with each updated estimate. Unfortunately, this is not generally the case. The project manager should devote a great deal of his effort to making sure that there are no surprises for the client or for his management in the budgetary process.

The project manager assures that there is only one control budget in use on the project at any time. Everyone working on the project should be advised when a change to the budget has been approved. Fortunately, most of the staff buildup is done after the final control budget is in place. This helps minimize confusion.

If the project is being released by phases, the current control budget may cover only that portion of the total project that is active at the time. Only under very special circumstances should any substantial amount of work be undertaken without a control budget even though it may be, difficult to subdivide the budget into corresponding segments. The responsibility for doing the work on each activity within the budget for that activity is assigned according to the work breakdown structure to a specific individual. For example, budgetary responsibility for the design of a structure to be included in a heat exchanger work package would be given to the lead structural engineer working in that area unless otherwise indicated. The cost of doing the design work as well as the cost of the structure would be his responsibility. Similarly, the cost responsibility for the equipment specification, design, and the purchase cost of the exchangers would lie with the lead mechanical engineer.

The responsibility for the total cost of the elements of that particular work package belongs to the area project engineer who coordinates all of the area work being done by the various disciplines. In some organizations, this responsibility might be given to an area project design supervisor. All or those individuals who have cost responsibilities should have a good understanding of the scope of the work and the budget for that work. They should have a detailed plan for doing, the work included for the money allocated As problems arise, they should be brought to the attention of the next level of supervision.

Scheduling Expenditures

When a project manager starts to schedule the expenditures for a project, he must immediately identify how that schedule is to be used by himself and also by others. From the project manager's standpoint. Once an order is placed, the project has committed the corresponding funds. Project cost management is concerned primarily with committed costs. In planning how to draw the cost curves for his project, the project manager will select those numbers that can be easily and meaningfully monitored. The numbers used for the curve should be comparable to those which will be used for the interim status reports. The planned project costs should be scheduled based upon, the budgets and the schedules for the WBS work packages. Projected costs should be summarized over the project life and the cost curves developed accordingly. Accounting on a project is based upon receipt of invoices from vendors, fabricators and subcontractors. The expense to the project is realized at that time. These "invoiced" or "billed" amounts represent another viewpoint of expenditures. These costs are the usual basis for project cost reporting and stress the importance of making commitments on time. The "invoiced" expenditures can trail the committed expenditures by as much as several months.

The point at which cash must be paid for equipment material or services is of primary importance to the owner's corporate financial organization. Depending upon the contract arrangements, the engineering contractor may be deeply involved with these expenditures. The cash disbursement expenditures normal trail the "invoiced" expenditures by from one to two months.

Both the owner's and the contractor's project managers should be aware of the difference in these three types of expenditure forecasting: *(1)* committed, *(2)* invoiced, and *(3)* paid. Whenever information of the type is furnished, the basis should be clearly identified. Unfortunately, each department is firmly convinced that the other instinctively knows what is wanted.

Construction financing may be a very significant element of project cost. Even a seemingly short delay in payment of invoices may benefit the project financially. On the other hand, the payment conditions for some invoices may include early payment incentives which might be overriding. The project manager must be aware of the importance of financial schedules in his area of responsibility. Where a contractor is called upon to make payments to his own employees, to vendors, fabricators, and subcontractors prior to receiving reimbursement from the owner, a serious financial burden may be posed for the contractor. This must be anticipated, evaluated, and compensated for in some manner. Advance payments for anticipated expenses or project payments from a zero balance bank account are ways to reduce the need for the contractor to finance the work. Some contacts provide no alternative except for the contractor to include his estimated "cost of money" allowance in his commercial terms when bidding the work.

❒

12

Purchase Management

Purchasing is the first phase of materials management. Purchasing means procurement of goods and services from some external agencies. The object of purchase department is to arrange the supply of materiais, spare parts and services or semi-finished goods, required by the organisation to produce the desired product, from some agency or source outside the organisation. The purchased items should be of specified quality in desired quantity available at the prescribes time at a competitive price. In the words of Alford and Beatty, "Purchasing is the producing of materials, supplies, machines tools and services required for equipment, maintenance and operation of a manufacturing plant". According to Walters, purchasing function mean's "the procurement by purchases of the proper materials, machinery, equipment and supplies for stores used in the manufacture of a product adopted to marketing in the proper quality and quantity at the proper time and at the lowest price, consistent with quality desired." Thus purchasing is an operation of market exploration to procure goods and services of desired quality, quantity at lowest price and at the desired time. Supplier who can provide standard items at the competitive price are selected. Purchasing in an enterprise has now become a specialised function. It was experienced that by giving the purchase responsibility to a specialist, the firm can obtain greater economic in purchasing. Moreover purchasing involves more than 50% of capital expenditure budgeted by the firm. According to Westing, Fine and Zenz "Purchasing is a managerial activity that goes beyond the simple act of buying. It includes research and development for the proper selection of materials and sources, follow up to ensure timely delivery, inspection to ensure both quantity and quality; to control traffic, receiving, storekeeping and accounting operations related to purchases. "the modern thinking is that purchasing is a strategic managerial function and any negligence will ultimately result into decrease in profits.

OBJECTIVES OF PURCHASING MANAGEMENT

The objectives of the purchasing department can be stated as follows:

(i) To ensure that proper quantities of materials are made available for a smooth functioning of the production department.

(ii) To procure the materials at reasonably low costs (not necessarily low prices) to the company.

(iii) To ensure that the desired quality of materials are supplied.

(iv) To select the proper source's of supply in order to ensure the above (i, ii, and iii).

(v) To do a study or research on the possible substitutes for the raw materials and bought out component parts; for this, the technique of Value analysis Value Engineering will be useful.

(vi) To keep abreast of the various substitute materials available in the supply marked, their prices and utility of the organisation; and to pass such information or discuss such information with the various other departments of the company such as Design, Production Sales, Finance, etc.

(vii) In order to ensure the continuity of the quantity and quality of the supply of raw materials (at competitive prices), to develop new vendors and develop goods relations with existing vendors. Vendor relations. vendor monitoring or vendor evaluation and development of new vendors is an integral part of the purchasing executive's job.

(viii) To develop good procedures and systems for the purchasing department, of that the various purchasing objectives do not remain personalised but become institutionalised.

(ix) To coordinate with other functional departments of the organisation and achieve as much continuity or information flow and integration between different departments as possible. For this purpose, it becomes essential for the purchasing executives to keep in touch with the various functions of the company such as Design, Production, Sales. Finance, etc.

The Wall Street Journal had quoted W.F Rockwell Jr., President of the Rockwell Manufacturing Company, USA as stating that a purchasing executive's job is not simply to buy a product at the lowest possible price: A Purchasing Executive should be one of the most knowledgeable managers in his company who should understand Design, Engineering, Production, Marketing and other related functions in sufficient detail. The Purchasing Executive should be brought into the picture in the earliest stages of design, engineering and production. In short, a Purchasing Executive's role is not restricted to procuring the requisitioned goods at a low price and at proper time, but is also to be knowledgeable and informed about not only what is being bought, but also about why it is being bought. So, the role of a Purchasing Manager is that of being well informed about the internal operations of the company as also about the external supply marked, and to combine these two in procuring materials at the right quantity, quality, time and cost, so that the organisation/firm as a whole benefits on a sustained basis.

MISSION OF PURCHASING

The purchasing department is a key player in the achievement of a company's strategic objectives. It can affect fast delivery of products/services, on-time deliveries, production costs; and product/ service quality, all of which are key elements in operations strategy. The mission of purchasing is to sense the competitive priorities necessary for each major product/service (low production costs, fast and on-time deliveries, highquality products/ service, and flexibility) and to develop purchasing plans for each major product/service that are consistent with operations strategies. One material, for example, may go into a product whose operations strategy calls for high volume, produce-to-stock production, and low production costs. For such a material, purchasing must emphasise developing suppliers that can produce the material at very low cost and in large quantities. On the other hand, another material may go into a product whose operations strategy calls for low volume, fast deliveries, high quality, and produce-to-order production. For this material, purchasing must emphasise fast response times by suppliers, very high quality, and dependable shipping schedules.

DUTIES OF A PURCHASING DEPARTMENT

The usual duties that are assigned to a purchasing department are:

(1) Finding and Approving Suppliers. In this context, suppliers must be taken to include both those who supply goods and those who supply services. This should be done not only by discussions with representatives and examination of catalogues and samples, but also by visits to the suppliers' premises. The technical approval of the vendor's product or service may be the responsibility of the quality or design departments, but the purchaser should be confident that the source of supply is stable, reliable and able to fulfil the demands made upon it. Visits to suppliers will not only help to give this assurance but will also allow the buyer to meet, in a direct manner, those people with whom he/she will be dealing and build up a spirit of goodwill between the two parties. Used with discretion, this goodwill can be of great value in times of difficulty.

Purchasing managers should try wherever possible to assign quantitative values to the factors which are desirable in a supplier. There are a number of schemes such as vendor rating, which is discussed later.

(2) Purchasing at Least Total Cost. While the quality and quantity of goods or services may be specified elsewhere, the purchaser must purchase these at the most advantageous terms. He must be prepared to assist in or lead all discussion on order quantities, and give advice on the imponderable—like anticipated service from the supplier—which can affect decisions on the choice of vendor.

Wherever possible, price should be fixed by competitive tender, if possible by comparison with a target purchasing price. It has been pointed out earlier that the lowest purchase price may not necessarily be that which is least costly to the purchasing company, since it may attract other costs (rectification, sorting progressing etc.) which increase the total cost of the purchased item. Any unexpectedly low price should be treated with caution.

A purchaser should obtain a list of satisfactory suppliers and should send out as many enquiries as convenient, requesting information on quality, delivery and price; these enquiries must be marked clearly FOR QUOTATION ONLY. Quotations should be examined for such items as delivery charges, discount structure (*e.g.*, discounts for prompt payment), supplementary charges and any restrictions. The use of the learning curve as a negotiating tool is advocated by some. while the practice of incorporating a purchaser into a value analysis team is well established and very useful.

(3) Ensuring Delivery of Goods and Services at the Right Time. This will involve contacting suppliers before the due dates and seeking assurances that these dates will be maintained. A formal 'progress' system may be set up to do this, and a convenient method is to log all delivery requirements in diary fonn, perhaps raising an equity before the due date, following this up by a final enquiry just before the due date to confirm. It must the realised that deliveries which are too early may fonn a source of embarrassment, not only because payment may be demanded early, but because excessive space might be occupied. In some organisations the delivery date and, indeed, time of day may require to be specified to avoid congestion. It is not unknown for goods delivered early to be refused or delayed entry. This is particularly important, of course, in the food preparation service industries.

(4) Warning all Concerned if Deliveries are not Going to be Met. If, as a result of the progressing action mentioned above, it is evident that a delivery date is not going to be met, the appropriate departments must be informed in order that work can, if necessary, and possible, be rescheduled.

(5) Organising all Discussions With Suppliers, Both Actual and Potential. It will be found that departments, such as design, will need to meet suppliers and discuss problems with them and, while in many cases the only persons competent to carry out 'technical' discussions with suppliers are within the technical departments, these discussions should never take place without the knowledge of purchasing. This will avoid arrangements on delivery and price being made which do not accord with the company's purchasing policy. In some organisations, a firm rule is laid down that all correspondence with suppliers must be signed by purchasing even if it originated elsewhere. This may appear restrictive, but it can save much misunderstanding later on, often at a time when the 'technical' departments have relinquished all interest in the purchase..

(6) Speculative Buying. Speculative buying is sometimes a duty of purchasing, and implies the purchase of goods, not from reasons of immediate need but because it appears that market conditions are particularly favourable. Thus, it may seem to the purchaser, from his intimate knowledge of the market, that a particular commodity is likely to become difficult to obtain or that its price is likely to rise sharply. Buying in the first case will guard against a hold-up, whilst in the second case it may pennit material bought cheaply to be resold at a profit. Speculative buying is both difficult and potentially dangerous, and can result in a company carrying stocks which are difficult to clear.

(7) Advising on Prices for Materials or Services. Advising on prices for materials or services to be used in new markets or in modified designes. This activity can be of substantial value since it may help to decide major policy questions—for example, the feasibility of meeting a marketing requirement on price, or the likely cost of re-equipping a unit.

MODES OF PURCHASING/PURCHASING SYSTEMS

(1) Forward Buying. Forward buying or committing an organisation far into the future, usually for a year is an vague. Depending upon the availability of the item, the financial policies, the economic order quantity, the quantitative, discounts and the staggered delivery. The future commitment is decided. This type of forward buying is different from speculative buying where the motive is to made capital out of the price changes, by selling the purchased items. Manufacturing organisation normally don't indulge in such buying. However, a few organisations do 'hedge", particularly in the commodity market by selling or buying contracts.

(2) Tender Buying. In public buying, all semblance of favouritism, patronage and personal preferences should be avoided. As such, it is common for government departments and public sector undertakings to purchase through tenders. Private sector organisations adopt tender buying if the value of purchases is more than the prescribed limits as Rs. 50,000 or Rs. 1,00,000. The steps involved are to establish a bidders list, solicit bids evaluate bids by comparing quotations and place the order with the lowest bidder. However, care has to be taken that the lowest bidder is a responsible party and is capable of meeting the delivery schedule and quality requirements. Open tender system or advertising the tender in newspaper is common in public sector organisations. As advertising bids is costly and time consuming. most private sector organisations solicit tenders only from renowned suppliers capable of supplying the materials.

(3) Blanket Order. This system minimises the administrative expenses and useful for "C" items. It is an agreement to provide a required quantity of specified items, over a period of time, usually for one year, at an agreed price. Deliveries are made depending upon the buyers need. The system relives the buyer from routine work, giving him the more time for focusing attention on high value items. It requires fewer purchase orders and thus reduces clerical work. It often achieves lower prices through quantity discounts by grouping the requirements. The suppliers under the system, maintains adequate inventory to meet the blanket orders, but he does not incur selling costs, once the negotiations are finalised.

(4) Zero Stock. Some firms try to operate on the basis of zero stock and the supplier holds the stock for these firms. Usually the firms of the buyer and seller are close to each other so that the raw material of one is the finished product of another, as for instance, Naptha in a fertiliser plant is one of the final products of the refinery. Alternatively, the system could work well if the seller holds the inventory and if the two parties work in close co-ordination. However, the price per item in this system will be slightly higher as the supplier will include the inventory carrying cost in the price. In this system, the buyer need not lock up the capital and so the purchasing routine is reduced. This also significantly reduces obsolescence of inventory lead time and clerical efforts in work paper work. Thus the seller can devote his marketing efforts to other customers and production scheduling becomes easy.

(5) Rate Contract. The system of rate contract is prevalent in public sector organisations and government departments. It is common for suppliers to advertise that they are on "rate contract" for the specific period. After negotiation, the seller and the buyer agree to the ıates of items. Application of rate contract has helped many organisations lead time as individual firms need not go through the central purchasing departments and can place orders directly with the suppliers. However, supplier always demand higher prices for prompt delivery, as rate contracts normally stipulate only the rate and not the delivery schedule. This difficulty has been avoided by ensuring the delivery of a minimum quantity at the agreed rates? This procedure of fixing a minimum quantity is called the running contract and is being practices by the railways and others.

(6) Reciprocity. Reciprocal buying means purchasing from one's customers in preference to others. It is based on the principle. "If you kill my cat I will kill your dog and do upto your customers as you would have them do upto you". Other things, like soundness from the ethics and economic point of view being equal, the principles of reciprocity can be practiced. However, a purchasing executives should not indulge in reciprocity on his initiative when the terms and conditions are not equal with other suppliers.

(7) Systems Contract. This is a procedure intended to help the buyer and the seller to reduce administrative expenses and at the same time ensure suitable controls. In this system, the original indent, duly approved by competent authorities, is shipped back with the items and avoids the usual documents like purchase orders, materials requisition, goods in words report, etc. The contract is invariably simple, covering only delivery period, price and invoicing procedure. Systems contracting is particularly useful for items with low unit price with high consumption profile and relives the buyers of the routine work.

(8) Negotiation. Negotiation particularly for prices has been accepted as a policy by some materials managers, since perfect competition does not exist in Indian situations and hence, the concept of lowest bid does not always work. Negotiation is indeed a battle of wits and an art of embodying sophisticated tactics and manoeuvre by both the buyer and the seller. Normally, buyers should not be opportunists and try to function as arbitrators between the factory and the suppliers. The buyer must enable his supplier to make a reasonable profit in the short run and survive as well as grow in the long run. He should remember that he is buying not only for today's price, but for tomorrow's cost as well. In this process, the buyers help the suppliers towards finding more economical ways of working rather than squeeing out the profit margin. Selling at a loss will drive the suppliers out of business reducing the sources of supplies. It is in this context that the art of negotiation is treated as a forum for exchange of views rather than cutthroat buying. In negotiating both the buyer and seller try to evaluate each other with regard to price and quality.

The parameters affecting the process of negotiation of an item are availability, number of sources, price, delivery, penality, discounts, package and transportation. The bargaining power will definitely be influenced by the preparedness of the buyer as well as the place and time of negotiation. It is not uncommon to find negotiations taking place over a cup of tea or beer. The known technique used for negotiations are price analysis, persuasion, discussion, interrogation, investigation, staging a walk out, prolonged silence, weighing pros and cons, offensive strategy, defensive strategy, blow hot and cold, suggesting complicated formula and learning curve. A successful negotiator has to possess the qualities of patience, persistence, persuasiveness, clear thinking, logical analysis, optimism, knack of getting along with the people, ability to plan and be 'thick skimmed' while negotiating, the buyer should hope for the best and at the same time be prepared for the worst. He should not adopt a strategy of hard choices and soft options. Care should however be taken to adopt negotiations on a selective basis as the seller will easily identify the individuals as Mr. five percent of Mr. Ten percent and inflate the prices accordingly.

FUNCTIONS OF PURCHASING DEPARTMENT

The main object of purchase department is to purchase items of specified quality and quantity at lowest price. To accomplish this, the functions of the department are :

1. Processing the Requisition. The department of the organisation communicate to the purchase department their requirement for various items through requisition form. The format of requisition form contains the details of the quality, quantity and other necessary specifications about the item to be purchased. The requisition is to be signed by the competent authority. The purchase requisition is prepared in duplicate and the original copy is sent to the purchase department. The purchase department processes and scrutinises the requisition and then proceeds to other operations for making purchases.

2. Location and Choice of Suppliers. The potential vendors are contracted through authorised representatives, their catalogues and sample of the items are inspected and examined either at the purchaser's place or at the vendor's place. On the basis of findings from inspection, examination of samples and analysis of the quoted prices, suppliers are approved for placing the orders. The criterion for the ultimate choice of a vendor is based on following aspects:

(i) ***Reliability of Supply.*** Past performance specially in the time of crisis as well as sound financial position of a supplier classifies him to be reliable.

(ii) ***Assurance of Timely Delivery.*** The punctuality pattern in observing the delivery schedule provide by the purchaser during past deals ensures the prompt supply by the vendor.

(iii) ***Other Considerations.*** After sales service, technical assistance attitude with regard to the goods rejected by the purchaser and cooperation in disposal of waste are some important guiding factors for the choice of supplies. Purchasing agents continually scan the market place in search of potential new suppliers. Continued monitoring and evaluation of the supplier performance is necessary and should be based upon actual result.

3. Placing of Orders. The purchase department tries to purchase the materials with desired quality and quantity at the most advantageous terms. All purchases should be made through a purchase order in a specified form and duly signed by some authorised person. The purchase order must contain the details about the supplier, description of the items required corresponding prices and amount required. The format of standard purchase order can be: as a rule original copy is sent to the supplier, one copy is retained by the purchase department and one copy is sent to the concerned department requiring the ordered items.

4. Follow up or Progressing the Purchase Orders. Receiving the ordered material at the right time is most important for an organisation. Late deliveries can close the enterprise. For this follow-up or expediting the purchase order after waiting for some reasonable time is essential. The priority of follow-up operations should be given according to the importance or classification of items *e.g.* 'A' class items are to be given top most priority. It is also necessary to review the outstanding orders at regular intervals.

5. Invoices Received from Suppliers are Checked and Verified with the Order Specification. The process includes the following activities: *(i)* The goods supplied are of desired specifications both in quality and quantity. *(ii)* comparison of quoted price and the price charged in the invoice. *(iii)* if some goods supplied does not confirm with the specifications or are damaged during transshipment then steps are taken for adjustments on claims.

6 **Some Other Functions of Purchase Department.** Some other functions of purchase department can be: *(i)* delay in availability of requisitioned material should be conveyed to concerned departments in time. *(ii)* to maintain records regarding supplier, their performance in past, products available with them, probable delivery period for each order etc. *(iii)* to dispose off outdated and scrapped items. *(iv)* control stores operation of receiving the items form vendors and issuing it to concerned departments of the organisation. *(v)* to evaluate the performance of the department. *(vi)* to collect information about trends in market regarding availability of improved goods and services and also about the substitute products in case of emergency. *(viii)* to handle damages and demurrage claims.

❐

13

Stores Management and Control

Two broad approches are normally adopted is establishing and organizing stores services. The first is characterized by a central store or warehouse that serves a number of user departments. The second is a decentralized approach where several independent stores are established to separately serve different departments and organizations. Each approach depends upon different circumstances, which may include:

(a) The size of the user department and the nature and scope of its functions; and

(b) The geographic spread of the department, indcluding the accessibility of its outstationed projects in relation to available transportation and communication facilities.

Generally the decentralized stores are common because user departments find them more practical in meeting their needs, especialty the requirements of projects located in remote and difficult-to-reach rural areas. Advantages claimed for the decentralized stores include easier access to supplies: familiarity with stores layout and consequent speed of action in processing requisitions; individualized security measures to cater to special departmental requirements; and the lower cost of storing high volume stocks. Despite its advantages, the decentralized stores system has proved uneconomic in certain cases. It generates unnecessary duplications of staffing, of the stocks held and of investment in buildings and operating machinery and equipment. The system also costs more in the aggregate in terms of the required supportive services and facilities.

Conversely a central storage unit located strategically to serve a number of different users is regarded in certain respects as more economic and practicable. The approach facililates co-ordination and prevents unnecessary duplication. It also fosters the maximum use of storage space as well as rationalization in the use of operating tools.

The centralized approach is more common for the storage and distribution of office supplies and equipment, housekeeping tools and furnishings, motor vehicles, common plant and machinery, standard spare parts and other common-use items. One arrangement is to establish several units or branches of a central stores organization to severe different groups of users located in contiguous geographic areas. Under another arrangement the service provided by the storage unit of one user department which has the greatest need for the items in question, as in the case of the storage unit of a ministry of health, provides common services to other ministries and departments for medical and health supplies. The latter approach is sometimes criticized on the groud that the subscribing user departments do not receive the same degree of attention and regularity in the services provided as the parent department.

STORES LOCATION AND LAYOUT PLANT

The nature of the goods to be stored, packaging specifications and units of goods received and distributed, their physical condition and storage characteristics, the site and frequency of usage, the reason for storage, the volume and quantity of items to be held, the speed of delivery' and the means of transportation are some of the basic factors that influence the size and type of the storage space to be provided as well as the form of storage that will be most appropriate. These and all other relevant factors should be carefully studied in making decisions on the siting of the stores; the indoor and outdoor space requirements; the type of bins, racks and shelves to be used; the specifications of band ling tools, the extent of air conditioning and other forms of temperature and environmental control; and the nature of security devices.

1. Location Factors

Factors influencing the siting of stores and warehouse fall into two broad categories;

Production Management

(a) Geographic factors, including the accessibility of the area to be served and such climatic conditions as temperature fluctuations, level of humidity incidence of dust and flood hazards; and

(b) The space required in terms of both indoor and outdoor storage.

The location of warehouses in relation to the site where the materials will be needed is an important factor in warehouse planning. It directly affects the flow of materials and consequently the speed of executing projects. Projects in remote rural areas often have serious disadvantages and limitations in warehouse facilities and distribution of goods. In many instances, projects located in the rural areas are not easy to access because of limited transportation facilities. This impedes the place of rural development as well as considerable increasing the cost.

The problem of distance is sometimes resolved by establishing district supply depots to feed a number of substations locacted within short distances from a main base. Although this approach has proved successful in some cases, it has often been characterized by duplication since different government agencies tend to set up separate supply bases in the same district even though their needs could be conveniently met from one store. This approach has been more wasteful when separate departmental district supply bases have been deliberately overstocked in anticipation of shortages that never happened.

One rational approach is to create in each district one or two common warehouse to serve different needs. This enables sufficient stocking of individual items to foster interorganizational transfers of stocks whenever the need arises. This system requires consolidation of stock item usage history, and procurement and inventory replenishment. Delivery of materials to different agencies within the same jurisdiction can be improved since better facilities are created for co-ordinated distribution.

2. Stores Plan and Environment

The layout should aim at facilitating the fast and smooth flow of materials to prevent unnecessary delivery holdups and work stoppages a project sites. Also, the plan should provide for the optimum utilization of space as well as the maximum protection against materials damage, deterioration and other forms of waste. It is generally recommended that at least 80 per cent of the available space be utilized. Where space requirements are increasing, surplus space should equal the lead time required to build or acquire additional facilities.

Proper lighting, adequate ventilation and noise abatement are other important factors that affect efficiency in storage operations. Poor physical conditions and unwholesome environment are not uncommon and these conditions have often contributed significantly to absenteeism and loafing in storage work in some countries. In some instances, good staff have left storage work for the same reasons, especially poor lighting and humidity.

Neither dimness nor glare are compatible with productive work in warehouses and storage facilities, as in other work places. Dimness and dark spots in stores impede the search for items on requisition and also encourage pilferage. Poor lighting in stores is a common experience developing countries where it is often taken for granted that sunlight or natural light is sufficient to meet all lighting needs during the day. It is generally not appreciated that the quality of natural light is impaired at a distance more than six metres away from windows and doors.

3. Layout of Bins

The flow of stores work and space utilization are directly affected by the design and layout plan of the bins, racks and shelves. Processing stores requisitions as well as placing incoming goods in their proper location is easier to carry out where the layout plan facilitates quick identification of the right bins and racks. A simple location code like CI7-D 12 will be usefulin tracing quickly bin 12 of shelf "D" in row 17 along bay "C". Shelf and bin labels and stock card folders are also important in facilitating efficient stock movement and in keeping records.

The type of shelving and other fixtures for storing goods contributes significantly to cost. Although wooden racks, shelves and bins have been found to be cheaper than metal ones, and are equally efficient, public officials a number of developing countries, including those where timber is cheap, often prefer to use the latter. Apart from the higher price of metal shelving, additional difficulties are created by the lack of sufficient foreign exchange resources to pay for the imports involved. Use of the wrong shelving of binning facilities also increase costs; by the same token, bins and racks in excess of requirements are wasteful.

Searching for requisitioned items can be a strenuos and sometimes futile exercise in an unplanned and disorganized store. Often the requisitioned items cannot be traced; this not only prolongs the time of search but sometimes creates a need for new purchases, while large quantities of the same items are mislaid somewhere in the store. Disorderly storage also wastes space and generates unnecessary work.

Usually, stock is received less often than it is disbursed; thus, in general, warehouse layout should be designed to facilitate "stock picking" for filling user requisitions. This is sometimes accomplished by arranging stock in the same location sequence as listed on stock requisitions or in a stock catalogue. For stocks that are disbursed in the same package units as received, *e.g.*, cartons or barrels, and that move in large quantities, random warehouse location can be used, if items are identified by lot.

MATERIALS HANDLING AND DISTRIBUTION

The pace of implementing projects and carrying out other government activities is influences cepsiderably by the flow of needed materials and equipment. The flow channels ard the material handling and distribution processes both of which increase the cost of operations. Therefore, offer, should be made to achieve the optimum movement of equipment and materials with minimum delay and at the lowest cost.

One important aspect of materials handling and distribution is that the design of operating tools must be adaptable to the available skills in order to maintain productivity. Other important aspects of material handling and distribution include the packaging of the requisitioned items, logistics planning and co-ordination, loading and unloading of carrier vehicles and documentation.

(1) Adaptability of Working Tools. Ergonomics is the technique concerned with increasing productivity by harmonzing the design of working tools and methods for operating them with the skill and capacity of these using the tools. The technique is also concerned with relating the size of tools and facilities to the average size of the operating staff. Another concern of the ergonomist is the reduction or avoidance of fatigue in the use of tools and in the process of handling goods.

The major objectives of ergonomics is to prevent both the waste of investment and the loss of productivity that arise from acquiring tools and equipment that are to be used by people who are neither trained and experienced, nor physically adjusted to use them effectively. This a common problem faced by many developing countries, but it can be avoided if attention is paid to making the design of the working tools compatible with available skills and other relevant human factors. Both supply managers and managers of user agencies in government should study and know the physical characteristics as well as the skills of their materials handling staff to be able to advise more meaningfully on the choice of proper tools and equipment.

(2) Packaging. Good packaging is essential for the protection of goods against physical damage, deterioration and pilferage. Different designs and construction methods match the requirements of different commodities. The basic requirements include the need to ensure that each container or receptacle is sturdy and of balanced construction. Bundling is often applied in the case of sawn timber, metal roads and other losse and bulky commodities that are not risky to expose. Sacks, bags, crates, cases, cartons, drums and kegs are used where the risk of damage or loss through ėxposure is great. Tensional strappings made of wire, steel or synthetic fibres are also used to bind the containers for extra strength and stability. Internal padding in the form of rubber, foam rabber, wood shavings, sawdust and other forms of cushioning are also applied as additional fittings to provide anti-shock protection for delicate and high-value materials. Although good packaging may require more money and effort to proxide, its benefits are far more rewarding. It prevents breakage or crushing often encountered in handling, storage and transportation activities. Proper packaging also provides security against pilferage, a common problem associated with supply management.

Another packaging guide is that the weight of each package must be suited to the capacity of the available tools and equipment. Bulky and heavy packages must as a rule be avoided, as they are expensive and difficult to handle. The risk of dropping and damaging the contents of bulky packages is generally high especially where they are handled manually.

Although lighter packages are easier to handle, their processing is not necessarily cheaper. On the contrary they create a need for more movement and loading. The larger the number of packages to be handled, the greater the need for more clerical action; more record-keeping is required in comparison to the limited clerical action generated by handling one bulky package. Small packages also induce pilferage. A midway approach, where the packages are neither too bulky nor too small or unnecessarily numerous, appears to be a useful guide.

Marking packages for easy identification is another important packaging requirement. Marking is done by branding, embossing etching, painting, printing, stenciling and other fast methods that do not rub-off easily. Each marking should incorporate the following basic data in order to expedite the required storage and delivery processes:

(a) The name and address of the consignee;

(b) Brief description of the contents of the package, including stock or code number. This information often attracts pilferage; to prevent it, some consignors pack the manifest, or list of contents, in the container;

(c) Instructions regarding: shelf-life of the package, the method of lifting and packing, possible dangers and limitations; and

(d) The package number and the quantity of packages making up the consignment;

(e) Date of dispatch;

(f) The name and address of the issuing warehouse or store.

In addition to external markings on the container, each article it holds should be also labeled. This additional requirement may cost more money and extra effort to satisfy, but it is useful for the purposes of control and speed of delivery.

Insufficient or improper labeling of out-going packages has been a major cause of property losses. In a number of cases, the post box address rather than the location address of the consignee is used in preparing the labels. The post box does not normally provide location directions; therefore, its use with out any additional guide creates difficulties for carriers, especially those who make deliveries in cities and larger towns. In some cases, the consigned packages are returned to stores because of failure to find the right location.

(3) Documentation. Effective documentation is also a critical factor in the distribution process. Proper documents are essential to ensure proper accountability and to prevent fraud as well as misunderstandings in case of disputes. Experience has shown that a major cause of loss in supply management is poor documentation.

Much material and equipment issued from stores and warehouses goes astray because of lack of supporting documents. Losses have also occurred because consignment notes, way bills or manifests are incomplete in that the consigned articles have not been sufficiently described or properly list.

PHYSICAL CONTROL MEASURES

Physical control measures embracing a regular and continuing programme of stock verification or audit and preservation of stocks contribute significantly to cost reduction in supply management. The aim of these measures is to ensure:

(a) accuracy in relation to the quantity of stocks used as well as the balance of stocks in hand;

(b) proper and correct record-keeping;

(c) optimum use of materials resources through inter-agency stock transfers and reallocations;

(d) unnecessary build-up of surplus stock; and

(e) the prevention of obsolescence and deterioration.

(1) Stock Verification and Audit

A periodic audit of stocks and storekeeping procedures is necessary to ensure that errors that occur from time to time are detected early and corrected before they cause serious damage. Periodic audits also enable appraisal and revision of stores procedures where necessary. The audit is usually undertaken by independent stock verifiers in the presence of the regular stores officials.

Broadly the objectives of stock verification include:

(a) Enforcement of rules and regulations to prevent waste and loss;

(b) Random selection and spot check of recorded transactions to increase the probability that records are accurate and up to date;

(c) Assurance that adequate security safe guards are provided to prevent unauthorized removal of items from the stores and warehouses. This is particularly important for high value, strategic and dangerous items;

(d) Evaluation of the condition and adequacy of the storage accommodation, storage layout, equipment, etc.;

(e) Assurance that enough separate checks and continuous controls are carried out regularly by the stores staff to detect and remedy any defects in the system;

(f) Advice on how to handle problems revealed in the investigations, and measures for appropriate follow-up on solutions.

(g) Identification of surplus and obsolete stocks and recom mendations on methods of disposal; and

The frequency and nature of stock verification should be established as a matter of policy, upon the collective advice of the head of the supply agency, the accountant or controll-ergeneral and the auditor-general; The two principal methods of stock vertification are:

(a) A periodic stock audit which entails checking the whole range of stocks held, or a substantial part of them, at one time. Where this method is used, it should be done at least once a year and preferably more frequently for very costly items or vital strategic breakdown spares, the physical holdings of which are unlikely to be large and can be checked whenever a review is triggered under the inventory or stock control system.

(b) Continuous or cyclical stocktaking, which entails a selection of items to be checked each day or each week, year-round, according to a programme that provides for each item of stock to be checked at least once in the programme established by management. Here again the programme must be framed to give the greatest attention to the most important items, according to the A-B-C evaluation system previously explained.

A stock audit is more than just verifying the accuracy of stock balances. It is more of an assessment of the assets of the organization, embracing periodic stock valuations in terms of prevailing market values or the original cost. The prime purpose of such valuation is to:

(a) Assess the total value of stocks held in an organization as part of its budget review process;

(b) Determine the value of obsolete and redundant goods and arrange for their disposal to prevent continuing loss of funds.

(c) Ascertain the extent to which the value of the stock has been diminished through deterioration and losses, and develop the necessary preventive measures for future control; and

(2) Prevention of Surplus Stocks and Obsolescence. The problem of obsolescence, obsolute, dormant and surplus goods is acute in many developing countries. Vast quantities of redundant and deteriorating goods have added significantly to the cost of government operations. To control or prevent such waste would contribute considerably to cost reduction.

Obsolute stocks are those items for which there is no further need by the user. Examples include spare parts related to modified or replaced equipment or machinery for which there is no further use. There are also items like food and drugs whose effectiveness or usefulness has lapsed with the passing of time. Items considered obsolescent are those for which there is continuing, but diminishing, demand. This may result from changes and improvements in machinery and equipment design. In many cases, old models are abandoned rather than being continued and used up before the new models are put into use. Obsolescence results from changes in products as well as the course of supply, which necessitates a gradual replacement of old stocks with new types and models.

Dormant or slow-moving stocks are those whose usage is infrequent. Stocks often become dormant when large quantities of spare parts held as safety stocks to support plan and machinery which break down less frequently than has been anticipated. There are several other reasons for slow-moving stocks, which must be identified and controlled. There are also surplus stocks, which include numbers of items in excess of requirements; these should be disposed of immediatety to avoid wasteful build-up. Surplus stocks often result from overordering and contribute significantly to the quantity of obsolescent and dormant stock items.

Holding obsolete, obsolescent are surplus stocks is costly but the cost is not always apparent. Whereas the cost of providing storage space for such stocks is obvious and easy to calculate, other not-so-obvious costs are equally significant. They include the following:

(a) The cost of periodic stocktaking and valuation:

(b) The cost of maintaining stock and accounting records;

(c) The loss of use of capital tied up in inventories;

(d) The cost of preservation and upkeep to prevent deterioration;

(e) The cost of security;

(f) The additional expenditure incurred in providing for extra storage place to accommodate current and active stocks during the period of expansian. Such expenditures would be unnecessary if the space were not occupied by the redundant stocks;

(g) Continuing depreciation or loss in the disposable value of redundant stocks.

(h) The cost of additional staff for stores work.

In views of the cost impact of redundant and obsolete stocks. special effort should be made to avoid them. This calls for constant vigilance not only by the supply manager and his staff but also by the management and staff of user departments whose demands and preference directly influence the quantity and diversity of redundant stocks. Technical preference in placing orders should be replaced by technical essentially 'to prevent extravagence and accumulation of waste. This requires close and cooperative collaboration among all user departments staff and control agencies and supply organizations in the government.

Obsolete and surplus goods should be disposed of as soon as practicable provided adequate steps are taken to ensure that such an action will not result in premature disposals which could in turn. result in stock-outs. Delays in disposing of redundant stocks not only increase the cost holding and maintaining the items involved but they also create the risk of deterioration and loss of sale value of the stocks in question. To insure that the highest utilization or value possible is realized from disposable obsolete and surplus stocks, the following factors should be taken into consideration:

(a) Valuation of the item in terms of its depreciated use for its scrap value;

(b) The advantage in transferring the item to another government organization or selling it to another government in a neighbouring country;

(c) The property of the item as a hazard; *e.g.*. it may be better to have redundant dangerous chemicals dumped at sea or buring in the ground than to transfer or sell them for use elsewhere;

(d) The possibility of breaking up the item into spare parts and refused for repair and maintenance.

(e) Method of sale. *e.g.*. competitive tenders, sale by auction. as limited negotiations and expected income; and

(3) Stock Preservation and Maintenance. Preserving or protecting stock items against deterioration and loss of value contributes to cost reduction. Unless items in stock are are inspected periodically and properly serviced, they can deteriorate rapidly. Deterioration is a serious problem in developing countries where the incidence of damage to stores through unfavourable weather conditions and attack by insects, rodents and other pests is high.

Rusting, evaporation, colour fading, body warping, cracking, swelling or shrinking, biological deterioration caused by mildew, fungus growth and rotting, and corrosion through chemical reactions are controllable forms of deterioration. Preservation methods that can be applied include those that are applied during the process of manufacture, those that are applied externally from time to time while the materials and equipment are in storage and special housing and storage requirements, such as refrigeration and homidity control. It is essential that the supply staff be sufficiently acquanted with the various preservation methods to be able to advise on which to apply in any given situation. They should be also acquainted with the sources of the necessary technical services.

Methods of preservation against rusting and corrosion include wrapping or "cocooning", together with the use of desiccants that absorb moisture. For wrapping purposes, there are various proprietary brands of plastic coverings that provide protection against rusting and corrosion and against biological damage. To complement this form of protection, the relative humidity in the warehouses and storage places must be controlled. Normally, corrosion and mildew damage can be prevented if the level of relative humidity is kept at 50 per cent or below. Air conditioning and other dehumidifying equipment is available, but such equipment can only be used where electrical power is available.

In many rural districts and outlying areas in developing countries the use of air conditioning and dehumidification equipment is impracticable because of the lack of electricity. Coating metallic items with grease, oil and other lubricants is a common alternative in such cases. Other protective measures and techniques include painting; plating with such metals as nickel, chrome, zinc and cadmium; chemical coating through the use of phosphates, oxide and sulphides; and coating with porcelain enamels, ceramics and plastic compounds.

One major disadvantage to applying coatings as antirust and corrosion protection is that the coating is usually hard to remove unless the article is meant to be used in its protected form. However, many proprietary cleansing processes are available to aid removal. The cost of removal may be high, and this should be borne in mind when coating is considered as a form of protection against material deterioration.

□

14

Statistical Quality Control

Statistical quality control is not to be thought of as a separate science or a unique theory of quality control. Rather, it is an integral part of total quality control, and provides a most valuable tool in this "total" approach. There is nothing new or unusual about the desire to produce a uniform product. It is the optimum condition in a process that attempts to eliminate variability among like units. As an ideal, this is commendable, but, just as there is no such thing as a perfect circle, it is impossible to achieve exact repeatability within a process. In everything in this universe, what we call chance, or random variation, is present. This variation is inherent, but there is also assignable variation that is directly attributable to specific causes.

In essence, statistical quality control investigates processes and locates and separates these two types of variation in order that meaningful steps can be taken to control "quality." When only inherent variation is at work in a process, we consider the process to be "under control."

Techniques of Statistical Quality Control

Statistical quality control is a fairly new concept in the United States. It wasn't until World War II, with demand for more material made to exacting specifications, that its methods were employed to any great extent. It has enjoyed extensive and expanding use ever since.

The economies enjoyed by industry through the use of statistical quality control are immense, as represented by reductions in "time and manpower requirements, in waste, scrap, rework, and inspection costs. Many problems in industry concerning the manufacture of a product, from its concept to its use by a consumer, lend themselves well to statistical treatment.

The two principal techniques of statistical quality control, the control chart and acceptance sampling, ensure that necessary quality standards are being met as economically as possible. In a general sense, though, statistical quality control embraces all statistical techniques associated with the manufacturing of the product, including process capability studies, used primarily in the research and development phase of new products.

The word quality in statistical quality control refers to some measurable property of a product, such as tensile strength, hardness, diameter, or weight, that can somehow be translated into numbers.

Many people are dumbfounded when told that there is no such thing as exact repeatability. It is impossible to duplicate exactly any given set of conditions. No matter how precise a manufacturing condition may be, it is still characterized by a variability due to chance, much like the variation we get by rolling a die many times (we realize, of course, that if we roll it six times we aren't going to get 1, 2, 3, 4, 5, and 6 in these six throws even though the law of averages says that, in the long run, we should).

This chance variation is inevitable in any process and can never be completely eliminated.

When the only variability present is chance variation (which can be determined with a certain degree of probability by statistical techniques), we say that the process is in statistical control. In this case, we must have already removed the other type of variation present-assignable variation through the use of statistical techniques such as control charts and the analysis of designed experiments. Through analysis of variance, we are able to locate significant variations due to differences in operators, raw materials, machine settings, etc.

Since no process is really immune to these troubles, it is necessary to have a continual method of data retrieval and analysis in order to detect deviations from statistical control when they occur or, if posible, before they occur. During in-process manufacturing the control chart covers this need just as analysis-of-variance techniques perform the investigative function in process capability studies, which determine the effects of changes in variables on the process.

By plotting sample results on a time scale, in a control chart. we can ascertain whether the variation from sample to sample is due to chance variation or to assignable causes. The criteria used to make these decisions are the control limit lines. Control charts are a type of process capability too, because they let us know the average level at which the process can operate, as well as the amount of chance variation present.

Control charts are a type of hypothesis testing. The hypothesis being tested is: The process is "in control." If we accept this hypothesis, we are in essence stating that the process is satisfactory and the only variability present is the random type. If, on the other hand, we reject the hypothesis, we presume that assignable variation is at work, and we set out to detect the source, or sources, of these variations.

Most of the common statistical techniques used in quality control are based on nonnal theory, a subject in itself, which we shall cover briefly later.

As in testing hypotheses, and as in inductive statistics, errors can be committed. Statistical quality control is based on the laws of probability. The errors we can make are:

1. If we reject the hypothesis that we are in control when indeed we are in control, we make an error (type I). The consequence of this is that we will look for non-existent trouble, and this search will cause an unnecessary increase in costs.
2. If we accept the hypothesis that we are in control when we are not in control, we make another error (type II). The

consequence of this is that we don't look for trouble when it is present and thus may produce and ship products that don't meet standards.

By using the nonnal theory involved with control charts, we are able to balance the risks associated with the above errors. In this country we use the so-called 3-sigma (3σ) control limits. This sets the risk of the first type of error at .003. The source of the second type of error is generally unknown, and more sophisticated statistical techniques must be employed for its detennination.

There are generally two types of control charts: control charts for variables and those for attributes. The latter type is generally a control chart indicating percentages of defective products.

Although control charts are the most commonly used statistical quality control technique, the probability theory behind makes them not applicable to every need. One area for which control charts are not suited is acceptance sampling, a method to determine overall quality of incoming or outgoing lots of goods.

Individual items are generally classified as defective or non-defective, depending on whether the unit possesses a certain characteristic or meets a particular specification. Rather than check each individual unit in a lot, sampling, with certain guarantees, is more economical.

"Screening," or 100 percent inspection, is impractical at best, and, because neither men nor machines are perfect, screening cannot guarantee that all defective items will be found.

Acceptance sampling involves deciding, on the basis of a sample, whether to accept or reject a lot; and there is always a chance that a good lot will be rejected and vice versa.

The probability of rejecting a good lot is called producer's risk and the probability of accepting a bad lot consumer's risk. In practice today, in the many sampling plans available, these two risks are generally present, built into the plans.

The most common sampling plans in use are described in military standard MIL-STD-I05D. This plan, which will be discussed later, is based on Acceptable Quality Level (AQL), the lowest quality at which the consumer is willing to accept a lot with a specified high probability (generally 92-98 percent).

Other plans are based on *(1)* Lot Tolerance Percent Defective (L TPD), the quality above which there is only a small specified probability that a lot will be accepted, and *(2)* Average Outgoing Quality Limit (AOQL), the maximum quality that can be expected in the long run when rejected lots are 100 percent inspected and all the bad items have been removed and replaced with good ones.

It is to be noted that there are no plans to guarantee perfect quality lots. First, this is almost an impossibility for high-volume items, and second, the only way to guarantee this is through 100 percent inspection, the disadvantages of which have already been mentioned.

The above paragraphs have presented a brief synopsis of the major aspects of statistical quality control with which we will principally concern ourselves.

PROBABILITY

Definition

The number of occurrences satisfying the probability statements divided by the total number of possible occurrences is the probability of that event.

Example

(a) The probability of throwing a 4 on a die. There are six possible occurrences 1, 2, 3, 4, 5, and 6, and one chance in six to throw a 4 in one roll. The probability is 1/6.

(b) The probability of drawing an ace from a deck of cards in one draw. There are four aces in a total of 52 cards. The probability is 4/52, or 1/13.

Multiplication Theorem

The probability (P) that two independent events will occur is the product of their individual probabilities. (Independence implies the probability that one event has an effect on the occurrence of the other.)

Example

To simultaneously throw a 4 on one die and to draw an ace from a deck of cards. These are independent events. Die: l/6 probability to throw a 4.

Ace: l/13 probability to draw an ace.

$$P_{AB} = P_A \times P_B$$

$$= \frac{1}{6} \times \frac{1}{13} = \frac{1}{78}$$

Addition Theorem

The probability that one of two mutually exclusive events will occur is the sum of the individual probabilities. (Mutually exclusive means that the occurrence of one event precludes the occurrence of the other).

Example

A box contains 100 balls. There are five colours distributed in the following manner:

A.	Red	30
B.	Green	25
C.	Black	20
D.	Blue	15
E.	Yellow	10

What is the probability of drawing a green or a blue ball in one draw?

$$P_{B+D} = P_B + P_D$$

$$= \frac{25}{100} + \frac{15}{100} = \frac{40}{100}.$$

Conditional Probability

If the probability of a second event is dependent on the outcome of the first event, we have conditional probability of the second event.

Example

Two balls are drawn on two draws from the box containing 100 balls of five different colors. What is the probability of drawing one green ball on the first draw and one blue ball on the second draw?

$$P_{BD} = P_B \times P_{B/D} = P_D \times P_{D/B}$$

$$= \frac{25}{100} \times \frac{15}{100-1} = \frac{15}{396}$$

Note. The conditional probability is shown by the fact that for the second draw, there are only 99 balls to choose from.

Permutations

The number of permutations of a group of items is the number of specific arrangements that can be made from these items. With N items, there are N! (N factorial) possible arrangements.(N! = N (N – l) (N – 2)...1).

Example

For the arrangement of three items A, B, and C, there are 3! (3 × 2 × 1 = 6) ways to arrange three items, specifically: ABC, ACB, BAC, BCA, CAB, and CBA.

Combinations

The number of combinations of a group of items is the number of permutations irrespective of order that can be made from these items. There are always more permutations for any group of items than combinations because permutations alone take into account the order of arrangement.

Example

For the group of three items A, B, and C, there is only one combination of all three, while there are six permutations.

Mathematics of Permutations and Combinations

Generally in using both permutations and combinations, a sample is drawn from the total group of item, so what we are interested in is the specific sample possibilities.

Permutations

$$P_{nr} = \frac{N!}{(N-r)!}$$

With a total of N items taken *r* at a time this expression gives the number of different possible permutations.

Example

With five letters A, B, C, D, and E, what is the number of permutations taking two letters at a time? Mathematically:

$$P_{5.2} = \frac{5!}{(5-2)!} = \frac{5!}{3!} = \frac{120}{6} = 20.$$

Specifically: AB, AC, AD, AE, BA, BC, BD, BE, CA, CB, CD, CE, DA, DB, DC, DE, EA, EB, EC, ED.

We have considered the permutation of different things to this point. However, if some of the things are identical, the number of possible permutations is reduced. Mathematically, this is expressed as

$$N = \frac{N!}{p!q!n!}$$

where p, q, and n are like things.

Example

Using the same five letters but changing the quantities to 3A's, 3B's, 2C's, ID, and IE, we now have 10 items but only 5 different values.

$$N = \frac{10!}{3!3!2!1!1!} = 50{,}400$$

If all 10 items were different, there would be 10! or approximately 3,638,800 permutations of all 10 items.

Combinations

We have previously defined the difference between permutations and combinations as the difference resulting from the arrangement of the tnings. Combinations do not require a specific order. It is also true that each combination could be calculated as to the number of permutations occurring within the combination. For mathematical purposes this fact is quite important, since the calculation of number of combinations is based on calculations of permutations. The total number of permutations equals the number of combinations times the number of permutations within a eombination. Using the same terminology as in the permutations, $C_{N,r}$ means the number of combinations of N things taken *r* at a time. The original definition of permutations stated that with N items, there are N! possible arrangements. Since we are now discussing the number of permutations within a combination, this is our figure *r*.

Writing the above expression in mathematical terms, $P_{N,r} = C \times r!$, we can also define a formula for combinations:

$$C_{N,r} = \frac{P_{Nr}}{r!}.$$

Or

$$C_{N,r} = \frac{N!}{r!(N-r)!}.$$

Example

What are the number of combinations with the five letters A, B, C, D, and E, taking three at a time?

$$C_{5,3} = \frac{5!}{3!2!} = 10.$$

Example

There is a box with 10 colored balls, 7 white and 3 red, from which we will draw exactly 3 balls. What is the probability of drawing exactly 0, 1, 2, or 3 red balls?

Total number of combinations is

$$C_{10,3} = \frac{10!}{3!7!} = 120.$$

In order to achieve this, we need to determine how many different combinations out of the total of 120 (the number of possible samples of size 3 we can select from the 10) satisfy the requirements of the problem.

Thus we must calculate the number of combinations of 0 red balls chosen from the 3 red balls in the box, and the number of ways (combinations) we can select 3 out of 7 white balls in the box. Thus:

0 red balls, 3 white balls

$$\frac{3!}{0!3!} \frac{C_{7,3}}{3!4!} = 35,$$

$$P_0 = \frac{35}{120} = 29.1\%$$

1 red balls, 2 white balls

$$C_{3,1} \times C_{7,2} \frac{7!}{2!5!} \frac{3!}{1!2!} = 63,$$

$$P_1 = \frac{63}{120} = 52.5\%$$

2 red balls, 1 white balls

$$C_{3,2} \times C_{7,1} \frac{7!}{1!6!} \frac{3!}{1!2!} = 21,$$

$$P_2 = \frac{21}{120} = 17.5\%$$

3 red balls, 0 white balls

$$C_{3,3} \times C_{7,0} \frac{3!}{3!0!} \frac{7!}{0!7!} = 1,$$

$$P_3 = \frac{1}{120} = 0.8\%$$

Note. 0! is equal to 1.

DATA DISTEMINATION

Normal Distribution

Individual characteristics of a part or product vary unpredictably. No two parts can be made perfectly identical, although the degree of variation can be minimized beyond our ability to measure. The inevitability of this variation is the reason for using tolerances on all measurable quantities. According to the laws of chance, individual measurements form distributions, and the distributions vary in a predictable manner.

The most typical means of summarizing and displaying data in distribution form is the frequency distribution chart (Table 1). In this type of chart, a series of quantitative measures is listed, and the frequency of occurrence is noted opposite each measurement. From the chart, we can compare the distribution visually with a known distribution shape. There are mathematical means for comparing a plotted distribution with an actual distribution, but they are time-consuming and require more sophisticated mathematical tools. Visual comparisons are more practical.

Table 1 : Typical Frequency Distribution Chart

<table>
<tr><th>Shaft length (inches)</th><th></th></tr>
<tr><td>4.96</td><td>|</td></tr>
<tr><td>4.97</td><td>||</td></tr>
<tr><td>4.98</td><td>|</td></tr>
<tr><td>4.99</td><td>||||</td></tr>
<tr><td>5.00</td><td>卌</td></tr>
<tr><td>5.01</td><td>卌 ||||</td></tr>
<tr><td>5.02</td><td>卌 卌 |</td></tr>
<tr><td>5.03</td><td>卌 卌</td></tr>
<tr><td>5.04</td><td>||||</td></tr>
<tr><td>5.05</td><td>||</td></tr>
<tr><td>5.06</td><td>|</td></tr>
</table>

The choice of intervals between measurements may influence our ability to determine a distribution shape. From 8 to 15 measurements seem to work quite well. A smaller number tends to bunch up the data so that only the central measurement has a significant frequency. A greater number tends to spread the data out so that no specific shape can be determined, and data are flattened out. Table 1 has 12 measurements, .01 inch apart.

The frequency distribution in our example has many uses in its present form. The following information can be determined: *(1)* most shafts fall in the area of 5.01-5.03 inches; *(2)* the present average is above 5.00 inches, or on the high side; *(3)* there is a possibility that some pieces will soon fall above the upper tolerance limit of 5.07 inches, as indicated by the distribution shape and spread; *(4)* if tolerances were reduced to ± 0.5 inch, there would be some rejected pieces on the high side of the tolerance; and *(5)* the spread for the present process is 4.96-5.07, or .11 inches. These types of observations, however, should only be made when sufficient data have been accumulated. A rule of thumb for the minimum amount of data would be 15 readings for a narrow spread and 25 readings for a wider spread.

In the numerous frequency distribution studies conducted by industry on product characteristics, it has been found that most of these shapes approach that of the normal distribution, or "bell-shaped," curve characteristic of the laws of chance. For this reason, most quality control statistics are really techniques developed and simplified for use in applications where the data are characteristic of the normal curve. However, it should be remembered that these techniques do not generally apply to other types of distributions, so that data should be visually checked through a frequency distribution chart before being subjected to mathematical analysis.

The characteristics of the normal curve that have significance are $\overline{X}$, the arithmetic mean (average), and σ the standard deviation (measure of dispersion). The formula for the normal curve is very unwieldy, but simplifying techniques have made the results usable in other forms. The formula is

$$y = \frac{1}{\sigma\sqrt{2\pi}} e \frac{-(X-\overline{X})}{2\sigma^2}$$

in which $\overline{X}$ represents the mean and 0" the standard deviation. Using the data in Table 2, the calculation of the mean in our example would be

$$X = \frac{\Sigma X}{N} = \frac{250.80}{50} = 50.016 \text{ in.},$$

in which N = Σ, F, F being the frequency of occurrence. The calculation of the standard deviation wou'd be

$$\sigma = \frac{\sqrt{\Sigma F(X-\overline{X})^2}}{N} = \sqrt{\frac{.024000}{50}} = .0219 \text{ in.}$$

Table 2 Data for Calculation of Arithmetic Mean & Standard Deviation

Length (inches) X	*Freq. of Occurrence* F	F_X	$X-\overline{X}$	$(X-\overline{X})^2$	$F(X-\overline{X})^2$
				10^2	10^2
4.96	1	4.96	–.056	.3136	.3136
4.97	2	9.94	–.046	.2116	.4232
4.98	1	4.98	–.035	.1296	.1296
4.99	4	19.96	–.026	.0676	.2704
5.00	5	25.00	–.016	.0256	.1280
5.01	9	45.09	–.006	.0036	.0324
5.02	11	55.22	.004	.0016	.0176
5.03	10	50.30	.014	.0196	.1960
5.04	3	15.12	.024	.0576	.1728
5.05	2	10.10	.034	.1156	.2312
5.06	1	5.06	.044	.1936	.1936
5.07	1	5.07	.054	.2916	.2916
	50	250.80			2.4000

As can be seen by the calculations, the number of figures to carry and the decimal points to be carried make for cumbersome mathematical manipulations. The first rule that any practitioner should learn is the art of coding the data for easy calculation. In our example. the difference in manipulation can be seen after the original data (length in inches) is multiplied by 100, and 500 is subtracted from each value (Table 3).

$$\sigma\overline{X}' = \frac{\Sigma FX'^1}{N} = 1.6, \quad \overline{X} = (500 + 1.6) \times \frac{1}{100} = 5.016,$$

$$\sigma' = \sqrt{\frac{\Sigma FX'^2}{N} - X^{22}} = \sqrt{\frac{368}{50} - 1.6^2} = \sqrt{4.80} = 2.19,$$

$$\sigma = \frac{1}{100}\sigma' = \frac{1}{100} \times 2.19 = .0219.$$

This is extremely time saving when readings have 4 or 5 digits (*e.g.*, 25.000 ± 0.0025 inches for shaft length) or when decimals are a factor (such as 0.0100 ± 0.0005 volts for a characteristic of an electric product). Since this coding is performed to allow easier calculation of squares and square roots, it must be remembered that the coded multipliers must be taken through the same steps to get the correct answer.

Table 3 Simplification of data in Table 2 for calculating arithmetic mean and standard deviation

X (100X–500)	*F*	FX^1	FX^2
–4	1	–4	16
–3	2	–6	18
–2	1	–2	4
–1	4	–4	4
0	5	0	0
1	9	9	9
2	11	22	44
3	10	30	90
4	3	12	48
5	2	10	50
6	1	6	36
7	1	7	49
	50	+80	338

A second step has been to convert the σ formula to an easier form to use, particularly with coded single digits. This new form, still mathematically identical, is

$$\sigma = \sqrt{\frac{\Sigma F \times 2}{N} - \overline{X}^2}.$$

This permits the elimination of one step, the calculation of $(X-\overline{X})$, and the simplification of the process of squaring where coding is used.

One of the most important characteristics of the normal curve is that the standard deviation is independent of the mean over limited ranges. Thus, from our example we could judge that the σ of .0219 inches would be the same for 4-inch or 6-inch shafts as for 5-inch shafts. The importance of this fact will be further explored in connection with other uses, such as process capability studies. It is also important to know other factors when using normal distribution data. Does the average tend to change through time, as would be the case with tool wear? Are there periodic adjustments on the process that will change either the mean or the standard deviation in an unplanned manner, such as dressing a tool? Are there eccentric, characteristics, such as changes in line voltage or air pressure, that affect the mean or the variations in the process?

Although we have limited the examples, to industrial applications, the normal curve had its first uses in other fields, such as agriculture, testing services, and biology. As first defined, the normal curve fits those applications that follow the laws of chance. In human characteristics, the heights of men (or women) follow a normal curve.

Sampling

Inspection is normally conducted on a 100 percent basis or by sampling, depending on such factors as desired quality level, quality level prior to inspection, and cost of inspection.

Unless performed automatically, 100 percent inspection is not 100 percent efficient, due to human factors such as inspector fatigue and the tediousness of repetitive operations. Frequently the quality of sampling inspection can be as high as or higher than that resulting from 100 percent inspection, and more detailed inspection is possible.

Sampling plans are based on the laws of probability. The phances are that, if a given number of defectives are in the lot, a certain number will appear in the sample. In this section I will attempt to explain the basic operation of sampling plans and their place in the manufacturing operation, without the use of mathematics.

Criteria for Selecting A Sampling Plan

For any sampling plan, the following criteria must be determined and stated as an integral part of the plan:

1 The conditions must be specified. Will material be accumulated in lots, or inspected by continuous sampling as it passes the inspection point?

   (a) If lots can be accumulated, the lot sizes, methods of selecting samples, and the conditions under which a lot will be accepted or rejected must be defined.

   (b) If lots cannot be accumulated, the production flow quantities and rates must be known.

2. The risks involved must be specified. These risks are defined as *(1)* consumer's risk, or probability of accepting or passing material which does not meet the requirements, and *(2)* producer's risk, which is the probability that material which does meet requirements will be rejected or fail to pass.

3. A set of rules must be available for disposition of inspected materials. These rules will specify the action to be taken following inspection.

4. The method of selecting samples must be specified. When sampling inspection is performed, it must be assumed that, if defects are present, they are randomly distributed throughout the lot, or that the lot is homogeneous. Any

piece of the lot therefore has an equal chance of being selected as part of the sample (the sample pieces must be chosen at random).

5. The characteristics to be inspected must be specified, and standards for acceptance of these characteristics must be defined.

Definitions of Sampling Terms

Consumer's Risk. The chance a "bad" lot will be accepted on the basis of the sample results. This risk is normally established at 10 percent probability on the operating characteristic curve. Also called the β risk.

Lot Tolerance Percent Defective (LTPD). The percentage of defectives a lot may contain with a 10 percent probability of acceptance; 90 percent of the lots exceeding the LTPD will be rejected.

Producer's Risk. The chance that a lot with fewer than the allowable percentage of defectives will be rejected on the basis of the sample results. This risk is normally established at 5 percent, or at the 95 percent probability of acceptance point of the OC Curve. Also called the a risk.

Acceptable Quality Level (AQL). The percentage of defectives a lot may contain with a 92-98 percent chance of being accepted on the basis of the sample results.

Process Average (p) of Material Inspected. The average percent defective of several lots of the material, computed by dividing the total number of defectives found by inspection by the total number of pieces inspected in samples taken from several lots. Lot sizes have no effect on the process average, other than the effect they may have on the size of the samples.

Average Outgoing Quality (AOQ) of Material Inspected. Average quality expressed in percent defective of material that has passed a particular sampling plan. Dependent on the process averaged of the material submitted to inspection.

Average Outgoing Quality Limit (AOQL). Maximum possible percentage of defectives after sampling inspection has been performed. Both the AOQ and AOQL are based on the assumption that all lots rejected by the sampling plan will be screened by 100 percent inspection and all defectives in the sample removed and replaced. As the process average of material inspected increases, the AOQ will increase to a point where a high rate of lot rejection and screening results in a reduced AOQ. The highest point of the AOQ curve is the AOQL. Beyond this point the AOQ decreases due to the large number of lots being 100 percent inspected following rejection.

Sampling Plans

Several different types of sampling plans and tables are available. They generally are divided into two classes:

1. **Lot Quality Potection.** This type of plan is used to evaluate the quality of individual lots of material on the basis of the Acceptable Quality Level (AQL) or the Lot Tolerance Percent Defective (LTPD). The AQL will ensure acceptance oflots 95 percent of the time, if the process average is below the stated level. The LTPD will ensure rejection 90 percent of the time if the process average is above the stated level.

2. **Average Quality of Several Lots.** This type of plan is used to evaluate the process average of several lots of material or to ensure that the outgoing quality from the inspection point is maintained. The Average Outgoing Quality Limit (AOQL) is used as the target for these plans.

Plans may be further subdivided into single, double, and multiple sampling plans:

A single sampling plan bases acceptance or rejection of a lot upon the units in one sample from the lot.

A double sampling plan allows the selection of one sample, with acceptance if the number of defectives is low, but a second sample must be drawn if the number of defectives is moderately high.

Double sampling is psychologically more popular from the standpoint of giving the lot of materials a "second chance." If the quality is good enough so that most lots are acceptable on the first sample, this plan is more economical than s1ngle sampling, since the first sample size is usually smaller, than the sample required by single sampling. This advantage is canceled, however, if too many second samples are required, because the defect level is too high or the part has excessive variation. Double sampling is most efficient when quality is much better than usual or much worse.

Multiple sampling plans are usually more difficult to administer and are therefore used infrequently. Savings in inspection cost is often offset by cost of administration. No further discussion of multiple sampling plans will be made-except for sequential sampling.

Sequential Sampling

Sequential sampling plans differ from single and double sampling plans in that they are usually "double acting" as regards the quality targets. Both the AQL and LTPD points are used as limits, and no decision is made until one or the other is exceeded. Thus, these plans specify the AQL and its associated producer's risk (or α risk) and the LTPD and its associated consumer's risk (or β risk). Sampling continues until either limit is reached, or it may be stopped at a

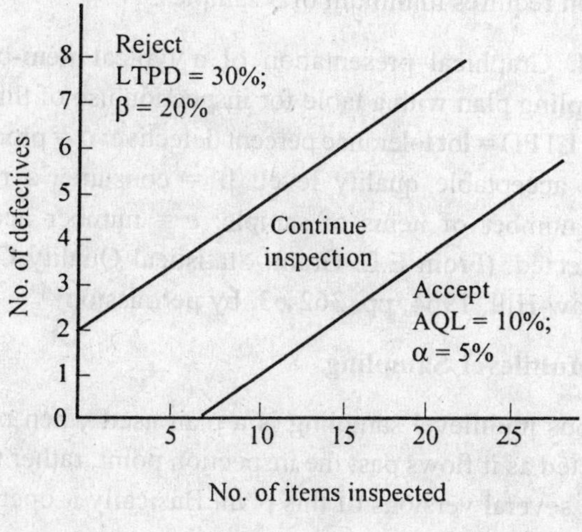

predetermined sample number and accepted. Figure 4 shows a sequential sampling chart, and an inspection table prepared from the chart. For each sample item inspected, if no more than c rejects have been observed, the lot may be accepted; if r or more rejects have been noted, the lot is rejected. If no accept or reject decision can be made, inspection continues with the next time.

n	*C*	*r*	*n*	*C*	*r*	*n*	*C*	*r*
1	*	+	9	0	4	17	2	6
2	*	+	10	0	4	18	2	6
3	*	3	11	0	5	19	2	6
4	*	3	12	1	5	20	2	6
5	*	3	13	1	5	21	2	6
6	*	4	14	1	5	22	2	7
7	0	4	15	1	5	23	3	7
8	0	4	16	1	6	24	3	7

* Acceptance requires minimum of 7 samples.

+ rejection requires minimum of 3 samples.

Figure 4. Graphical presentation of a typical item-by-item sequential sampling plan with a table for inspection use of this plan. In the diagram: LTPD = lot tolerance percent defective: α = producer's risk : AQL = acceptable quality level: β = consumer's risk. In the table: n = number of items of sample: c = number accepted: r = number rejected. (From E.L. Grant, Statistical Quality Control, 3rd ed., McGraw-Hill, 1964, pp. 362-63, by permission).

Continuous Multilevel Sampling

Continuous multilevel sampling is a plan used when material must be inspected as it flows past the inspection point, rather than by lots. There are several versions of this plan. Basically it operates by inspecting all of the items until i consecutive pieces have been accepted. Sampling is then started with a given fractional sample size f_i until an additional i consecutively inspected pieces have been inspected and passed without a rejection. The sample may then be further reduced to a fraction, until another i consecutively inspected pieces have passed, and so on. The plans vary in the number of levels or sample divisions that are allowed before the sampling fraction becomes fixed, and in the action taken when defective pieces are found. For example, one plan may require that inspection revert immediately to 100 percent if a defective is found, and start over; another may require that inspection revert to the next highest sampling level when a defect is found; still another plan may require 100 percent inspection of a given number of pieces when a defective is found.

A Standard Cell Variables Data System

In the production of many of today's complex products, constantly increasing emphasis on quality control and reliability, plus a rapidly advancing state-of-the art, results in more stringent test and inspection efforts in all phases of development and manufacture. This increased effort generates increasing quantities of two types of data: attributes (go or no go, pass or fail) and variables (quantitative measurements). As the quantity of data increases, it becomes more difficult to use conventional methods of review and analysis to isolate problems, potential problems, and trends, and to compare actual product performance with the specifications.

When it is necessary to handle large quantities of data, obviously the most efficient method will involve the use of automation. In some cases, the means for automatic recording is built into the test equipment to produce readouts on punched cards, paper tape, magnetic tape, or in some other form. The standard cell system herein described bridges the gap between such sophisticated (and very expensive) equipment and the more frequently used data sheet on which data are manually recorded.

Variable-type data should be collected only for specific purposes, of which the foremost are : *(1)* to fulfil contractual obligations, *(2)* to isolate and correct problems (and evaluate corrective action), and *(3)* to quickly detect changes that may occur in the product. Such data, when collected only for documentation or review on a unit-by-unit basis, are generally of little value, and can often be replaced by attribute-type data, which require considerably less effort to produce and maintain.

All data collected should be reviewed periodically, and the collection of data that do not contribute directly to such objectives as contract obligations and problem isolation should be discontinued. Data for data's sake is an expensive and time-consuming luxury. By eliminating unnecessary data, attention can be focused on the critical parameters, and faster feedback loops can be established. If enough data can be eliminated, it may be feasible to record the few parameters that remain by means of control charts or by techniques which require no records other than charts used directly at the data source.

Description of Conventional System

The test record most commonly used to collect variables data is data sheet on which each of the parameters to be evaluated is listed with its specifications. Specifications may take the form of *(1)* the nominal value with plus and minus tolerances or *(2)* a simple statement of minimum and maximum limits. The actual measurement obtained for each parameter must be recorded in the space provided.

When a group of completed data sheets is delivered to the statistical group for analysis of test results, three steps should be followed: *(1)* extract the data from the data sheets and regroup it by parameters, *(2)* classify the data into cells, and *(3)* code the data to simplify arithmetical calculations. When there are many parameters, step 1 is difficult and tedious and, due to its repetitious nature, highly susceptible to errors of transcription and classification. Its completion can require the full-time efforts of several clerks, and it is at this point that the data analysis system often breaks down-due to lack of clerical assistance, to accumulation of backlogs, and to belated outputs. Many data analysis programmes are abandoned at this stage. The following system for data collection will overcome this bottleneck.

SAMPLING PROCEDURE

Applications

One of the most popular and useful statistical tools available is sampling. The sampling used in industrial applications takes many forms, from the spot-checking technique and the lot percentage sample to standard table adaptations and more sophisticated techniques. All these methods apply to specific situations, but it is more typical for a single method to be used in all applications without the user being aware of its limitations or cost. It is the responsibility of the quality engineering department to determine the requirements for the sampling plans, including administrative planning, selection of the plan, and determination of the cost of implementing it and the potential cost of expected rejects.

The philosophy of sampling is to make an accept-reject determination on a lot of material through measurements on a predetermined sample of this lot. This determination involves risks. What must be known before devising a sampling plan? It might be easier to visualize some of the characteristics of sampling plans in general if an example with known parameters is first described.

Example

A box contains 100 balls—4 red, 8 black, 88 white. Reject the box if one red ball is found in the sample. Use combination theorem

$$C_N = \frac{N!}{r!(N-r)!}$$

A. Sample size = 5. Total combinations.

$$C_{100,5} = \frac{100!}{5!95!} = \frac{100\times99\times98\times97\times96}{5\times4\times3\times2\times1} = 75,400,000.$$

Accept no red balls (100–4 = 96 balls):

$$C_{96,5} = \frac{96!}{5!91!}$$

Probability of no red balls:

$$\frac{C_{96,5}C_{4,0}}{C_{100,5}} = \frac{\dfrac{96!}{5!91!}}{\dfrac{100!}{5!95!}} = \frac{96!95!}{91!100!} = 81\%.$$

B. Sample size = 10. Total combinations:

$$C_{100,10} = \frac{100!}{10!90!}$$

Accept no red balls:

$$C_{96,10}C_{4,0} = \frac{96!}{10!86!}$$

Probability of acceptance:

$$\frac{\dfrac{96!}{10!86!}}{\dfrac{100!}{10!90!}} = \frac{96!90!}{100!86!} = 65\%.$$

C. Sample size = 25. Total combinations:

$$C_{100,25} = \frac{100!}{25!75!}$$

Accept no red balls:

$$C_{96,25}C_{4,0} = \frac{96!}{25!71!}$$

Probability of no red balls:

$$\frac{\dfrac{96!}{25!71!}}{\dfrac{100!}{25!75!}} = \frac{96!75!}{100!71!} = 31\%.$$

D. Let us now define the black balls as rejects. (100–8 = 92 acceptable balls.) Sample size = 5. Total combinations:

$$C_{100,5} = \frac{100!}{5!95!}$$

Accept no red balls:

$$C_{92,5}C_{8,0} = \frac{92!}{5!87!}$$

Probability of no black balls:

$$\frac{C_{92,5}C_{8,0}}{C_{100,5}} = \frac{\dfrac{96!}{51!87!}}{\dfrac{100!}{5!95!}} = \frac{95!92!}{100!87!} = 65\%.$$

E. Sample size = 10. Total combinations:

$$C_{100,10} = \frac{100!}{10!90!}$$

Accept no black balls:

$$C_{96,10}C_{8,0} = \frac{92!}{10!82!}$$

Probability of no black balls:

$$\frac{\dfrac{92!}{10!82!}}{\dfrac{100!}{10!90!}} = \frac{92!90!}{100!82!} = 42\%.$$

F. Sample size = 25. Total combinations:

$$C_{100,25} = \frac{100!}{25!75!}$$

Accept no black balls:

$$C_{92,25}C_{8,0} = \frac{92!}{25!67!}$$

Probability of no red balls:

$$\frac{\frac{92!}{25!67!}}{\frac{100!}{25!75!}} = \frac{92!75!}{100!67!} = 9\%.$$

G. Summary of example. Probability of acceptance:

Sample size	*Red(4)*	*Black(8)*
5	81%	65%
10	65%	42%
25	31%	9%

This example, with calculations from probability and combination theory, shows two effects. First, the difference in sample size does affect the probability of accepting the lot when the criteria for acceptance do not change. Second, the inherent unacceptable percentage affects the probability of accepting the lot as shown in the differences between the red and the black balls. Another effect, which is not fully demonstrated but which is applicable, is the effect of a specific lot size, 100 balls. The same percentage of defective balls in lot sizes of 50, 100, 250, 500, 1000, etc., will affect the probability of acceptance. For example, 2 red balls in 50 will produce the following results, which are compared to 4 red balls in 100:

Sample Size	*Lot of 50*	*Lot of 100*
5	80%	81%
10	63%	65%
25	25%	31%

This last effect of lot size will diminish as the lot size becomes larger and the ratio N/n (lot sizes/sample sizes) goes above 10. The factors of lot size, sample size, acceptance number, percent defective, and probability of acceptance will now be applied to industrial applications, in which the percent defective of the lot is not known beforehand.

But first, why do we sample, and what are the advantages of sampling?

First, because of the savings in cost, which will vary depending on setup time and unit inspection time, but will always be less than the cost of inspecting the lot 100%. The application of sound sampling plans is one method of reducing quality costs in the appraisal area.

A second reason, also related to economics, is the fact that a 100% destructive test would leave no product to ship. The selection of sampling plans represent a balance between the accuracy of results needed and the amount of product needed. This particular application is usually reserved for variable-type sampling versus attribute (accept-reject), because the decision can be made with fewer pieces destroyed.

A third reason for the use of sampling is related to the effectiveness of the inspection effort. Historical studies have proved that sorting, or 100% inspection, is only 65-98% effective, because of the judgment required in making an accept reject decision in the visual inspection of a product, for instance. Moreover, there is the danger of making a wrong decision, of accepting a reject or rejecting an acceptable piece, which also applies to inspections other than visual. A third, and primary, factor is inspector fatigue. Because of inability to concentrate over long lengths of time, an inspector doing the same inspection routinely will miss rejects and will reject good pieces.

❑

15

Quality Assurance and Maintenance Management

The reputation attached to an organisation for the quality of its products and services is accepted as a key to its success and the future of its employed. To prosper in today's economic climate, any organisation and its suppliers must be dedicated to never-ending improvement, and more efficient ways to obtain products or services that consistently meet customers' needs must constantly be sought. The consumer is no longer required to make a choice between price and quality, and competitiveness in quality is not only central to profitability, but crucial to business survival. In today's tough and challenging business environment, the development and implementation of a comprehensive quality policy is not merely desirable—it is essential.

Quality is often used to signify. 'excellence' of a product or service we talk about 'Rolls-Royce quality' and 'top quality'. In some engineering companies, the word may be used to indicate that a piece of metal conforms to certain physical dimension characteristics, often set down in the form of a particularly 'tight' specification. If we are to define quality in a way which is useful in its management, then we must recognise the need to include in the assessment of quality, the true requirements of the 'customers'.

There is another word that we should defined properly—'reliability'. 'Why do you buy a Versa car?' 'Quality and reliability' comes back the answer. The two are used synonymously, often in a totally confused way. Clearly, part of the acceptability of a product or service will depend on its ability to function satisfactorily over a period of time, and this aspect of performance is given the name 'reliability'. It is the ability of the product or service to continue to meet the customer requirements.

Our definition of quality requires that both the needs of the customer and his/her perceived needs are explored. Frequently, a choice of product or service is made upon apparently irrational grounds; identical offerings, presented in different ways, will sell in vastly different quantities, and will have different qualities ascribed to them. The detergent which sells better in a blue box than a red one, the bank account which has a higher status because of the leather chequebook wallet are well known. Similarly a quality judgement is often related to the price paid without any regard to the discernible properties being purchased. The reasons for a purchase may be difficult to identify, yet their reality must not be denied.

The quality of products and services is important not only for users but also for suppliers. For manufacturing, quality deficiencies result in additional costs for inspection, testing, scrap, re-work, and the handling of complaints and warranty claims. In the so-called service industries, errors, checking, enquiries and complaints accounts for losses in efficiency and productivity. Repeat sales and future market share will also be affected, with significant effects on profitability and survival. Quality must, therefore, be taken into account throughout all the areas of marketing, design, purchasing, production or operations, and distribution. It must be controlled in all these functions, and their activities co-ordinated to achieve a balanced corporate quality performance. Quality performance will not just happen; effective leadership and team work is the only sure recipe for success:

A quality policy then requires top management to:

(a) Establish an 'organisation' for quality;

(b) Identify the customer's needs and perception of needs;

(c) Assess the ability of the organisation to meet these needs;

(d) Ensure that supplied materials and service reliably meet the required standards of performance and efficiency;

(e) Concentrate on the prevention rather than detection philosophy;

(f) Educate and train for quality improvement;

(g) Review the quality management systems to maintain progress.

OBJECTIVES OF QUALITY CONTROL

The objectives of quality control may be stated as follows :

(i) To establish standards of quality that are readily acceptable to the customer and economical to maintain.

(ii) To analyse the trend and extent of quality deviation in a part of product during manufacture, and to determine the cause of such deviation by statistical techniques when it cannot reasonably be attributed to chance.

(iii) To take the necessary corrective steps to keep the quality of the product from dropping below the desired level during manufacture.

(iv) To avoid as far as is reasonably possible, having products reach the customer which are lower quality than that which to considered acceptable.

COST OF QUALITY

There are costs associated with product and service quality. Some costs are associated with preventing poor quality, and some costs occur after poor quality occurs. These costs include:

(i) **Scrap and Rework.** When products are found to be defective while in production, they must be either scrapped or repaired. The costs include the costs of producing the items that are scrapped; the cost of repairing, reworking, and recasting defective products; and all the costs of delays, paperwork, rescheduling, and other hassles caused by defective products.

(ii) **Defective Products in the Hands of Customers.** When products are shipped to customers, the costs can be enormous and difficult to measure. These costs can include warranty costs, product liability suits or settlements, the cost of returns or recalls, and lost business and goodwill.

(iii) **Detecting Defects.** The cost of all the activities aimed at finding products and service that do not confirm to specification before they are shipped to customers. This includes the cost of inspection, testing, and other quality control activities.

(iv) **Preventing Defects.** The cost of training, charting of quality performance to study trends, revising product designs, making changes to production processes, working with suppliers, and other activities aimed at improving quality and preventing defects.

While each of these costs can be high, it is a generally accepted fact that the first three of these costs, the cost of finding and dealing with defective products, may account for as much as 25 per cent of the cost of sales in many companies. Emphasising the activities of finding and dealing with defects has been the traditional approach to quality management.

DIMENSIONS OF QUALITY

As customers evaluate quality, they consider several different aspects of products and service.

Companies have to look to customer as they set standards for measuring quality. Customer surveys and suggestions can be used to obtain inputs from customers about quality. Customer expectations of quality are affected by many factors including competitors' products and are likely to change over time. Products and services must therefore be improved with time to meet the changing expectations of customers.

Customer's expectations of quality are not the same for different grades or classes of products. For example, customer do not ordinarily expect construction nails to be masterpieces that are designed and produced to the same exacting standards of excellence as Rolls-Royce auto mobiles. But nails should serve their intended purpose and be better than the competition. This point is an important one. It is the objective of many companies today to become what is called a world-class company. Becoming a world-class company in terms of quality means that each product and service would be considered best-in-class by its customers. Best-on-class quality means being the best product or service in a particular class of products or services.

DETERMINANTS OF QUALITY

A key issue is how to achieve quality. Several activities or accomplishments are necessary.

(i) **Quality of Design.** After first identifying who its customers are, a company must determine what its customers want from its products and services. Then products and services are designed to exhibit the attributes necessary to meet its customer's expectations.

(ii) **Quality Capability of Production Processes.** Production processes must be designed and build that have the capability of producing products with the attributes wanted by customers.

(iii) **Quality of Confirmance.** Production facilities must than be operated to produce products and services that meet the quality expectations of customers.

(iv) **Quality of Customer Service.** All contacts between customers and companies must be managed so that customers perceive that they have been treated fairly and courteously with their needs attended to promptly and with care and concern.

(v) **Organisation Quality Culture.** The entire organisation must become energised to doing what is necessary to design, produce, and service products and services that meet customer's expectations. Mechanisms must be in place to continuously improve every facet of the organisation toward the objective of building ever-increasing levels of customer satisfaction.

STATISTICAL QUALITY CONTROL

Statistical quality control is applied by taking samples and drawing conclusions by means of some mathematical analysis. It has already been explained that variation in the quality of the product is an inherent characteristics of a manufacturing system. Irrespective of all possible precautions and quality measures there are always a larger number of random disturbances responsible for deviations in the quality of the product from the set standards. The sources of these disturbances are known as chance causes, *e.g.*, movement of the machine due to passing traffic, sudden changes in temperature etc. The presence of these causes in the system is due to a multitude of reasons which are difficult to identify an uneconomical to estimate.

BENEFITS OF STATISTICAL QUALITY CONTROL

(i) The use of statistical quality control ensures rapid and efficient inspection at a minimum cost.

(ii) It minimises waste by identifying the causes of excessive variability in the quality of product.

(iii) A SQC exerts more effective pressure for quality improvement than 100 percent inspection. Statistical quality control is systematic as compared to guess work of haphazard process in inspection. Application of statistical techniques further minimises bias and judgmental errors. Modern techniques of statistical quality control and acceptance sampling have an important part to play in the improvement of quality creation of consumer confidence etc.

TECHNIQUES OF STATISTICAL QUALITY CONTROL

The statistical quality control techniques used in SQC can be divided into two broad categories:

(i) Control Charts

(ii) Acceptance Sampling

I. CONTROL CHARTS

Control charts are used to control quality of products and parts during the course of their actual manufacture. A control chart may be defined as a graph with lines which indicate the tolerances *i.e.*, limits within which variations from the average quality are to be permitted. It consists of three horizontal lines:

(a) Control line indicating the desired (standards) level of quality.

(b) An upper line indicates the upper quality level while.

(c) The lower line shows the lower quality level. The middle line represents the standard quality. A randorm sample of output is taken periodically art frequent intervals and the results are plotted on the control chart. A graphical comparison of measurements with acceptable limits will show the capacity of the production process to produce desired quality level. Any deviation from the limits will mean that the process is influenced by external causes. The upper and lower control limits serve as the decision criteria. When a sample points falls beyond these limits, steps are taken to locate and eliminate the sources of assignable variations, otherwise the process is left free.

Thus a control chart helps to separate out chances variation from assignable variation. It detects 'out of control' situation gives warning of implementing trouble as a running record of quality a control charts provides continuous monitoring of the production process. Control charts can be used for other purpose also. Such charts can indicate the average level at which a process under control is capable of operating and the magnitude of chance variation inherent therein. Some suppliers send control charts with each shipment so that the buyer himself can judge the quality level supplied.

Types of Control Charts

There are two main types of control charts:

(i) Control charts for variables

(ii) Control charts for attributes

(i) Control Charts for Variables

Control charts for variables (measurable characteristics) are designed for the following objectives:

(i) To analyse the production process with a view to establish or change specifications, production procedures and inspection procedure.

(ii) To provide a basis for decision as to when to leave the production process alone and when to look for assignable causes.

(iii) To provide a basis for decisions on acceptance or rejection of a manufactured or purchased product.

Control charts for variables are of three types:

(a) Mean or ($\overline{X}$) chart;

(b) Range or (R) charts; and

(b) Standard deviation or (σ) charts.

(ii) Control Charts for Attributes

Control charts for attributes (Non-measurable characteristics) can also be of three types:

(i) Control charts for proportion of defective units or **(*p*-chart);**

(ii) Control charts for number of defective units or **(*np*-charts)**; and

(iii) Control charts for number of defects or **(*c*-chart)**.

It may be noted that ($\overline{X}$, **R**, σ) control charts can be used when the quality is measured numerically. In order situations quality has to be expressed in terms of attributes, *e.g.*, good or bad. In such a situation a percent defective chart **(p-chart)** or number of defective chart or **(np-chart)** is used. The defects per unit chart **(c-chart)** is used when the number of possible defects is very large but the expected occurrence is small *e.g.*, number of risks on the refrigerator. The **c-chart** is also useful for typing errors and in process control of defects per unit of cloth from a look.

There are many manufacturing systems where the quality characteristics is not capable of direct quantitative measurements. Here the items can be classified either good or bad with respect to the quality characteristics *i.e.*, the item can be classified only as defective (when quality specification does not hold good). Attributes are of yes or no characteristics. This is done by simple examination of the items of the lot. The items may be classified as defective due to a number of reasons and a separate record for each cause may be out of question.

In such situation, we calculate the proportion of defective items in each subgroup or lot. This is defined as

$$P = \frac{\text{Number of defective items found in the lot}}{\text{Total number of items inspected in the lot}}$$

P = fraction of defective in the lot.

In repeated sample size of 'n' the distribution of fraction defectives is found to be Binomial with mean = P and standard deviation = $\sqrt{(pq)}$ / in the case of fraction defectives and with mean = xP and standard deviation equals $\sqrt{(npq)}$ in the case of number of defectives. Here q = 1 – P

As with other distributions, the behaviour of binomial samples can be assumed to follow a normal distribution and normal tables can be used to determine the control limits.

II. ACCEPTANCE SAMPLING

Any inspection procedure involving 100% inspection needs huge expenditure of time, money and labour. Expenditure on inspection is always considered as 'dead weight cost'. Moreover due to boredom and fatigue involved in the repetitive inspection process there is always a possibility to overlook some defective item even by most competent and efficient inspectors. Also the nature of items may be such that these may be completely destroyed during the process of inspection *e.g.* life of a candle. Evidently in such cases 100% inspection cannot be planned. The alternative is statistical sampling inspection method. Here from the whole lot some items are selected for inspection and a decision regarding the quality of the whole lot is taken on the basis of the sampled items. The items can be selected by various sampling methods. Here the whole lot is accepted if the sample items confirm to the specifications otherwise it is rejected. Thus the sample items are considered to be the representatives of the whole lot. The method of rejecting or accepting a lot on the basis of a samples is known as Acceptance sampling or Sampling inspection. Acceptance sampling is the process of evaluating a portion of the product material in a lot for the purpose of accepting or rejecting the lot as either confirming or not confirming to quality specifications.

ADVANTAGES OF SAMPLING

The advantages of sampling inspection can be listed as follows.:

(i) Items of destructive nature during inspection can be inspected by sampling only.

(ii) Economy of time and money in comparison to 100% inspection.

(iii) Problem of inspection fatigue occurring in 100% inspection is eliminated.

(iv) Small inspection staff required.

(v) Due to quick insoection, scheduling and delivery times are imoroved.

(vi) Can exert more effective pressure on quality improvement than the rejection of individual items.

QUALITY AT THE SOURCE

The concept of quality at the source aims to put the production worker in the driver's seat in controlling product quality. Toward the goal of having each worker produce parts that are of perfect quality, quality at the source follows these principles:

(i) Every workers' job becomes a quality control station. Workers are responsible for inspecting their own work, identifying an defects and reworking them into non-defectives, and correcting any causes of defects.

(ii) Statistical quality control techniques are used to monitor the quality of parts produced at each work station, and easy-to-understand charts and graphs are used to communicate progress to workers and managers.

(iii) Each worker is given the right to stop the production line to avoid producing defective parts.

(iv) Workers and managers are organised into quality circles, or QC circles, small groups of employees who analyse quality problems, work to solve the problems, and implement programmes to improve product quality.

This set of arrangements does four things: first, it assigns responsibility for product quality to production workers and the production function, where it belongs. Second, it can lead to production workers who are more committed to high product quality. Third, rather than checking on others, quality control personnel can do work that has a direct impact on producing products of high quality; working with production personnel to remove the causes of defects, training workers in quality control, and working with suppliers to improve their product quality. Fourth, it removes an obstacle to cooperation between quality control personnel and production workers so that they can better work together for higher product quality.

PURPOSES OF QUALITY CIRCLES

Zero defect programme promotes motivation individually on invites suggestions individually. Quality circle is a collective effort 3 to 5 voluntrees from the worker from a group and meet regularly weekly or bi-weekly or about an hour in order to identify, analyse and search for solutions to work related problems and the way of implementing the solutions. The meetings, which are generally supervised (usually the foreman), address themselves to technical problems and follow a strict problem solving approach (worker and management are trained in it) so that the meetings do not fritter the time away and become forums to handle grievances.

The problems addressed are not limited to quality alone but deal with all "technical" problems that affect productivity.

Every department can have its quality circle and this should depend largely on the initiative of the workers themselves, with the support and encouragement from the management.

Quality circle should encourage participation by all members and should faster creativity. The idea is to develop the talents of the people and to develop leadership besides getting a bunch of good ideas to solve problems by tapping the collective intellect and creative genius of the working staff.

FACTORS INFLUENCING THE SUCCESS OF QUALITY CIRCLES

Quality circles is a case where the leadership in bringing about changes is taken by workers themselves leaning the management with the new role of an advisor, a catalyst, a facilitator. The labour unions also have to change their traditional concept of leadership style. This change in attitude and in the style of leadership takes time. The management has to get over its phobia of losing the management prerogative of decision making, and likewise unions have to rid themselves of the fear the management are tring to undercut their power through this new gimmick. These fears may be far fetched, because quality circles are not just a modified, version of the old 'suggestion box'; far from it.

For the good work done by such circles, some organisations believe in giving tangible recognition such as monetary incentives. Although recognition is essential, monetary incentives pose tricky problems such as How much of incentives and how to distribute it amongs the workers ? More over monetary incentives may be unnecessary. As a worker from BHEL has pointed out, in quality circles the work itself is a reward besides having a safer and improved work environment.

The concept of quality circles is also reportedly being experimented in various non-industrial sectors such as hospitals, banks, educational institutions etc. in India. Professional bodies such as the national institutional for quality assurance and the Indian association for quality and reliability have been helpful. The quality circle forum of India has been active in the propagation of knowledge, gained from experience, about the methodology for starting an establishing quality circles in the Indian environment.

Finally, quality management is a total organisational activity. One has to be quality conscious at every step of the functioning of an organisation, if the organisation desired to ensure the quality of its products or services. Quality management is neither an activity involving anyone functional area nor is an activity which ends with the control of the process and the proper selection of raw materials. It is a process encompassing the total management effort of the company, unless the latter is understood and imbibed, ensuring product quality may not be possible.

MEANING OF RELIABIUTY

Reliability is defined as the probability of a plant to give satisfactory performance in particular period of time under specified operating conditions.

The subject of reliability which is fairly new, is becoming more and more important because the complexity of equipment and plants is growing day by day with increasing sophistication, failures have become more critical and some times catastrophic as in the case nuclear reactors, superthermal power stations, automated chemical plants etc.

It is becoming necessary to forecast or predict the life of plant and equipments the availability of plant and equipment and thereby the expected maintenance work required. The amount of maintenance work either preventive or break down will depend upon the reliability of the system and the system components. If the reliabilities of the system and the system components are known and calculated ahead of time, then the work load for maintenance can be fairly well estimated and allocated with respect to time and with respect to different machinery and equipments. This reliability estimates will provide guidance in stocking the spare parts and standby machines. Reliability figures will help in deciding when to replace machines and components. Reliability calculations will tell what improvements in the design of equipment and total plant system would make the probability of failure low enough for acceptance.

Reliability of equipment depends much upon the design of the equipment. Of course. It also partially depends on how the preventive maintenance for the equipment is carried out. Reliability of a plant depends upon the design of the plant system, that is, the way various equipment are linked with each other.

QUALITY DRIVES THE PRODUCTIVITY MACHINE

The traditional view of quality control was that it cost more to get higher product quality. But this is no longer the prevalent view. Japanese manufacturers are credited with popularising the notion that quality drives the productivity machine. This means that if production does it right the first time and produces products and services that are defect-free, waste is eliminated and costs are reduced. In this new way of thinking, when operations managers work to eliminate defects, the quality of products and services is improved and at the same time productivity also improves. Costs are reduced as product quality improves because there are fewer products lost to scrap, fewer products returned for warranty work, and fewer intrusions to production. It has been estimated that 20 to 25 per cent of the overall cost of goods sold in the United States is spent on finding and correcting errors. Quality managements programmes today are, therefore, viewed by many companies as productivity improvement programs.

DESIGNING FOR PRODUCTION

Designing and Developing Products and Production Processes, illustrated that product quality can be improved by designing products for ease of production. And in Production Technology, we discussed the principles of designing products for automated assembly. When products are designed accordingly, products typically have fewer parts and can be assembled quickly and easily. Designing products for production can vastly reduce the sources of error and improve overall product quality.

DESIGNING FOR RELIABILITY

Each part of a product is designed for a given level of component reliability, the probability that a type of part will not fail in a given time period or number of trials under ordinary conditions of use. Components reliability is usually measured by: liability (CR), failure rates (FR und FRn), and mean time between failures (MTBF):

$$CR = (1 - FR)$$

where:

$$FR = \frac{\text{Number of failures}}{\text{Number tested}}$$

$$FR_n = \frac{\text{Number of failures}}{\text{Unit - hours of operation}}$$

$$MTBF = \frac{\text{Unit - hours of operation}}{\text{Number of failures}}, \text{ or } \frac{1}{FR_n}$$

For instance, for a particular type of automobile tyre with an expected life of 30,000 miles, if only 1 percent of the tyres fail within the 30,000 mile. span, we would say that a tyre has a reliability level of .99.

When component parts are combined into a product, the combined reliability of all the components forms the basis for product or system reliability (SR). When independent critical components—those that can directly cause the product to fail—are combined into a product. the system reliability is determined by multiplying the liabilities of all the interacting critical components. For example, four automobile tyres, each with a reliability of .99, would have a system reliability of:

$$SR = CR_1 \times CR_2 \times CR_3 \times CR_4 = .99 \times .99 \times .99 \times .99 = .961$$

The concept of system reliability is further demonstrated in Figure. If the critical components of a system have a reliability of 90 per cent, the system reliability is almost zero if there are more than 50 critical components parts. Similarly, when components parts have a 99.5 percent reliability, system reliability falls to 60.6 percent when there are 100 critical component parts.

Considering the concept of system reliability, what are some of the ways that operations managers can increase the reliability of products? There are three practical ways. First, overdosing of component parts to improve reliability may be a viable strategy in holding product reliability at acceptable levels. Overdosing means enhancing a design to avoid a particular type of failure. Let us say that if a part tends to corrode, overdesigning the part could mean machining the part out of stainless steel to reduce corrosion. Or if a part tends to weak over time, making the part out of forged steel that has been hardened could improve its wearing quality. Similarly, manufacturing parts to closer tolerances, may improve fit of the parts during assembly and reduce the likelihood of improper meshing of parts during use.

When products are relatively simple (have only a few critical interacting component parts), overdesign may be a reasonable alternative for improving system reliability. But when products are complex (have many critical components parts), overdesign of components parts may not significantly improve system reliability. Even if overdesign of critical component parts warrants consideration, the cost of designing, testing, and producing overdesigned parts may be exorbitant. Thus other alternatives must often be considered.

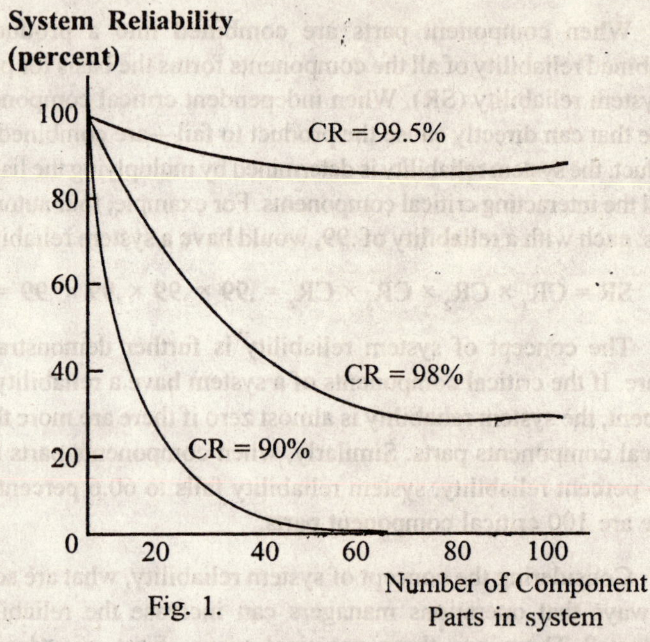

Fig. 1.

Second, design simplification, the reduction of the number of interacting parts in a product will ordinarily improve system reliability. Two examples of this approach from the 1980s are well known. In the IBM Proprietary, the number of parts was halved to about 64. Similarly, the number of parts in the Ford Taurus and Mercury Sable autos was reduced by about one-third. One of the main reasons for such design simplification is to improve the system reliability of the products.

Third, another practical approach to improving product reliability is to provide redundant components. In this approach, a component with low reliability may have a backup build right into the system; thus, if the first component fails, its backup is automatically substituted. The electronics industry commonly employs this approach.

MAINTENANCE MANAGEMENT

When buildings and equipments break down, malfunction, or are otherwise damaged so that normal operations are hindered, they are repaired, mended, overhauled, and put back into operating condition.

Repair activities are reactive; that is, they are performed after a malfunction has occurred. A malfunction is indicated when a piece of equipment will not operate, operates at a less than normal speed, produces products below quality standards, or when workers think that the equipment is about to malfunction. Repair crews and repaid shops work together with production workers to get the machine or building back into operation as fast as possible so that the interruption to production is minimised. Stand-by machines and spare parts are often used to speed this process.

PREVENTIVE MAINTENANCE (PM)

Regularly scheduled inspections of buildings and all pieces of equipment are performed. At these times, machine adjustments, lubrication, cleaning, parts replacement, painting, and any needed repairs or overhauls are done. These activities are performed before the buildings or machines malfunction. The inspections and the needed repairs are usually performed during periods when the buildings and equipment are not needed for production. The inspection for a piece of equipment could be scheduled at a regular time interval, say, once a month, or after a certain number of operating hours, miles, or another measure of usage.

Repair Programmes

Operations managers implement repair programmes to achieve the following objectives:

(i) To get equipment back into operation as quickly as possible in order to minimise interruptions to production. This objective can directly affect production capacity, production costs, product quality, and customer satisfaction.

(ii) To control the cost of repair crews, including straight-time and overtime labour costs.

(iii) To control the cost of the operation of repair shops.

(iv) To control the investment in replacement spare parts that are used when machines are repaired.

(v) To control the investment in replacement spare machines, which are also called stand-by or backup machines. These replace malfunctioning machines until the needed repairs are completed.

(vi) To perform the appropriate amount of repairs at each malfunction. The decision about how far to go with a repair ranges from a Band-Aid and bubble gum fix to a complete overhaul. Some parts can be replaced early to extend the time until the next repair is required.

PREVENTIVE MAINTENANCE (PM) PROGRAMMES

In the case of machine breakdowns, operations managers have no choice—repairs must be made. On the other hand, the decision to have regularly scheduled inspections, machine adjustments, lubrication, and parts replacement as a part of a preventive maintenance (PM) programme is discretionary. Operations managers do not have to have PM programmes, but most do have them because they want to:

(a) Reduce the frequency and severity of interruptions to production caused by machine malfunctions. This objective can directly affect production capacity, production costs, product quality, employee and customer safety, and customer satisfaction.

(b) Extend the useful life of production machinery.

(c) Reduce the total cost of maintenance by substituting PM costs for repair costs.

(d) Provide a safe working environment for workers. Worn-out machines in poor operating condition create safety hazards for workers.

(e) Improve product quality by keeping equipment in proper adjustment, well serviced, and in good operating condition.

PM and Operations Strategies

PM can be an important factor in achieving operations strategies. For example, a PM programme can be essential to the success of a product focused positioning strategy. In product-focused positioning strategies, standardised product designs are produced along production lines where there are little if any in-process inventories between adjacent operations. If a machine breaks down at one operation, all other downstream operations will soon run out of parts to work on. An extensive PM programme in such systems will reduce the frequency and severity of machine breakdowns.

Automation and the Prominence of PM

In automated factories, PM programmes are essential. Consider the concept of workerless factories. In this concept, systems of automated machines operate continuously without the need for production workers. In such an environment, a larger number of maintenance workers would be needed to keep the machines adjusted, lubricated, and in good operating condition. Although many of our factories will never become workerless, they will become more automated and we shall see a shift from large to smaller production work forces, but we shall also see a shift from small to larger PM work forces. Some of the production workers who will be displaced by automation will need to be retrained to become a part of the growing maintenance work force.

Scheduling PM Activities

At some Ford, Toyota, General motors, and other plants, production is scheduled on two 8-hour shifts per day along with one 4-hour minishift for PM activities. At other factories that produce on three shifts per day, the capacity of each machine used for production-planning purposes (master production scheduling and capacity requirements planning) is reduced to allow time for each machine to undergo its regular PM inspection, adjustment, lubrication, and parts replacement. Regardless of the arrangement devised to schedule PM activities, PM and production are increasingly viewed as being equally important, and therefore PM and production must be regularly scheduled on each machine.

PM Data Base Requirements

For an effective PM programme, detailed records must be maintained on each machine. An ongining history of the dates and frequency of breakdowns, descriptions of malfunctions, and costs of repairs is fundamental to determining how often to schedule PM for each machine. Equipment specifications and checklists are needed for PM inspections and early parts-replacement decisions. These records form the basis for improving PM programmes, and the amount of data for a large factory can be great. Computers are often used to maintain a data base for maintenance departments to access as needed. Also, much of the data can be kept in a plastic pocket on each machine; then, as repairs or preventive maintenance is performed, the cards in the pocket can be updated.

Modern Approaches to PM

In JIT, in-process inventories and production lot sizes are reduced to very low levels. This forces the attention of workers and managers to be focused on machine breakdowns. If a machine breaks down, all downstream machines will soon be out of parts and the whole production system will soon stop. Machine breakdowns simply cannot be tolerated in JIT systems; this is why manufacturers strive for perfect machine maintenance. We have discussed earlier how these manufacturers speed up repairs so that interruptions to production are minimised. Here we want to emphasise how they strive to eliminate machine breakdowns through PM.

A cornerstone of PM programmes is worker involvement. Just as in the concept of quality at the source (placing the responsibility for product quality on the production worker), U.S. producers must also similarly apply the concept of PM at the source. In this approach, workers have the fundamental responsibility for preventing machine breakdowns by conducting preventive maintenance on their own machines. Workers must develop an aircraft mentality toward PM. You know how pilots and air crews go down checklists before an aircraft can take off? This meticulous attention to each small detail of the performance of the aircraft is to avoid the unthinkable—an air crash. Workers must also go down a PM checklist every morning, inspecting, lubricating, and adjusting their own machines with the same dread of the unthinkable—a machine breakdown.

IMPORTANCE OF MAINTENANCE

Plant and equipment are the heart of a production system. Therefore, proper maintenance of plant and equipment is essential for keeping them in good working condition. This ensures optimum utilisation of production facilities and resources. All production equipment is designed to give a predetermined quantity and quality of output. This objective can be realised only when the equipment is supported by proper maintenance. In the absence of timely up keep, even the best machines will ultimately break down. Regular use over a period of time causes wear and tear. Gears become loose, bolts tear off valves get chocked, parts crack, pipes leak, lubrication dries etc. Therefore, regular inspection, lubrication, repair etc. must be undertaken to maintain the reliability and efficiency of equipment.

Proper maintenance helps to maximise production performance by preventing break downs and by minimising the loss caused by break downs. In a developing country like India maintenance has special significance. The capital is a scarce resource and its best possible use is essential. Moreover, the natural conditions like tropical climate, and extreme humidity requires special up keep of equipments. Proper maintenance results in better performance and longer life of machinery. It helps to improve reliability of plant and equipment. Maintenance is essential in all manufacturing concerns because machines breakdown, parts wear out and tools deteriorate.

MACHINE RELIABILITY

Out interest here is in machine reliability, the likelihood of a machine breaking down, malfunctioning, or needing repairs in a given time period or number of hours of use. If machine reliability can be increased the incidence of machine breakdowns and the cost of the havoc caused in production by breakdowns can also be reduced. The exception that the world machine is substituted for product. For you see, our machine that we want to be more reliable was another department's or another company's product when it was designed and produced.

There are three approaches to improving machine reliability-overdesign, design simplification, and redundant components and all three take place when a machine is designed. Overdesign means enhancing a design to avoid a particular type of failure. If a machine has only a few independent critical interacting parts, then overdesign may be an effective way to increase machine reliability. Design simplification means reducing the number of interacting parts in a machine. Because there are fewer parts that can fail, machine reliability increases when the number of interacting parts is reduced. Redundant components means building backup components right into the machine so that if one part fails, its backup is automatically substituted. These approaches can be used together or separately to design more reliable machines.

Secondary Maintenance Department Responsibilities

All maintenance departments are responsible for the repair of buildings and equipment and for performing certain preventive maintenance inspections, repairs, lubrication, and adjustments. Additionally, certain secondary responsibilities have traditionally been assigned to these departments.

Housekeeping, sanitorial, window washing, groundskeeping and painting services are usually performed by maintenance departments. These activities usually include all areas of the facility, from restrooms to offices to production departments to warehouses. In some plants, however, the area around each production worker's immediate workplace is cleaned by the worker, and the appearance and cleanliness of all other areas are the responsibility of the maintenance department.

New construction, remodelling, safety equipment maintenance, loss prevention, security, public hazard control, waste disposal and transformation, and pollution control responsibilities have been assigned to some maintenance departments.

TRENDS IN MAINTENANCE

Production machinery today is far more complex than it was a decade or two ago. Computerised controls, robotics, new technology in metallurgy, more sophisticated electronic controls, new methods in lubrication technology, and other developments have resulted in many changes in the way complex machines are maintained.

Special training programmes have sprung up to give maintenance workers the skills necessary to service and repair today's specialised equipment. An example of this training is found in the field of life-support systems in hospitals. The engineers and technicans who design and perform maintenance programmes for this sophisticated medical equipment must be involved in continuous training programmes to stay abreast of new equipment develcpments. These training programmes are conducted by individual hospitals, by cooperative health care groups, and by public and private educational institutions.

Subcontracting service companies have developed to supply specialised maintenance services. Computers, automobiles, office machines, and other products are increasingly serviced by outside subcontracting companies. Their specialised technical training and their fee structure, which is usually based on an as-needed basis, combine to offer competent service at reasonable cost.

Other technologies are developing that promise to reduce the cost of maintenance while improving the performance of production machines. An example is the network of computerised temperature-sensing probes connected to all key bearings in a machine system. When bearings begin to fail, they overheat and vibrate, causing these sensing systems to indicate that a failure is imminent. The massive damage to machines that can happen when bearings fail-snapped shafts, stripped gears, and so on-can thus be avoided.

As computers have been almost universally absorbed into management information systems in all types of organisations, maintenance departments have also been affected by this development. Five general areas in maintenance commonly use computer assistance today:

(i) Scheduling maintenance projects;

(ii) Maintenance cost reports by production department, cost category, and other classifications;

(iii) Inventory status reports for maintenance parts and supplies;

(iv) Parts failure data; and

(v) Operations analysis studies, which may include computer simulation, waiting lines (queuing theory), and other analytical programmes.

Information from these uses of computers can provide managers in maintenance with the necessary failure patterns, cost data, and other information fundamental to the key maintenance decisions discussed in this section.

Although computers, robotics, and high-tech machinery are important concerns in maintenance management today, people concerns may be at the heart of better maintenance. One important trend is the involvement of production workers in repairing their own machines and performing PM on their own machines. By enlarging production workers' jobs to include maintenance of their machines, not only is maintenance likely to improve, but many side benefits open up as well. Restrictive union work rules seem to be falling away at a record pace.

Maintenance today in POM means more than simply maintaining the machines of production. As POM has broadened its perspectives from minimising short-range costs to other, long-range performance measures such as customer service, return on investment, product quality, and providing for workers' needs, so also has maintenance broadened its perspectives. Today maintenance means that the prompt supply of quality products and services is what is maintained, and not merely machines.

TYPES OF MAINTENANCE TECHNIQUES

The following alternative methods may be employed to ensure uninterrupted operation of plant and machinery in case of breakdown maintenance.

(i) Stand by Machines

In some cases, the loss and inconvenience due to breakdown of an equipment is so high that a stand by equipment is kept as soon as the original equipment fails, the stand by facility is employed to avoid interruption and down time. Stand by machines are often kept to reduce the loss due to the breakdown of a key machine. Break down maintenance also requires use of standby machines.

The main question here is how many stand by machines to keep and how long. In order to decide this, a cost benefit analysis of stand by machines is to be done. First, there is interest cost on capital investment. Secondly, space is needed to keep stand by machines. Thirdly, there is depreciation in the value of stand by machines. Fourthly, periodic checking and servicing is necessary to keep the stand by machines in new condition.

The benefits of stand by machines consists of protection against a complete shut down of operation. It avoids loss of production and therefore, it is necessary to estimate loss of future failures. A table of expected costs and benefits can be prepared.

(ii) Shifting Production During Break Down

Under this method spare capacity is maintained not also in the form of stand by machines but also by allowing rest to running machines at intervals and by rotation. If one machine in a production line requires shut down, the output is maintained by shifting to under utilised machines in other lines. For such application, the capacities of different machines must be properly matched.

Disadvantages of Break Down Maintenance

(i) Break down generally occur at importunate times. This leads to poor, hurried maintenance and excessive, delays in production.

(ii) Reduction of output.

(iii) Faster plant deterioration.

(iv) Increased chances of accidents and less safety to both workers and machines.

(v) More spoilt material.

(vi) Direct loss of profit.

(vii) Break down maintenance practice cannot be employed for those plant items which are regulated by statutory provisions, for example, cranes, lifts, hoists and pressure vessels.

OBJECTIVES OF PREVENTIVE MAINTENANCE

(i) To minimise the possibility of unanticipated production interruption or major break down by locating or uncovering any condition which may lead to it.

(ii) To make plant, equipment and machinery always available and ready for use.

(iii) To maintain the value of equipment and machinery by periodic inspections, repairs, overhauls etc.

(iv) To maintain the optimum productive efficiency of the plant equipment and machinery.

(v) To maintain the operational accuracy of the plant equipment.

(vi) To reduce the work content of maintenance of jobs.

(vii) To achieve maximum production at minimum repair cost.

(viii) The ensure safety of life and limbs of the workmen.

❐